WARNING

THE ENEMY WITHIN
CONTAINS ADULT LANGUAGE,
ADULT CONTENT, PSYCHOLOGICAL NUDITY

READER DISCRETION ADVISED

THE ENEMY WITHIN

THE ENEMY WITHIN

SAVING AMERICA FROM THE LIBERAL ASSAULT ON OUR SCHOOLS, FAITH, AND MILITARY

MICHAEL SAVAGE

Published by
THOMAS NELSON™
Since 1798

www.thomasnelson.com

Scripture quotations are from THE NEW KING JAMES VERSION. Copyright © 1979, 1980, 1982, Thomas Nelson, Inc., Publishers.

Published in Nashville, Tennessee, by Nelson Current, a division of a wholly-owned subsidiary (Nelson Communications, Inc.) of Thomas Nelson, Inc.

Nelson Current books may be purchased in bulk for educational, business, fundraising, or sales promotional use. For information, please email SpecialMarkets@ThomasNelson.com.

Library of Congress Cataloging-in-Publication Data

Savage, Michael.
    The enemy within : saving America from the liberal assault on our schools, faith, and military / by Michael Savage.
        p. cm.
    ISBN-10: 0-7852-6102-8 (hardcover)
    ISBN-10: 1-5955-5013-5 (softcover)
    ISBN-13: 978-1-59555-013-2 (softcover)
    1. Liberalism—United States. 2. Social values—United States. 3. United States—Moral conditions. 4. Conservatism—United States. 5. Savage, Michael. 6. Radio broadcasters—United States—Biography. I. Title.
JC574.2.U6S27 2004
320.51'3--dc22   2003022812

Printed in the United States of America

07 08 09 RRD 10 9 8 7 6 5

For Janet
who helped slay the Dragons

A nation can survive its fools, and even the ambitious. But it cannot survive treason from within. An enemy at the gates is less formidable, for he is known and carries his banner openly. But the traitor moves amongst those within the gate freely, his sly whispers rustling through all the alleys, heard in the very halls of government itself.

For the traitor appears not a traitor; he speaks in accents familiar to his victims, and he wears their face and their arguments, he appeals to the baseness that lies deep in the hearts of all men. He rots the soul of a nation, he works secretly and unknown in the night to undermine the pillars of the city, he infects the body politic so that it can no longer resist. A murderer is less to fear.

—MARCUS TULLIUS CICERO
Roman orator, statesman 42 B.C.

CONTENTS

PREFACE

Who is the Enemy Within?

Are there names to be named? Yes.

There are enough names to fill this entire book. Perhaps we should put our own names in this book. Why do I say that? Because most of us have failed our own democratic system by not being vigilant. Most of us have looked the other way while our borders, language, and culture have been diluted.

There is also an ideological divide as to an "enemies list." Both Left and Right have created operatives who are enemies of our way of life; enemies of firm borders, English as a national language, and a common cultural glue. The question really becomes whom do you fear most? The vast "right-wing conspiracy" or the vast "left-wing conspiracy"?

Analyzing both sides of this equation, you will come to see the right-wing supports God, country, family, the military, and has far higher moral standards than the Left. The Left operates specifically to undermine God, country, family, and the military. They use the courts to undermine the popular will. What they cannot gain through the ballot box they gain through the gavel. In California we recently saw how the ACLU with three leftist judges tried to *stop* an election to recall a failed, corrupt governor.

Analyzing recent Supreme Court decisions on sodomy and affirmative action, you will see the vast left-wing conspiracy at its worst, legitimizing the use of race as opposed to achievement and destabilizing family values. Left-wing operatives have come very far in their plans.

It is clear to me if God could vote, He would be a member of the vast right-wing conspiracy. In fact, to the mad dog leftists in the ACLU, The National Lawyers Guild, and the Democratic party, God is the enemy.

In this sense then, this book is not so much about naming names as it is about defining terms. The extreme Left has attempted to redefine family and patriotism among other clearly evident concepts: to redefine marriage to conform to their own perverse worldview and to redefine patriotism to mean stabbing our troops in the back while they are under fire.

In this book I hope to reaffirm the meaning of the most basic concepts of family, nation, and morality. By pointing out how internal enemies are undermining our religion, schools, courts, military, media, and police, I hope to continue to act as Paul Revere did in his time.

If I were given to comedy in this serious battle for the future of America, I might say my "midnight call" would be, "The liberals are coming, the liberals are coming." Unfortunately, these times do not lend themselves to comedy. Moreover, the liberals aren't coming—they're already here.

The damage they are doing and have done is very difficult to calculate. The precise connection between extreme liberal pressure groups and outright criminal activity is difficult to determine. But I assume it does exist. Why do I say this?

Many of you are under the impression that civil libertarians are sincere in their desire to protect our liberties from an oppressive government. At least that's the message they have sold you for decades. If that were the case, how would you explain the following?

The U.S. Justice Department has been using the USA PATRIOT Act not only to fight terrorists but also to catch child pornographers, drug traffickers, blackmailers, spies, money launderers, and even corrupt foreign leaders. Now, who would argue that any tool that can be used to trap drug traffickers and child pornographers is a bad tool?

The answer is the Red Diaper Doper Babies in groups such as the People for the American Way (PAW). For example, Elliot Mincberg, legal director for PAW, a radical, leftist "civil liberties" group often critical of America, especially the police and military, said the following: "What the justice department has really done is to get things put into the law that have been on prosecutors' wish lists for years. They've used terrorism as a guise to expand law enforcement powers in areas totally unrelated to terrorism."[1]

I would ask Mr. Mincberg if he feels child pornographers, spies, and drug dealers deserve the special protection they have been enjoying for decades thanks to "liberal" judges and laws.

This front group from Hollywood has another spokesman by the name of Ed Asner who is often seen bumbling on television. Asner both blasted America and displayed his utter contempt for the president's anti-terrorism effort, saying, "[The people of America] are sheep. They like [Bush] enough to credit him with saving the nation after 9/11. Three thousand people get killed, and everyone thinks they're next on the list. The president comes along, and he's got his six-guns strapped on, and people think he's going to save them."[2]

While Asner may appear a buffoon, the damage he and the People for the American Way have done to our law enforcement agencies is ines-timable, as you can see by the Mincberg statement in which they oppose the government's ability to capture the worst domestic criminals imagi-nable; criminals who have often been able to evade the law owing to clever lawyers and the liberal judges they plant on the courts.

Also chiming in on the government's use of the terror law to pursue a variety of other crimes is Anthony Romero, executive director of the American Civil Liberties Union. He said, "Once the American public under-stands that many of the powers granted to the federal government apply to much more than just terror, I think the opposition will gain momentum."[3]

Which side is Mr. Romero on? The law, or that of the child pornogra-pher and drug dealer?

Joining these extremists is Democratic Senator Patrick J. Leahy of Vermont. He said the Justice Department's secrecy and use of these laws made him question whether "the government is taking shortcuts around the criminal laws"[4] and invoking intelligence statutes with differing stan-dards of evidence to gain access to surveillance and records—as though this is a bad thing.

Leahy stated, "We did not intend for the government to shed the tra-ditional tools of criminal investigation, such as grand jury subpoenas gov-erned by well-established precedent and wiretaps strictly monitored"[5] by federal judges. In other words, federal judges controlled by the radical Left and their criminal cohorts.

This is why child pornographers and drug dealers have been able to get away with their vile crimes for so long. Because of the Enemy Within our courts and our Fifth Column civil liberties organizations.

What is equally astonishing is the headline *The New York Times* ran, "U.S. Uses Terror Law to Pursue Crimes from Drugs to Swindling." Again, I must ask, which side is *The New York Times* on? Surely not the side of the drug dealers, swindlers, and child pornographers. I hope they are on the side of law enforcement, which has been hobbled by extremely liberal interpretations of what freedom is.

But I don't think so. The left-wing establishment believes that a "corrupt, racist American state deserved to be attacked and destroyed."[6] That is their *modus operandi*. It can be heard and it can be seen as practiced by civil liberties lawyers.

For example, one prominent leftist civil liberties lawyer stated in his autobiography that one of his clients, who had participated in bombings in the 1960s and who has recently been released from a twenty-year murder sentence, had a just cause even though her means were "tragically wrong." To most leftists today, the sixties aren't dead by any means. All you have to do is listen to their rhetoric.

Whenever there is a rally against our attempt to pacify Iraq and bring it into the family of man, speaker after speaker at these Communist-organized "protests" attacks America with more viciousness than they direct at the former regime of the murderous sadist Saddam Hussein.

I hope this book will act as an awakening to you, the reader. And I hope you will use what I disclose in these pages to clearly see America as it is. Infinitely great, and infinitely corrupted by liberalism.

America is crying for those who will defend her against the Enemy Within.

—MICHAEL SAVAGE

ONE

FREEDOM:
THE SAVAGE AMERICA

A near-death experience taught me one of the most important lessons of my life. I was seventeen years old and working as a busboy in the Catskill Mountains in upstate New York. One afternoon my friend Harry suggested we take a break and drive around the narrow mountain roads for an hour or so to relax before serving the hotel guests another meal.

His car, his idea. Off we went.

At one point Harry started speeding, like kids will do, down a steep, two-lane stretch of mountain blacktop. On our right, the jagged rocks threatened to puncture the car like a giant can opener. On the left, just to the other side of the oncoming traffic, was a cliff falling about a hundred feet into a dark, cold river.

I'll never forget it. I started to yell at him, "Harry, you're going too fast." That's when I saw his eyes. He was crazy. He went completely insane. His hands gripped the wheel so hard his knuckles turned white.

Me? I'm thinking maybe Harry's never been down this road before. Maybe he's clueless about joyriding on the edge of a mountain. Could be he was drunk or a suicidal maniac. Whatever the reason for his maniacal behavior, I figured we were both dead.

I shouted again, "Slow down, idiot!"

In that moment, looking at his glazed-over, dilated eyes, he looked like a deranged psycho. This half-wit wouldn't hit the brakes. He sped down the hill while I'm screaming, "Stop the car . . . *Stop the car!*"

The idiot lost control.

Have you ever been in an out-of-control car? Even for a few seconds on the ice? It's a terrifying experience. Back then, unlike today, cars didn't have airbags. Only a few models had seatbelts. We had neither.

We were crash test dummies without a prayer.

No matter what Harry did with the wheel, it was too late. We careened out of control. Like a pinball, we first slammed into the side of the mountain. A split second later we shot across the road and flipped over. That's when my head smacked the dashboard with a boom.

It's a miracle I'm alive.

There's a lesson about the future of America in that story. America is the car. Whoever is in the driver's seat determines whether we as a nation will crash and burn or survive and hand the keys to the next generation. You better read that again.

It all boils down to the heart and soul of the driver.

Does the driver respect the laws of the land? Or does he take the law into his own hands to do as he pleases? Will the driver exercise some modicum of common sense? Or will he disregard the warning signs that clearly show desperate corrective measures are needed? Will he preserve what was passed down to him? Or will he selfishly squander what he inherited?

Today, the liberals have seized the wheel.

They're speeding down the pathway of good intentions. Their mantra: Celebrate perversity, embrace ultra-tolerance, pay rape-a-nations (so-called reparations), support affirmative racism, provide government subsidies for every illegal who sneaks across the border, and do so through the judges if they can't win at the ballot box.

In their haste to push failed socialist ideals, the libs have placed us on a crash course of total destruction.

But some people can't see that, can they? They're sitting in the backseat with headphones on, or watching TV, or hooked on the Internet. I say it's time to sit up, wake up, and take notice while there's still time to apply the brakes.

America is headed for a fatal social crash.

Am I overstating the danger here?

With these sanctimonious zealots driving public policy, the homeless are the sacred cows of the streets. The sexual perverts are the teachers' pets. The lawyers twist the system in favor of the criminal class. The churches are silenced while the courts legislate immorality. And patriots and police are censored while dung-slingers are subsidized.

These diehard, irreligious lefties are also the driving force in re-education. The professors at the institutes of lower-living shove failed Marxist ideology down our children's throats. Students are required to open up and just say "Ahhh"—if, that is, they want a passing grade. And, if the extremist National Education Association has its way, children as young as first grade will undergo homosexuality sensitivity indoctrination.

I can't speak for you, but I'm not going to watch TV while the leftists drive America over the cliff. I've already been down that road. What's beyond me is how anyone can sit by while America is being overrun. My love for America and my fears for my children and for my future grandchildren compel me to speak out.

To name names.

To call it as I see it.

You see, the Enemy Within is an octopus. In its mind is liberalism, and its eight tentacles are strangling the government, the church, the courts, the schools, the media, the military, the police, and health care. You might say this book is a call to awaken—it's time we break the death grip that liberalism has on these institutions of American life.

After all, as I pointed out in my national bestseller *The Savage Nation*, extreme liberalism is a mental disease. It is a destructive contagion more deadly than any force this country has ever faced. As you will find later in these pages, it is also a canker sore that seeks to silence anyone who dares to speak the truth. It is a sickness that would have us dismantle our borders, language, and culture.

Did you get that?

Modern distorted liberalism is the Enemy Within.

I PLEDGE ALLEGIANCE

I don't want my children's children to inherit a broken nation. I don't want my grandchildren to inherit a land whose people fled tyranny only to bring tyranny here. Everything so many backward migrants run from they bring with them.

Their hatred.

Their bigotry.

Their small-mindedness.

Their religious extremism.

America wasn't built on those values. She was built on the backs of immigrants who knew how to work, not how to work the system. On immigrants who learned the language, not corrupted it. They embraced a hard work ethic.

A love for God.

A desire to build, not tear down.

By the way, why do we have so many negativist immigrants today? Nobody screened them under Bill Clinton, that's why. For eight dark years the Demoncats handed the keys to the country to any and all. Clinton, the most scandalous president in our history, let the dregs of humanity invade America. It wasn't "give us your tired and your poor." No, under Clinton it was "give us your loafers and your free-loaders."

Do I suffer from xenophobia?

Not in the least. I'm the son of an immigrant. But there's a right way and a wrong way to handle immigration. What happened to the days when people coming to this sacred soil pledged to make "America first"? What happened to working toward a common good, not a common handout?

Unless the conservatives who hear my voice grab the wheel and put a stop to this twisted joyride, your grandchildren will not inherit the paradise you inherited. A paradise, I might add, that was secured by the blood of Eddie. Eddie, lest you forget, a soldier who is lying in a shallow grave buried all over Europe, paid for your freedom.

What are you going to do with the legacy handed to you by Eddie, who bled to death on Omaha Beach . . . in the skies of Europe . . . who died all across the chain of islands in the South Pacific . . . who risked his life and lost it. Will you preserve it, cherish it, and pass it on to your children's children? Or will you, in good left-wing fashion, snub your nose at Eddie's sacrifice because he wasn't culturally diverse?

I ask you, why did honorable men and women like Eddie, serving in our military, sacrifice their lives?

So you could suck white powder up your nose?

So you could molest the Boy Scouts?

So you could ogle porn?

So you could tax the tax on my last dollar to pay for some socialist government program? That's the position of the Red Diaper Doper Babies.

Where has six decades of radical, mad dog liberalism brought us? I'll tell you where: America is teetering on the cliffs of insanity. Lady Liberty is about to have a mental breakdown if it gets any worse, and the leftists will be the ones with the padlock on the straitjacket. Need proof? In this book, you'll see what rotten fruit liberalism has produced:

- The YWCA hires Patricia Ireland, a bisexual, pro-abortion feminist, to head the 145-year-old Christian-based young girls association.[1]

- The United Way de-funded more than fifty Boy Scouts of America chapters over the Scouts' refusal to offer special homosexual counseling for gay youth.[2]

- A Princeton University professor advocates the murder of disabled babies for up to several weeks *after* they have been born.[3]

- The "Founding Fathers" are out. The "Framers" are in. The feminists say this new generic label in textbooks will be less sexist and more tolerant.[4]

- Leading psychiatric groups such as the American Psychiatric Association are contemplating the normalization of pedophilia—sex with children.[5]

- An appellate court rules recitation of the Pledge of Allegiance by students is unconstitutional. The inclusion of "under God" is offensive to atheists.[6]

- Members of the ultra-left-wing activist organization, MoveOn, are now planted in the newsrooms of ABC, NBC, MSNBC, CNN, and CNBC to manipulate news coverage.[7]

- Affirmative racism[8] and sodomy are normalized by a radical Supreme Court.[9]

That's just for starters.

As you read these words, a flood of human contraband is gushing over our southern states. Some are hidden in the back of trucks. Others waltz across the two thousand miles of mostly unpatrolled borders. Has the government stopped this invasion?

No.

Not even in the wake of 9/11.

Instead, the liberal socialists, who believe in open borders,[10] are pressuring the Immigration and Naturalization Service to place water stations in the desert. Why? So lawbreaking migrants sneaking their way into this great land can have a Coke and a smile.

More than ever, we have to be vigilant. We must remain alert and aware of the people and institutions that encroach on the values we hold dear as Americans. I'm not just speaking of the terrorists in dirty nightshirts who will use any means to attack us.

No. We must fight for our freedom on many fronts, including on our own soil, within our own government, within our educational system, within our courts, and especially within the media.

Whether you know it or not, we have a lot of internal enemies in this country. They hate our freedoms. Some of them are representatives, some of them are lawyers, some of them are state senators, some of them are mayors, some of them are just plain psychotic street thugs, but we have plenty of homegrown haters of America.

For instance, just as the Founding Fathers sought independence from British tyranny, today you and I must seek independence from the judicial tyranny of the Supreme Court. The Stench from the Bench has stepped in it once again with its endorsement of moral degradation which, as you'll see in a later chapter, was a complete reversal of what they ruled just seventeen years ago.[11]

Yes, there is much to do—or undo as the case may be. But, as John Adams said so well, "Liberty, once lost, is lost forever." That is why I, Michael Savage, refuse to toss in the towel. Not now. Not ever.

Not on my watch.

DEAD MAN'S PANTS

Growing up in the Bronx, as I did, the man-child in the Promised Land, I didn't have many of the luxuries most kids with their hat on backwards take for granted today. My father was a first-generation immigrant. He worked his fingers to the bone. We simply didn't have the money to afford more than the basics. So, as you might expect, I cherished and took care of the things I had.

As a kid, I'd line up my shoes under my bed at night, neat, like in the military. I made sure they were polished, too. I'm sure some shrink today would say I suffered from ADD or some obsessive-compulsive disorder and should have been put on an immediate regimen of Ritalin.

I wonder what a shrink would say about the fact that through most of my youth I wore secondhand pants from dead men. I'm absolutely serious. Many of the pants I wore as a preteen came off of stiffs and were cut down to fit me.

Don't get me wrong. My father was a good man. He ran a small antique store with mostly nineteenth century stuff. On the side, at least in the beginning, he sold used goods as well. A man's got to do what a man's got to do to make ends meet, right?

Occasionally, he would go to an auction where a man had died and buy the entire estate. The clocks, the dishes, the mirrors, whatever the man had. The pants. The shirts. The whole deal. You get the picture.

Back at the store, as he sorted the stuff for resale, my father would take a closer look at the suit. Once he got a Hart Schaffner & Marx suit from a dead man. Now, what's he going to do? Toss it in the garbage like they do today? In those days, it wasn't in him to throw out a good worsted fabric. Instead, he brought home the pants to me.

I remember my father showing them to me like the head tailor at Nordstrom's department store. He'd say, "Now, Michael, get a good look at the fabric." I wanted to vomit. I got a migraine because I knew what was coming.

"Take a look at the quality of this fabric." He's working me like a salesman. He's unrolling the pants on the bed. I can see it to this day. He unrolls them like he's selling me a bolt of hand-woven cloth. He would say, "You can't get fabric like this just anywhere."

I wanted to say, "Of course not, Dad. They only sell stuff like that for men who died." You know, it was like special clothing for the undertaker.

Even if I had said something, that wouldn't have changed one thing. He'd go downtown, and the pants would come back fit for me, you know, without the legs taken in properly. They ended up baggy like a pair of Charlie Chaplin's pants. Even if they had fit me properly, there was something repugnant about the whole idea.

Here's the connection.

Today, almost daily, the leftists from both political parties come into our homes peddling some new entitlement program or some new right or a new educational initiative. As they roll out their One World, socialist ideals that went out of fashion decades ago, we feel nauseated. Why? These posers are offering us nothing more than dead man's pants—ideas history has demonstrated don't work.

Un-American ideas.

Socially dangerous ideas.

Ideas that should have been buried long ago.

Or, in fact, were.

The next time a Democrat proposes an expansion of government-funded health insurance for all lower and middle income families[12] . . . think *Dead Man's Pants.*

When Tom Daschle blasts a tax cut as a means to boost the economy while proposing to provide non-working persons health-care benefits[13] . . . think *Dead Man's Pants.*

When the Rev. Jesse Hi-Jackson spouts off about the U.S.'s obligation to invest in Africa's development[14] . . . think *Dead Man's Pants.*

When the National Education Association pushes "school-based support groups" for gay and lesbian students[15] . . . think *Dead Man's Pants.*

When Congresswoman Nancy Pelosi advocates providing government-funded health-care coverage for every child in America[16] . . . think *Dead Man's Pants.*

You see, every one of these ideas may look good on the surface—until you consider their roots. Let me put it this way. These concepts are based on the notion that it's the government's job to provide a chicken in every pot, a pot and a bed in every house, and the key to a house in every pocket.

What does that sound like?

How well do you know history?

This is nothing short of socialism. The Dems are creating a state wherein the sheeple, the ignorant incompetents, are dependent on the government. Their view of utopia is the creation of a nanny state. That's precisely what communism is about.

Here's how it works: Let's say these libs are dangling the dead man's pants in front of your face. You *know* what they really are, but you figure it's "Take them or wear nothing at all." You figure you have no other options. After all, nobody else is presenting you with a better option. So you talk yourself into believing that dead man's pants can't be all that bad.

That's when they've gotcha.

Once you empower the government to provide these so-called initiatives (a power you won't find granted to them in our Constitution) then they can start to regulate what you must *do* with your dead man's pants.

For instance, a private Christian college whose student body is funded, in part, by government loans might now suddenly be required to hire a multi-culti dancing transsexual to teach their Bible classes or face de-funding along with a lawsuit.

Or a private Catholic school that enjoys a tax-exempt status might be required by the government to teach students "Talking about Touching," a sex-ed and personal safety program designed by advocates of prostitution.[17] Are you beginning to get the big picture? Give the government an inch, and they'll take you to the cleaners.

THE BULLY PULPIT

But there's another part to this story of my dead man's pants. Let's spin the clock forward; I'm in junior high now. By the seventh grade, my mother took pity on me, so she spends the money and buys me some expensive pegged pants. I'll never forget how beautiful they were. It was Elvis Presley time, you know, with the saddle stitch and all of that.

I was now the style-setter of my class!

One day at school, this big punk a few grades ahead spots me wearing my new pants. He's maybe seventeen; I'm all of twelve. He works his way towards me in the hall and starts to get in my face. Why? He didn't like my pants because he had a pair like them, too.

Before I know it, this bully starts to smack me around a little. With a shove to my chest, this mean SOB knocks me down and takes off. When I get up, my pant knee is ripped. My heart is broken.

The rest of the afternoon my heart is pounding all through my classes—I didn't know what the teacher was saying. All I was thinking was, "My mother's going to kill me. I ripped these pants."

So the pants are ripped, and I can't focus on math or world history. I'm too preoccupied wondering, *How am I going to tell Mother?* I walk home in the ice cold, and all I can think about is the rip in the pants and the shreds over my knee. I get home and break the news to my mother.

She was really very nice about the whole thing. She takes them to a tailor, and the word comes back two days later that he can weave the pants. Weave? I asked, "What does 'Weave the pants' mean"? It was a huge family discussion. Of course, not in front of my father!

The women—it was like a conspiracy—always sat with the bread knives over the plastic table cover, moving the breadcrumbs around as they talked, sorting them. I loved those days. She explained how the tailor could weave the threads of the fabric into almost as good as new shape.

I felt like a life sentence had been lifted from my heart. I rejoiced inside that I hadn't ruined this great present given to me. By the time the crumbs were sifted, the pants were more or less consigned to where they belonged to begin with.

Unfortunately, if you rip your pants today as a kid you'll probably come home to an empty house, thanks to the feminists who devalued the high calling of motherhood. Instead of coming home to a mother who'll hug and greet you and serve you a cookie while you pour out your heart, your best friend is now a TV or some Internet stranger in a chat room half way around the world—or some pervert in the next town.

What kind of life are we offering kids today? When a child is hurting, a widescreen TV never bakes her cookies—and it sure doesn't listen to or care about her problems. I guess I was lucky. I had a mom who was there for me. So my heart was healed, and we all went on with our lives.

I don't care if you think I'm being sentimental. Those were the good old days. When women had time to drink a cup of coffee together and sift the breadcrumbs on the tabletop. What's wrong with that? Wouldn't we all be better off with that kind of support? Here's the tie-in to modern liberalism and the Enemy Within.

When I said there doesn't appear to be many options on the table of politics, besides the liberal dead man's pants, there are a number of reasons for this, but one primary reason.

Let's say you have a new, conservative idea for improving education, like providing vouchers so all students can pick a school where real education takes place. The moment you put that idea into action, a bully comes along and knocks it down.

Perhaps you have a faith-based, skill-equipping outreach to the homeless bums on the street. The second this bully learns you've used a garage on church property to house bottled water and blankets for the program, he screams "separation of church and state" and slaps you with a restraining order to close the thing down.

Or let's say you want to raise the American flag on the front lawn of the local library and tie a ribbon around the old oak tree in honor of the troops abroad. The same bully who tears the crosses off of war memorials shows up and drags you into court to remove those "divisive symbols of patriotism."

Who is this bully?

The Red Diaper Doper Babies of the American Un-Civil Liberties Union, that's who.

They start by intimidating you with their legalese.

They smack you around with their bogus lawsuits.

They wrap themselves in the Constitution and shut you down like a criminal. I'm telling you, my heart is breaking. We're losing control of this country. I can't stand the way these self-righteous ambulance chasers are raping America with their neo-socialist worldview.

You might be wondering, how did we get this way? How did this happen? It seems everywhere we turn some lib is dictating and selling us dead man's pants—or suing us if we don't put them on. I thought America was a superpower.

As I'll explain in a moment, the answer is found in two words: soft spot.

THE JUNGLE

I was flipping channels on television one night. I came across a guy who raised otters and cried every time he put them back in the river. I thought,

"Our whole country is going insane." A grown man and his wife rescuing river otters. God bless them. I have nothing against river otters.

But I'm watching the guy petting the otter and calling him Howie. He says, "Howie, have a nice life," and releases him into the river. He starts bawling. The wife pats him on the shoulder. I didn't know whether to laugh at or cry with this guy. We're talking about an otter—it looked like a rat to me, with whiskers.

Believe me, I know you could get attached to a spider if you're a lunatic. But, you know, where does attachment to pets begin and end? I don't know anymore. Our country is crazy. Our young ones throw babies into an incinerator and go back to a disco dance five minutes later.

The old hags, the harridans in the Senate who make a living off the abortion racketeers, get up and scream that we should continue to rip babies out of the womb and sell the skin for women who have wrinkles.

So I'm watching this sixty-year-old guy getting choked up over a river otter. I couldn't understand it. I changed the channel to a National Geographic special about water buffalos. Turns out the lions were hunting for food, and they found a water buffalo.

Lions are smart. They culled one of the large water buffalos from the herd, and then this beautiful, strong creature, the water buffalo, stands there stoically as the pride of lions starts to rip at her. First, they tear out her nose. Then, the others tore at her anus.

The once glorious water buffalo stood there bleeding and looking straight ahead bleeding from both ends—the whole scene disheartened me. Why? Listen to what I'm about to tell to you. It's an analogy even you liberals can follow for a moment.

The lions attacked at the weakest point of the strong, thick-hided water buffalo. They knew once they ripped out her anus and nose and entrails, she's finished. She falls down, and then they tear her to pieces and eat her.

America is somewhat like this large water buffalo. If you want to know how things got this bad, it's because our enemies knew where to hit us. They first hit us in the nose. That was the sixties. The anti-capitalist, neo-socialists—or, as I like to call them, neo-socs—hit us in the nose with their free love, free sex, anti-family, anti-marriage, anti-God, and party 'til you puke celebration of decadence.

We are still bleeding from it.

Stunned, we didn't unify as one giant organism and fight back against the attack. That's when the radical rats started gnawing on the other end. The anus. Once inside, they attacked our president from within; they attacked our wars against evil; they attacked our police and military, the flag, God, the family, the Church, our memorials . . . everything that makes us strong and holds us together. The glue of Western Civilization has been undone by the radical Left.

I have no gray zone when it comes to this.

Nor should you.

THE SLOW ROAD TO RECOVERY

You might find it interesting that I didn't always see things this clearly. I wasn't always an independent conservative. As I've said before, I was raised in a Democrat, blue-collar home. My first job out of college was as a social worker in the Upper West Side of New York City. All of my so-called clients were minorities.

Now, I was a good liberal at the time, having had my brain washed at one of the city universities of New York by a whole slew of European emigrants who, instead of kissing the ground when they got here, urinated on the sacred soil and the flag and immediately sought to instill communist philosophy in the minds of the young.

I didn't know that at the time. I was just a wide-eyed liberal kid with an eye on changing the world. There I was, fresh out of college. I took a job as a social worker to save the oppressed minority. I was always an idealist; I still am, as a matter of fact.

But the abuses of the welfare system that I saw back then nauseated me and started me on my slow road to recovery. Day after day I found people who had jobs but who claimed they didn't so they could get their government handout. They were ripping off the welfare system without batting an eye.

Here's when the scales started to drop from my eyes.

As a young social worker, I made something like $5,500 a year. I was fresh out of college, and I had no furniture in my apartment. I had a mattress on the floor and orange crates for lamp tables. But I wasn't complaining. It was a start.

I'll never forget the day I visited one of the so-called welfare clients and what happened when I came back to my supervisor in the New York City Department of Social Welfare, or whatever it was called, to file my report. She wanted to know if they had furniture. When I said they didn't, she tells me to take out a pen and paper.

She said, "Write this down: They're setting up an apartment, Mr. and Mrs. Whomever. Every civilized family needs a bed. Write down $350 for a bed. They need two lamp tables. Write down $120 each. In the living room, they need a coffee table. Write down $120. They'll need a sofa. Write down $300." This went on for a few minutes.

By the time she was done, the bill was something like $3000-$4000. I was supposed to authorize a check to Mr. and Mrs. Whomever to furnish their welfare apartment so they could lead a standardized life. Me? I went home to a mattress on the floor and two orange crates. I was the professional.

That's when I knew the system was broken.

That's when I knew the system was sick.

Now, my observations didn't radicalize me overnight. I just left the welfare department and moved on to teaching. I saw certain excesses in teaching, but I loved the children. I taught at an all-black school and happened to love it. I got along great with the kids, and they got along great with me. So far, so good.

But the moment I decided to go to the top of the teaching profession, that's when I slammed into a rude awakening. I left teaching and went back to school where I laboriously got two master's degrees and then a Ph.D. from a great university. I had written six or eight books by the time I had graduated.

When it was time to get my teaching job, I was told, in effect, "White men need not apply." That's when the worm turned. That's when I became radicalized. That's when I saw the true colors of liberalism. Here I had two young children. I had killed myself to get that degree, but because of the social engineering of the radical Left, I was told to put aside all of my aspirations.

The rest is history. I will not bore you with the details or whine. I do very well indeed today, but the government didn't hand it to me. It's been a long road of crawling on broken glass. Everything I ever achieved has been won with hard work, dedication, sweat, tears, and pain. But the fact of the matter is that was the slow road to reality for me to explore conservatism.

What about you? Are you prepared to handle the Savage truth that liberalism is destroying your country?

THE SOMINEX GENERATION

Then again, maybe you're listening to rap music, and your next stop is a tattoo parlor. As you see it, the only problem you have is whether there's money to buy your "medical" marijuana. You care more about whether or not your satellite dish is working than the steady stream of lies the Left dishes out on your big screen.

Friend, I ask you, how bad must it get in this country before you get the picture? At what point will you see that your world is falling apart? What will it take before you understand that there are forces (both within and without) that hate your nation?

Forces that want you silenced.

They see you, the infidel, as the enemy.

They will stop at nothing until America is nothing more than an ash heap on par with any of the Krapistan countries in the Middle East.

And another thing. In this battle for the heart and soul of America, you may think you're not involved. You may believe you don't have a dog in this fight. But hear me well: There are no neutral players. Either you love this country, her freedoms, her opportunities, her beauty, and her place in history, or you don't.

Period. End of story.

I am going to make a prediction. The day will come, and very soon, when you nay-sayers and leftover leftists are going to become the target of the wrath of America. You will ultimately be seen for who you are. Especially you radical leftists who love to put your agenda before the nation. Don't you understand there's only so much that a people can tolerate until they fight back?

That day is not here.

That day will be here very soon.

When the Sominex Generation wakes up and sees what you've done to our borders, language, and culture, not to mention what you've done to our courts, churches, military, and schools, I predict you will be tried for your crimes against America.

AMERICA THE BEAUTIFUL

My radio studio is about two hundred feet in the air in downtown San Francisco overlooking the Bay. The other day it was foggy, and I was up there having a coffee and fruit salad. During a break I looked out the window and saw a white cruise liner just slipping out of the harbor.

As it glided past Alcatraz Island, my heart started to soar. I thought, "My God, this world is beautiful. What a great country we have. We have heaven on earth. We have paradise. We have so much to be thankful for. We are so blessed. No wonder everyone wants a piece of us."

Then my thoughts drifted to the maniacs, the psychotics on the Left, who continue to denigrate this great country. Here we have had more freedom than man has ever known in the history of the world, and all these Marxist-Leninists want is *more* freedom.

They're anarchists of the soul.

They're imprisoned by their own chains.

George Orwell put it another way. He said whenever he hears people screaming freedom, freedom, freedom, give us more freedom, he says he hears their chains rattling. Well, that's exactly how I see it.

The leftists are rattling their chains. You see, they're still slaves. They'll never have freedom. They don't need freedom from America. They don't need freedom from the patriarchy. They don't need freedom from heterosexuality.

No, what they need is freedom from their own dungeons.

I know what I'm talking about, and I'll continue exposing them because I don't live in Nazi Germany or Stalinist Russia. That's all. Simple as that. If you want to squelch my free speech, go ahead and try it.

By doing so, you'll reveal your true colors.

You'll be acting exactly like the Brown Shirts that you really are.

ORAL TRADITION

One way I blow off steam after my radio program is to get on my bike and ride until the sun sets. The other night I did something I had never done before. I didn't feel like doing the bike thing, so I took my wife's kayak out on the bay for the first time. I never was into kayaking. I sneered at them. "Not me," I thought. "I'm Mr. Power Boater. Only hippies use kayaks."

But then I took the thing out for the first time, and it was incredible. You glide right over the surface of the water because of the genius of the technology. You know, a flat bottom. No rudder. No keel. You just snap your wrists left-right-left-right.

I'm telling you, out there in the water, I felt like a Native American. For those few inspired moments, I was the Nanook of the South skittering across the high seas. The experience started me thinking about the Native Americans. If you look at the native peoples of America, you know, the various Indian tribes, some had a continuum of twelve thousand years living in the same territory, in the same locale.

That's twelve thousand years. No small accomplishment, especially when you figure we've only been a nation less than 250 years. How did they do it? What enabled them to pass on their values, their skills, their nobility, and their unique tribal identity on to so many generations?

It was one major element, in addition to all their keen survival skills. This may surprise you, but it was their oral traditions.

When I say oral traditions, I'm not referring to the particular variety that rose to international prominence under Bill Clinton. What we're talking about is very different.

It was the job of the *storyteller* to preserve the text of their tribal history for younger generations to hear, to learn, and to apply to their lives. The storytellers told tales of the glory of their warriors, their courage, and their victorious battles. They celebrated the purity of their women and the sanctity of their elders. They told tales of the nobility of their people. The Native Americans survived because they *glorified* their own people and their nation.

Not us. We have a nation of whacked-on-weed storytellers who debase our people everyday. They make us look dirty and treasonous and evil. No nation on earth can ever survive with such negative tales about itself. Ever. How do I know? Think about it. What family can survive if it harps on its frailties?

Or what individual can survive if he looks back only on his failings, his blunders, his missed opportunities? What man can take that kind of self-debasement? He can't. He'd commit suicide first, or die of a stroke or heart attack.

Likewise, what nation can survive that continues to focus only on its shortcomings? None.

You see, we have a Hollywood Mob that tells us stories of the weaknesses and the cowardliness of our warriors, the treason of our leaders, the corruption of our police, and the evils of our business leaders, as if the exceptions are the rule. All around us we're seeing the telltale signs that these stories have darkened the minds of Americans.

They have darkened our souls.

They have darkened our sense of patriotism.

And that's why, as a storyteller, I choose to tell about my vision of an America that rises above these attacks. It is irrelevant whether my vision of America existed exactly the way I see it. What is important is that it can exist—must exist—or we'll cease to exist.

Yes, the Hollywood Mob have become the de facto storytellers of our age. However, their vision of America is a distorted, perverse, yes, even obscene vision of our nation. With them, everything is upside-down. The criminal is the hero. The cop is the traitor. The soldier is the mass murderer. Every war we ever fought was unjust.

What kind of tribe could have survived for twelve thousand years that had such perverse storytelling? That's the question. Even if there have been—and there are—excesses within all of our militant professions, be they soldiers or the police, the fact of the matter is you don't emphasize your shortcomings in your oral tradition. You *de-emphasize* them if you love your country!

Hear me. I'm not saying you put on rose-colored glasses and sweep the mistakes under the rug. But it's one thing to recognize these excesses exist. It's quite another to zero in on the occasional abuse and call it the norm. The tail doesn't wag the dog, unless it's a tale told by Hollywood and the liberal media.

Instead, you emphasize the *greatness* of your nation, your leaders, your police, your soldiers, your religious leaders, your way of life. The storytellers of today are the Hollywood idiots who have made a perverse view of America the norm, whereas I as a storyteller choose to paint pictures of what makes us great.

Now, if both I and the Hollywood idiots err to some extent in our storytelling, I ask you, which viewpoint has more survival value for a nation? The story that errs on the side that America is a great nation? That our soldiers are heroes, and our police are brave? Or the pied piper who says our nation is evil, only founded on slavery, and all of the police and soldiers are corrupt?

Again, which story has more survival value for America?

Let's take it a step further. I ask you, which story *must* be told and which storyteller *must* be heard?

How much of Hollywood's twisted vision can a nation take until it snaps? Until it becomes an executioner of its own soul? I'm convinced that, thanks to these chronic rehab cases in Hollywood, America now suffers from amnesia.

We've forgotten our heritage.

We've forgotten our legacy.

We've forgotten what made us strong.

We've forgotten that the super glue which holds us together is composed of our borders, language, and culture.

THE AMERICAN DREAM

I remember an America that was beautiful, free, and safe. Sure, some of the politicians may have been just as corrupt as now. But somehow you could tell they still loved America. That's the difference I've discovered over time. There has always been a tension between Democrats and Republicans, but there were no traitors like there are today; it was unheard of.

Indeed, something has settled into the political structure, mainly on the Demoncat side which, frankly, is traitorous and anti-American.

Let me take you back to an earlier time in America.

When I was seven, I remember being taken out of school on a Wednesday for the Thanksgiving weekend. Mom would come for me at noon. I would wait all morning with my little heart pounding. My hands were sweating because I knew we were going away on the train. Trains were a big deal back then.

Mom would take me downtown on the subway. We traveled all the way into the bowels of Manhattan to go to Penn Station. Dad worked seven days a week. He never came with us. Now, picture me. I'm seven years old, Mom's got me by the hand—she's happy to be going to Pennsylvania to visit her brother and sister-in-law. I was thrilled because I was getting out of school and out of New York, which I hated as a kid, in a way, to visit my cousins, my aunt and uncle, and their dog (whose fur was always cold and soft from living on the closed-in back porch).

We'd get to Penn Station, and what was down there? Huge, black locomotives surrounded by all of the hustle and bustle of a train station. In those days, train stations were safe. Graffiti wasn't plastered all over the place like filthy wallpaper. Litter wasn't drifting under foot. And everywhere you walked, you didn't have to worry about stepping in fresh urine from a homeless bum panhandling to the passengers.

To me, the conductor could have been a general in the U.S. military because, as a kid, I respected anyone in a uniform, even a conductor. When you're seven years old, you figure this guy is General Patton. And he's yelling, "Alllll aboard!"

You get on that train, take a seat, and chug-a-chug-chug out of the station. Before you know it, you've traveled under the Hudson River, and you've come out in the light of New Jersey. The engine starts belching black smoke. It's billowing back through the train. What did I care? To me, that smoke represented freedom. I didn't see pollution. I saw a powerful train taking me to the freedom and adventure of Pennsylvania.

Oh, and I'd get that ham sandwich with the white bread. I'd sit back, and I'd read a comic book or maybe watch the scenery slip by. Then, before we knew it, we'd get into that station in Pennsylvania. I'll never forget the chaotic scene as long as I live. When we arrived, everyone would get off the train and merge into a sea of humanity hustling and running around looking for relatives.

Me? I'm wondering, *How will they ever find us? Will they even show up?* You don't know for a few seconds. Meanwhile, they're searching the faces on the platform, too. My doubts, like a thick cloud, start to settle on me. You just don't know if you're going to connect in such a gigantic, strange place. All of a sudden, your heart leaps. It's them. The hugs, the kisses, and in an instant, you're transported into the paradise of your relatives' embrace.

Those days are gone.

As I observe the ever-changing American landscape, I'm starting to wonder if the America I have in my mind was really a fantasy. I'm beginning to doubt that it was real. I don't know if the imaginary America I carry around in my heart ever existed. I'm starting to think that it was all a figment of my imagination. A trick of the mind. Why? Just look around you at what we've become as a nation—what the liberals have done to us.

Granted, I'm an idealist who dreams of a purer time.

I dream of a purer country.

I dream of a purer political system.

I dream of a purer people. I dream of a purer self.

Did the America of my dreams ever exist? If it did, could it ever exist again? That depends. Again, it all boils down to one thing: Who's sitting in the driver's seat? A social engineer with a neo-Marxist agenda? Or a people determined to fight for the principles that made this country the envy of the world?

I do know this: Just when I'm overwhelmed with second thoughts, I come to the microphone and find that many other Savages and Savagettes, from Boston to Bakersfield, have had this same dream.

Maybe you are one who has such memories tucked away in some dark, unused corner of the mind. You, like me, long for a better place. We wonder if there will ever be an America that maintains her borders; that respects her language, English; and that respects her cultural attributes.

Maybe the words of President Abraham Lincoln resonate with you as they do with me, when Lincoln said, "But we have forgotten God. We have forgotten the gracious Hand which preserved us in peace, and multiplied and enriched and strengthened us; and we have vainly imagined, in the deceitfulness of our hearts, that all these blessings were produced by some superior wisdom and virtue of our own."

We also know *now* is the time to ferret out the Enemy Within.

I cherish my memories of this different America. A purer America where your mother and sister could safely walk the streets at night. Where the cops were pillars of authority. Where neighbors treated neighbors with courtesy and respect. Where national pride and a sense of patriotism went hand-in-hand with mom and apple pie and the smile on your face.

Did that America really exist? I believe it did. And I pray to God that we will one day return America to her glorious roots of freedom, faith, and family. Yes, this book is about the America that once was and the

America that could be again—*if* you have the will to stand and fight against the Enemy Within.

If you refuse to back down when they sue you.

If you refuse to back down when they accuse you.

If you refuse to back down when they bruise you.

The fact of the matter is every time these Lilliputians spin their spider webs around our brains, we must speak out. We must sue and accuse *them!*

Then, and only then, will we have a prayer of steering America back on course, a course set forth by courageous men and women who gave their lives so that we, too, might dream freedom's dream.

Where do we start? By fastening your seatbelts as I strip away the veneer of deceit to bring you the naked reality of the liberal body politic. It isn't always pretty. You might even at times become uncomfortable. But as you read on, you'll find these pages always contain the Savage truth.

That is how to fight with the Enemy Within.

TWO

COURTS:
STENCH FROM THE BENCH

ederal courts and judges in America today are to be more feared than al-Qaida. These unelected, unaccountable radicals have twisted our laws to advance their own extremist agenda. They compromise our borders, language, and culture as they melt Lady Liberty down into a golden calf of their own making.

Let me be clear. Judges who enjoy unfettered judicial power control the courts. These liberal lifers act as if they are above the law, choosing to *make* law rather than *interpret* the law. Worse, they don't give a damn about what you, I, or other freedom-loving Americans cherish:

Our unique constitutional approach to government.

Our national Judeo-Christian heritage.

Our distinctive American way of life.

Our safety from alien invaders.

Our desire to openly and freely express personal faith.

What's more, the hard left-wing liberals in the Senate are relentless in their politics of personal destruction over moderate and conservative appointees. Look no further than the recent case of Miguel Estrada, nominated by George W. Bush to the United States Circuit Court of Appeals, the second most important court in the land next to the U.S. Supreme Court. The treatment of Estrada is a prime example of the inexcusable obstructionist position of the Left.

Demoncat Senator Charles Schumer, himself a minority, launched a broadside, anti-Catholic, bigoted attack against Estrada, a minority who happens to be Hispanic. Why? This God-fearing, pro-family nominee was not liberal enough for the goons on the Left. Evidently, the Left's celebration of diversity stops at the doors of the court.

Miguel Estrada is a perfect example of the American dream. A Honduran immigrant, he came here with nothing, worked his way up through law school, became a successful lawyer, clerked for Supreme Court Justice Anthony Kennedy and then joined the Department of Justice as assistant to the solicitor general. This man should have been the poster boy for *legal* immigration. Yet the rabid mad dog Left, using the yapper Charles Schumer as their lead attack dog, viciously assailed him as unqualified.

Why was Estrada alleged to be unqualified? Why was he hounded until he withdrew his name from consideration? Simply because he could not be trusted to be a useful stooge of their internationalist agenda.

But we've seen this before.

They did it to Judge Robert Bork, one of the most brilliant constitutional minds of our time. The AFL-CIO, the National Organization of Women, the American un-Civil Liberties Union, Common Cause, and the NAACP joined forces with liberal Demoncats Edward Kennedy, Paul Simon, Howard Metzenbaum, and Joey Biden to smear a good man because he believed in "judicial restraint."

Edward Kennedy unloaded both barrels just forty-five minutes after Reagan nominated Bork. Kennedy claimed, "Robert Bork's America is a land in which women would be forced into back-alley abortions, blacks would sit at segregated lunch counters, rogue police could break down citizens' doors in midnight raids, children could not be taught about evolution."[1]

Inflammatory lies, every last one of them.

Read Robert Bork's new book *Coercing Virtue* for yourself. You'll see the kind of "judicial restraint" he supports, as well as the alarming practice of "foreign jurisprudence" he cites. That's what we're seeing in law. Bork demonstrates when the Left cannot get what they want immediately through our court system, they take their issues to other countries, secure a favorable ruling, and then point to such cases as the basis for law here at home.

The radical Left is fighting so fiercely to block the appointment of all moderate judges to any court in the land because they have lost the support of the electorate—the American sheeple. The Left has discovered they can only control the country through the courts. Judge Bork said, "'The left wing of the Democratic Party relies upon the fact that they can get courts to legislate much more liberal laws than they can get through Congress or state legislatures."[2]

That's why Schumer misuses his power on the pivotal Senate Judiciary Committee to thwart presidential appointees, especially those who hold traditional Catholic values. Imagine if a senator tried to filibuster a candidate for the court who happened to be a Muslim. The media would launch a jihad of their own against such a senator.

Schumer said of Estrada's faith, "It's hard to believe that the incredibly strong ideology of this nominee won't impact how he rules if confirmed."[3] Hey Chucky, here's a tip since you obviously misinterpreted American government in junior high. Read the U.S. Constitution. Specifically, Article Six, which says, "[N]o religious test shall ever be required as a qualification to any office or public trust under the United States."

What's most saddening about the attack on Miguel Estrada by the leftists and their cohorts in the media is this: the Republicans were all talk. Republicans failed to act on their convictions for two years. At the first sign of resistance, these cowardly checkpants Republicrats ran for cover with their collective tails between their golf bags. They could have played hardball with the Schumer squad. They could have forced an end to the Dems filibuster. But not one person stood up against this character assassination.

Instead, the Republicans did the same thing as when Bill Clinton nominated neo-Marxist Ruth bad-girl Ginsburg in 1993 to the U.S. Supreme Court: *Nothing!* The Republicans permitted her to sail right through the approval process. In fact, even "conservative" Senator Bob Dole joined the Enemy Within by praising her nomination and actually voting to approve her.

I maintain Ginsburg's appointment should have been blocked by the spineless Republicans. Why? Ginsburg had been the general counsel for the most rabid mad dog leftist group in the history of America: The American un-Civil Liberties Union. Her work on behalf of the ACLU should have immediately disqualified her for an appointment to the U.S. Supreme Court. Period.

Do you have any idea how subversive the ACLU is?

The ACLU's nationwide army of more than 275,000 ultra-leftist members uses its $35 million dollar budget to attack the Ten Commandments, strip the mention of God from our schools and our public buildings, silence the Pledge of Allegiance and our National Motto ("God Bless America"), attack the Boy Scouts of America, and redefine marriage while, on the other hand, their network of more than 300 chapters works to defend the rights of pornographers, terrorists, advocates for homosexual adoption, and even child molesters.

And Ginsburg was the general counsel—not the janitor.

In fact, in her capacity as the ACLU's top legal dog for the better part of a decade, Ruthie co-authored a misguided and dangerous report ("Sex Bias in the U.S. Code") which actually recommended the age of consent for sexual activity be *lowered to just twelve years of age.*

Here's what this whack-job wrote: "Eliminate the phrase 'carnal knowledge of any female, not his wife, who has not attained the age of 16 years' and substitute a federal, sex-neutral definition of the offense . . . A person is guilty of an offense if he engages in a sexual act with another person . . . [and] the other person is, in fact, less than 12 years old."[4]

That's just for starters.

This militant leftist believes prostitution should be legalized, writing, "Prostitution as a consensual act between adults is arguably within the zone of privacy protected by recent constitutional decisions." She argues all-boy and all-girl groups should become sexually integrated, and women should be part of the military draft and assigned to combat duty.[5]

Tell me she's not a menace to society.

Tell me she's not a threat to our freedoms.

Tell me she shouldn't be impeached.

To have permitted Ginsberg's appointment is akin to appointing the general counsel of the Ku Klux Klan to the bench—only with one difference. Her robe was black. Certainly nobody in his or her right mind would favor approving a lawyer for the KKK. And yet we have the correlative of that on the Left band of the spectrum sitting on the High Court today.

By all appearances, Ginsburg's radical internationalist position is now the prevailing force on the Supreme Court. Just ask Robert Bork!

SUPREME SODOMY

The illiberal in-justices on the Supreme bench are dragging us down the road to deviance and degeneracy. I'm talking about the 2003 High Court decision (*Lawrence v. Texas*) to legalize sodomy. Of course, that's not the technical language of the case, but that's the truth of it.

The Court says anti-sodomy laws "demean" people. But doesn't legalizing sodomy demean our culture even more? Let me level with you. The *Lawrence* decision is like a loaded gun pointed at the heart of traditional marriage. I feel as if we're living in the last days of the ancient Roman Empire, which, as historian Edward Gibbon noted, fell when this kind of degenerate behavior was allowed to take over the public and then the military.

I fear America is on the same path.

While I think we can all pretty much agree the Texas sodomy law was an antiquated law at best, for the Supreme Court to decide to review the case is an example of their having their heads up their robes. Why would they decide discussing sodomy was a "significant" issue while saying Judge Moore's Ten Commandments case in Alabama did not rise to the level of their consideration?

The Supreme Court rejects a lot of cases when they don't want to be bothered. They might claim a particular case is not worth hearing or it does not fit their activist agenda. So, just by agreeing to hear this case they've acknowledged the power of the radical homosexual lobby.

Besides, the U.S. Supreme Court already settled the question of the constitutionality of sodomy cases seventeen years ago. In the 1986 Georgia case *Bowers v. Hardwick*, the High Court said, "The Constitution does not confer a fundamental right upon homosexuals to engage in sodomy."[6]

Really? What changed their minds?

From time-to-time in very rare instances the Supremes will reverse themselves. Yet in the wake of *Bowers* there were no other cases brought before the High Court that would have warranted such a U-turn in the road. So, what accounted for this sudden and radical departure from a relatively current decision?

There are two explanations. The first one borders on treason. The Supreme Court has abandoned their role as *interpreters* of our Constitution in favor of studying foreign jurisprudence when shaping their opinions. Ruth Ginsburg addressed this trend in a speech before the hard-Left American Constitution Society. She opined, "Our island or Lone Ranger mentality is beginning to change [as justices become] more open to comparative and international law perspectives."[7]

Likewise, Justice Stephen Breyer is openly questioning the relevance of our Constitution—the oldest governing document in the world—in what he sees as an age of globalism. Breyer exposed his true colors on national television. He said:

> Through commerce, through globalization, through the spread of democratic institutions, through immigration to America, it's becoming more and more one world of many different kinds of people. And how they're going to live together across the world will be the challenge, and whether our Constitution and how it fits into the governing documents of other nations, I think will be a challenge for the next generations.[8]

Did you catch this treasonous distortion?

He's wondering how *our* Constitution will fit into the documents of Zimbabwe. While he's at it, let's make sure our Constitution fits in with the Taliban's governing documents. Or maybe Cuba's government under Castro. What is Breyer saying? Are we, in the name of globalism, supposed to permit the mutilation of the genitals of women? Are we to throw all females into hooded straitjackets with eye-slits just because some backwards nation governs that way?

Despite what Ginsburg and Breyer might babble about global implications, America is not governed by a potpourri of international thinking. We are a sovereign nation governed by our *own* Constitution. Judge Bork warns about this trendy approach to law, saying, "By creating novel new international laws, the New Class hopes to outflank American legislatures and courts by having liberal views adopted abroad (by foreign governments and organizations such as the United Nations) and then imposed on the United States."[9]

Secondly, at the heart of the reversal of the 1986 sodomy ruling, I believe, is the invisible hand of Ruth Ginsburg at work behind the scenes. She's doing her best to bring an end to American democracy and to establish an oligarchy (ruled by the few) through the illiberals on this activist Supreme Court that ignores the text of the Constitution.

Contrary to how they are acting, these nine justices are not our high priests. And nothing poses a greater threat to our liberty and freedom than having a black-robed minority running roughshod over the Constitution. Need proof? Look how the high court in Israel has snatched power and authority from other branches of government.

According to Judge Bork, Israel is well on its way to "judicial imperialism." He writes, "The Israeli Supreme Court is making itself the dominant institution in the nation, wielding an authority no other court in the world has achieved. It has (among other things) gained the power to choose its own members, wrested control of the attorney general from the executive branch, and exercised the authority to override national defense measures."[10]

Unless the current move by our Supreme Court toward judicial imperialism in America is reversed, the day is coming when judicial enemies within will declare our Constitution "unconstitutional."

YOUR HONOR, I OBJECT!

If you go through your family pictures and look at your deceased male relatives, you'll find pictures of them sitting on a sofa after dinner, no doubt holding their stomachs with their pants open. I don't mean in a perverted way. I'm talking after a family dinner maybe with a few close friends, the men usually loosened up their belts, right? They'd sit back and sigh, "Ahh," as if in pain, like someone had beaten them up.

If you're Italian or Greek or Jewish, you know I'm telling the truth. The women always cooked eight, maybe ten dishes. It wasn't good enough to just eat one of them. If you didn't sample all of them, the women took it as an insult. So, just as you're cleaning your plate, they are piling on another portion. The dishes were so fatty that if you wanted to design a cardio-toxic diet to kill males, you couldn't have done any better than those ethnic cuisines.

When I was a little kid in the Bronx, that's how I sometimes remember my dad and several of his friends. They would sit on our sofa for an after-dinner meeting with their belts open. On more than one occasion, I listened as they discussed my future as if I weren't in the room. You know what? They all agreed I'd make a good lawyer. I guess I had a good command of speech even then.

But me, a lawyer? Frankly, as I thought about it back then, the idea of memorizing tons and tons of books in order to trick people just didn't appeal to me. Not in the least.

Ironically, years later, when I was about seventeen and had my driver's license, a friend of mine got a ticket for going through a red light. I went with him to traffic court. It was decided on the way that I would be his lawyer. Maybe it was fate. You know, my big break.

When I got up in front of the judge, I started to shake. I began by saying,

"Your Honor, my friend did not know he had to stop for the red light once his car was already through the intersection and the light had changed."

The judge looked down upon me with his stern face. With his gavel he slammed, "Ignorance of the law is not a defense!" My friend was fined $50 bucks and I knew my career as a lawyer was over. As you'll see, we need to expand on what that judge said that summer afternoon. Today, my verdict would be: "Distortion of the law is not a defense."

SILENCE THE COURT

I'll tell you exactly why we're losing the country from within. Just dig into the history of activist judges on the bench. Many have prior history with the ultra-Left ACLU. Every morning these radicals wrap themselves in their black capes and act like some sort of socialist superheroes. They swoop down on unsuspecting Americans and twist laws to suit their agenda.

For example, Prop. 209, the California Civil Rights Initiative, had been approved by 55 percent of voters and would have ended affirmative racism in state hiring. But the ACLU joined several other militant groups including the feminist Equal Rights Advocates organization in filing a lawsuit against the measure.

A lone ranger federal magistrate, Chief U.S. District Judge Thelton Henderson, a Jimmy Carter appointee, heard the case and denied the wishes of nearly 5 million Californians by single-handedly overturning Prop. 209. Oh, did I mention Judge Henderson was a former board member of both the ACLU and Equal Rights Advocates?[11]

Or, take the case in Washington State where voters overwhelmingly approved a statewide referendum, which validated the state's statute banning assisted suicide. The provision in question prohibited all persons from "knowingly causing or aiding other persons in ending their lives." Five years later, in *Compassion in Dying v. Washington*, Judge Stephen Reinhardt of the Ninth Circuit Court of Appeals cited public opinion polls as a basis for overturning the will of the people.

His closing comments blasted people with "religious convictions" saying "they are not free . . . to enforce their views, their religious convictions, or their philosophies on all the other members of a democratic society."[12] Why am I not surprised to learn Reinhardt's wife, Ramona Ripston, is the executive director of the Southern California chapter of the ACLU?[13]

In similar fashion, there's no better example of how one man tried to work the system than what we saw in California in the fall of 2003. Gray Davis, failed governor, tried to block the democratic process of a recall by the people. In the eleventh hour of the recall campaign, he granted driver's licenses to illegal aliens primarily from Mexico in order to get votes.

What is doubly absurd about this move is the fact that immigration is a federal, not a state matter. Davis's own office has said that numerous times. For example, the radicals in California once fought a ballot initiative, Prop. 187, which would have denied funding for illegal aliens in terms of education and medication. Voters in the state overwhelmingly approved the measure at the ballot box.

The radicals shopped the outcome to a federal judge arguing immigration is a federal matter and must be decided by a federal court. U.S. District Court Judge Mariana Pfaelzer overturned the votes of 6 million Californians, forcing them to pay valuable tax dollars to support medication and education for *illegal* immigrants.

Now, when the shoe is on the other foot, Californians get dismissed again. Showing his twisted mind, Gray Davis turned around and stated that granting driver's licenses to illegal aliens is a *state* matter!

Here's where our federal government is failing us.

George Bush has the power to overturn Davis's decision either under immigration laws or the Homeland Security Act. Because only God knows how many terrorists will now be getting driver's licenses in the state of California and a full set of IDs, if not citizenship, as a result of this backdoor asylum of illegal aliens.

VEILED JUSTICE

Judicial tyrants represent one side of the coin. On the other side we find a host of opportunistic, obnoxious, and obstructionist lawsuits. I'll give you several choice examples. You've probably heard about Sultaana Freeman, the Muslim woman in Florida who refused to remove her *niqab* for a driver's license photo. Sultaana, previously known as Sandra Kellar, converted to Islam in 1997. She was unwilling to uncover her face because of her interpretation of her religion, Islam. She says the Koran forbids her to remove the veil.

Guess what? You live in America, honey, and American law forbids having your face covered on your license. It should be pretty obvious why there are photos on driver's licenses—so law enforcement officials can see your face and make sure it's really you driving the car.

For all we know, it could be Osama bin Laden hiding behind a veil!

What if I'm a member of the Ku Klux Klan and I say it's my religious belief to wear the hood? Can I wear my white sheet and hood for my license photo? How about those sadomasochists in the dungeons around San Francisco? What if they argue sadomasochism is their religion? Could they wear a leather bondage mask in the photo?

Where does it stop?

Isn't this a matter of national security? Isn't the safety of our nation more important than one woman's religious beliefs? I say, if she doesn't like it here, move to *niqab*-friendly Saudi Arabia. Then again, even the Arabs insist women take off their veils for official photos.

By the way, according to news reports this same woman used the same phony religious defense when Child Protection Services officials tried to examine one of her two twin foster children for bruises and a broken arm in 1998. She claimed her brand of Islam forbade the three-year-olds to disrobe. Talk about a cover up. A year later, she was convicted of aggravated battery and went to the slammer for eighteen months.[14]

But we're supposed to feel sorry for Sultaana. The libs say we need to be more *seeennnsitive* to her plight. After all, she said she can't even drive to the store to buy diapers for her son. Naturally, the ACLU is defending her in court. Big surprise there. They love to twist both common sense and our laws beyond recognition.

I find it interesting in this particular case that the ACLU has sided *with* religion. Remember, the ACLU are the same mad dogs who don't want the words "In God We Trust" displayed in public places because that might offend non-religious folks. And yet, they seem to have no problem defending a distortion of Islamic law instead of Florida law.

While the judge hearing this case saw through Sultaana's veiled argument, I must point out the sect of Islam with which she aligns herself (that forbids her to remove her veil and disrobe her children) also *forbids women to drive!*

Are you seeing a pattern of deception here?

Again, let me be clear. I don't care what religion you embrace. But when you come and live in America, you must observe American laws, especially when our national security is at stake.

OUT TO LUNCH

I don't know about you, but every day seems to bring another crazy experience my way. Normally, around lunchtime, I begin to walk around the streets of San Francisco looking for that special meal. I'm scanning the stores trying to find something to consume which will give me the energy for a good radio show.

Recently, I changed things up. I ate in the suburbs. I took the risk of eating with the flaming liberal psychos in the area of Sausalito, just over the bridge. As you well know, I happen to love food, and I especially love a good buffet. This particular day I settled on an Indian buffet. Maybe it was the curry. But something called to me from the streets and I just followed the fragrance.

It might surprise you I actually prefer a buffet to so-called fine dining. The truth is I get very antsy waiting for food. I hate it. I hate nothing more in life than sitting around while the guy with the nametag launches into a speech, like, "Hello my name is Fredrick and our chef's special is a pan-seared, fresh water trout presented with new potatoes and a sprig of . . ." You get the picture. By the time he gets through with the specials, I want to run out and eat a fishburger.

So I prefer a good buffet now and again. In my view, the whole point of going to a buffet is you're in and out quickly and you get to pick what you like. This particular afternoon, I walk in the door, and I'm ready to eat right away. Right? Wrong. Not in liberal Sausalito.

Let me tell you something. I manage to attract liberals like a magnet. And I don't mean the nice ones. I get the real cheap ones. The real stinkers. The real RDDBs on trust funds. The retired professors out on disability. Happens all the time.

Anyway, I'm feasting my eyes on the spread. I grabbed a plate and made a huge mistake. I was nice for a second. I let my guard down. I let this liberal-looking college girl cut in front of me. The truth was, she didn't even ask if she could—she just jumped the line. Normally, my instinct might have been to tell her to get in line. But I was nice.

Immediately I felt as though I was behind an old lady at the supermarket. Know what I'm saying? This liberal girl with a pierced lip is taking her sweet time at the buffet. I glance over my shoulder and watch the line backing up in the restaurant. She's clueless. She's personally examining every piece of food. Every grain of Basmati rice.

The whole time she has that smile, that coy smile liberals get in ethnic restaurants. I could see her pea brain trying to pinpoint the origins of each spice used by the Indian chef. I'm standing there boiling. I'm tempted to ask, "Have you ever eaten at a buffet?" I can see this great liberal education she received was going to good use. She doesn't even know the basic etiquette of a lunch line.

But I was being patient as the line moved at snail speed. The people behind me are wondering if she's even past the rice yet. I began to fume. The canned background music with the Indian sitar was getting on my nerves and the tempura was building up inside me. All I wanted was that chicken jalfrezi, the prawn bhuna, and the rice. Maybe a piece of garlic naan.

But she, of course, positioned her fat behind so I couldn't even maneuver around her in the narrow hallway. At this point I know she's doing it on purpose. I know liberals in general do these things on purpose. Why do they do it? Just because they can. Just because they seem to enjoy jerking our chain and pushing our limits.

Whether it's in the buffet line, or a court of law, the liberals by their nature go to great extremes to work us over. Or, as you'll see, to work the system. In the end, our ability to maintain law and order and justice is emasculated.

SHOCKING COURT CASES

You won't believe the kinds of things people are getting away with in American courts thanks to the liberal judges and a newly manufactured legal loophole some slimy RDDB lawyer invented called the "cultural defense." This defense tactic is nothing more than a subversive strategy used by the snake oil ACLU-types to slither around the law.

The cultural defense goes something like this: "Your Honor, I know my client killed his wife here in America, but she cheated on him. In the village in China where my client was born, it's actually okay to kill your wife if she cheats on you. My client was just acting in accordance with his culture."

You might think I made that up. I didn't. That was an actual case tried in the New York State Supreme Court. I am disgusted to report this cultural defense strategy worked in *People v. Chen*.

According to court records, Doug Lu Chen, a Chinese immigrant, lived in New York for a year when he learned his wife, Jian Wan Chen, had an extramarital affair. Several weeks later, on September 7, 1987, Chen whacked his wife in the head eight times with a hammer.

During his defense, a professor of anthropology from Hunter College, whose name is not worth mentioning, offered this gem. According to Professor Nutcase, Chen's wife's infidelity would be viewed in the traditional

Chinese culture as a sign of Chen's weakness. Murdering her could be explained by *understaaaaanding* his cultural background.

Mind you, nobody claimed Chen was insane or irrational under pressure. His lawyer stuck with the ludicrous "cultural differences" argument, which supposedly diminished his capacity. Justice Edward K. Pincus bought this gibberish. In the wake of this so-called expert testimony, Pinhead Pincus argued, "cultural factors lessen the defendant's responsibility for certain crimes."[15]

Chen ended up with a charge of manslaughter in the second degree and was sentenced to only five years *probation* after murdering his wife in cold blood.

Why should we be surprised?

I wish I could say this was an isolated, far-fetched exception. But it's not. Not even close. Consider these backward distortions of our legal system by the Red Diaper Doper Babies who are leading the charge:

- A Hmong immigrant forcibly took a young Laotian-American woman from her job at Fresno State University. He sexually assaulted her against her will. Facing rape and kidnapping charges, he maintained his behavior was nothing more than the "customary" way of choosing a bride. While it sounds like this creep should have gotten thirty years, evidently the judge bought his "capture the bride" cultural defense. He was sentenced to a mere 120 days in jail and was required to pay a small cash fine. (P.S., NOW did not comment on this case.)

- In Anaheim, California, on New Year's Day in 2002, a five-year-old boy stole a pack of gum from a local store. His father, Wellington Soto, was a Guatemalan immigrant who decided to teach his boy a lesson. Did he give him a spanking? Time out? No. As punishment, Soto held the kid's fingers over an open gas flame. Noticing the burns, the boy's teacher reported the abuse. The case went to Orange County Superior Court Judge James Perez who could have thrown Soto in jail for upwards of six years upon conviction of child abuse. Instead, citing the "crosscurrent of customs and habits"[16] of the Latin culture, Judge Perez fined Soto a measly $100 for torching his kid's hand.

- A pair of Cambodian refugees in California killed and ate a German shepherd. The thirty-year-old men claimed they didn't *know* eating dog meat was illegal. Besides, they did it all the time in their country of origin. Eating dog meat was part of their cultural heritage. A judge agreed and dismissed the charges of animal cruelty.[17] I thought ignorance of the law was no excuse.

I must mention one last cultural defense case. It centers on Fumiko Kimura, a Japanese woman in California. Kimura, ashamed and despondent upon learning of her husband's affair with another woman, headed for the ocean. She took a bus to Santa Monica with her two kids and proceeded to wade into deep waters. She fought against their protests to catch another breath, to survive, to see another day. She held those innocent children under water until they had both drowned. She was about to drown herself when she was spotted and prevented from her suicide.

Kimura was initially charged with first-degree murder in *People v. Kimura*. During her trial, her lawyers claimed her behavior could be explained in light of a traditional custom called *oyako-shinju*, "parent-child suicide." Once again, this absurd cultural relativism argument won the day. Kimura was sentenced to time served (one year) and probation.[18]

Today, she's a free woman.

Not so for Susan Smith. Remember her? Just like Kimura, Smith drowned her two kids. The only difference between these two lunatics is the method they used—and their nationality. Smith, instead of using her hands, used a car to dump her kids into a South Carolina lake.

The end results were the same. Two dead children. At present, Susan Smith is spending the rest of her life behind bars, as well she should. After all, Smith couldn't hoodwink the courts by appealing to some clever cultural strategy.

Mind you, I am not arguing Smith should get off because Kimura copped a break. Rather, these two cases demonstrate what happens to American justice when we allow liberal lawyers and clueless judges to "customize" the law. Such legal schizophrenia is astounding. When will we learn multiculturalism is a complete and total fraud? How long will we give lawbreakers a free pass when they eat dogs?

When they rape young women?

When they burn a child's fingers?

When they drown their children?

When they murder their spouse?

What's next?

How much more of this can America take before it snaps? Activist ACLU lawyers and the judges who ignore our laws and invent new ones are like termites. Case by case, these vermin are eating away at our nation's foundation. It's just a matter of time before this house of cards collapses. Am I the only one who understands this insanity must stop?

Let me remind you about the three most important words in the Savage Nation: Borders, Language, and Culture. It's that last word, culture, which applies in each of these cases.

LAWYERS FROM HELL

Among *all* internal enemies, in my opinion, the ACLU has done the greatest damage to our nation. My heart breaks when I see this dangerous pack of maniacs tearing at the heart and soul of freedom. Books have been written on their outrageous litigation. As far as I'm concerned, the ACLU is the KKK on the Left. While they don't wear hoods or burn crosses, they are more dangerous. They don't need to wear hoods because they no longer fear being found out.

Why Republicans continue to cater to them as though they're a branch of government is beyond me. That's the crux. Who the hell elected the ACLU to office? Who made the ACLU the fourth branch of government? And why does the media always turn to the ACLU for an opinion on any significant legal discussion in the United States of America?

While many well-meaning American citizens support civil liberties groups like the ACLU and the National Lawyers Guild, they're doing so not understanding the true agenda and nature of these organizations. To be redundant, they are using the courts to advance their internationalist, anti-God, anti-traditional family, and hate-America ideals.

In communities throughout the country, the ACLU membership is fighting to expunge all signs of faith. Aside from their countless attacks on the Ten Commandments, this band of militants is operating on many fronts to rob you of your faith and freedoms.

- They have threatened the National Parks Service to remove three small bronze plaques, each bearing a Bible verse, from a display in the Grand Canyon National Park.

- They fought and successfully prevented the Boy Scouts of America from maintaining their 50-year-old lease of Camp Balboa in San Diego over the Scouts policy regarding homosexuals and their core belief in God.

- They are fighting to block a voluntary faith-based initiative in Harvey, Illinois, a crime-infested suburb of Chicago, because in their warped view it's government promotion of religious values.

- They are fighting to overturn Florida's ban on gay adoption.

- They asked the Virginia Supreme Court to legalize cross burning on public property. In their view, the current state ban suppresses the freedom of speech for the Ku Klux Klan and like-minded pyromaniacs.[19]

- They are fighting to prevent students from reciting the Pledge of Allegiance at Cherry Creek High School in Colorado.

- They led the assault to recall the recall vote of California's failed Governor Gray Davis.[20] Using their usual tricks of distortion and obstruction, the ACLU once again tried a legal coup to overturn the will of millions of voters.

- They are defending, pro bono, the North American Man Boy Love Association (NAMBLA), a despicable group of child molesters.

You better read that last one again.

Here's the sad story.

In October of 1997, 10-year-old Jeffrey Curley was playing at his home in Cambridge, Massachusetts, when two homosexual lovers decided to lure Jeffrey into a sexual encounter. Charles Jaynes, one of the gay men, had been a member of NAMBLA for about a year. NAMBLA is an organization that advocates sex with children.

Jaynes wrote in his personal diary, discovered by police, that finding NAMBLA "was a turning point in [the] discovery of myself. NAMBLA's Bulletin helped me to become aware of my own sexuality and acceptance of it."[21]

I'll give you just two sentences from the NAMBLA publication he's talking about. Tell me this isn't outright pedophilia propaganda: "Call it love, call it lust, call it whatever you want. We desire sex with boys, and boys, whether society is willing to admit it, desire sex with us."[22]

According to trial records, the men secretly stole Jeffrey's bicycle and then offered to help him find it. After a bogus search, they told Jeffrey they would buy him a new bicycle. What did Jeffrey know? He was just an innocent kid who took them at their word.

On the way to the store the men tried to pay Jeffrey for sex. When he refused, they suffocated him with a rag soaked in gasoline, dragged his lifeless body back to their apartment and sodomized his corpse. They zipped his body into a plastic container before they dumped him in a nearby river.

The Cambridge police found NAMBLA literature and a manual published by NAMBLA called "Rape and Escape" that, according to one eye witness, graphically details how pedophiles might lure, befriend, and rape a child, then avoid detection and prosecution. Understandably, the parents of little Jeffrey have sued NAMBLA for its role in what amounts to an accessory to murder.

Who in their right mind would defend NAMBLA?

What kind of person or organization would defend such a beastly scab on the face of society?

The ACLU, that's who. Free of charge, too.

John Roberts, executive director of the American Civil Liberties Association of Massachusetts, had this to say about the case. Listen to this genius: "While we join with all others in deploring the heinous crimes committed against Jeffrey Curley, two people have been convicted of his murder and are serving life sentences."[23]

Okay, stop right there. Don't you just love the way the ACLU always offers such a moving tribute to the victim? You'd never know he was talking about the rape and murder of a ten-year-old boy.

This vacant soul makes me so angry I'd like to break something. Is he implying justice has been served? The bad guys are in jail, right? Wrong. Not all of the bad guys are behind bars. The reprehensible beasts of NAMBLA are still peddling the same kind of material that contributed to Jeffrey's death. And if you can believe this, Amazon.com is selling subscriptions to NAMBLA's official periodical on their website even as I write.[24]

ACLUM legal director John Reinstein, who's in bed with NAMBLA as their legal defense, puts the proverbial free speech spin on Jeffrey's death. Reinstein had the nerve to say, "I think it is fair to say that most people disagree with NAMBLA and that many would find its publications offensive. Regardless of whether people agree with or abhor NAMBLA's views, holding the organization responsible for crimes committed by others who read their materials would gravely endanger important First Amendment freedoms."[25]

Why don't you give that canned speech to Jeffrey.

Tell Jeffrey about being in a grave!

Tell Jeffrey about losing his precious freedom.

Tell Jeffrey about abhorring NAMBLA.

Or did you forget Jeffrey was tortured, raped, and murdered at the hands of two grown men who just happened to fill their minds with NAMBLA's material?

Are you ready for the kicker? The ACLU asked the judge to impose a gag order on the case. How amazingly ironic the ACLU, those self-appointed, self-righteous, high-and-mighty defenders of free speech (remember, they are defending NAMBLA on the grounds of free speech) would want to prohibit the details and truth of this trial from ever becoming public.

Maybe you're now beginning to see why Americans must impeach Ruth Bader Ginsburg from the Supreme Court. After all, at the core she is one of them, having been their chief counsel for years. What further proof do you need before you recognize the ACLU is the epitome of evil and the Enemy Within?

NO MORE MONKEY BUSINESS

My dad's small antique store was on the Lower East Side of New York. He specialized in nineteenth century French bronzes. They were fascinating to me as a kid. I learned a lot about art in those days because I stared at the bronzes all day long. I remember how the figures would come in with a brown or black patina, which had accumulated over the ages.

To me, the patina was gorgeous. But the nouveauxs who were buying them wanted to turn them into lamps or bookends. They wanted them to look golden, because underneath the patina was the original bronze color. So they'd say to my dad, "Okay, Ben, I'll take that and turn it into a lamp, maybe mount the thing on the wall."

They'd make their purchase and a certain number would be left for me to clean over the weekend down in the store basement. Down I'd go into the pit, the dirty, horrible, dank, Ludlow Street subterranean cellar filled with huge old wine barrels. And, a toilet from hell with a mirror on the wall that had been speckled from chemicals.

I'm down there from about age twelve, thirteen, fourteen, armed with a toothbrush. There was only one other guy, Louie, from the Bowery who helped out once in a while. Nobody else in the history of the world would do this. I'd get those rubber gloves pulled up to my elbows, and I'd drop some white pellets into water and turn it into a cyanide solution. Then I'd take the brush and rub the figure until the patina came off the bronze.

It would take me an hour or two of chemical scrubbing to make just one bronze figure into a golden prize. So I'm rubbing off the patina thinking about where I'm going to go that night, on a date, or hang out with my friends, or drag race, or whatever. Meanwhile, my face would be blotched from the chemicals. And I'm rubbing and cleaning, and it's like a Dickens basement.

The funny thing is, one day I go to my chemistry class and tell my teacher what I was doing. You know, that I was using cyanide balls as a cleaning solution (my father had a huge chemical supply). You should have seen the look on her face. She said, "What? Michael, they use cyanide balls at San Quentin to kill people. But don't get too worried, there's a sodium cyanide and a potassium cyanide."

"Really?" I asked.

For a moment I'm thinking this is very much like when Abraham almost slew Isaac. So I went to my dad and said, "Do you know they use cyanide to kill people with the gas?" He smiled and said, "Yea, but that's the other one. I'm giving you the correct ion." So back to the dungeon I go. The time usually went by faster when Louie stopped by.

Louie, I remember, was a tall, thin guy. I came to like Louie very much because he was a bright man, although he was an intermittent alcoholic who was known to go on long binges and get beaten up. Don't get me wrong. He wasn't a bum with urine-stained pants and strong breath. No. He just let the alcohol get the best of him from time to time. Still, he was an intelligent and kind man.

Louie lived alone in a cold-water flat in the Williamsburg section of Brooklyn. One day, Louie purchased a pet monkey. Not just a petite, spider monkey, but a large wooly monkey, the kind you might see at a circus. Almost overnight, Louie became a different man.

He would come to my father's store with a smile on his face talking about his monkey, Charlie. He would tell us Charlie did this and did that.

How Charlie rode on his back, how he sat on the sofa. How Charlie would hang out with him when he'd drink and when he'd smoke.

He'd tell us how Charlie would sleep next to him and how much he loved that monkey. This went for some weeks. And then, out of the blue, Louie came in all bandaged up with a dark, depressed look on his face. I said, "Louie, what happened?" Turned out Charlie had attacked Louie one day and Louie had to give Charlie away.

Here's the connection.

Civil liberty groups like the ACLU and the National Lawyers Guild are like Louie's monkey. You think they're your friends. You welcome them into your towns, homes, schools, and churches. And sure as it happened to Louie, the day has already come that the monkey of civil liberties has torn your face and body politic wide open.

It's time to cut your ties to the civil libertarians and get the monkey off of your back. But how, you ask? Read on.

WE CAN BEAT THEM IF WE UNITE

Over the years, Louie became somewhat of a work friend, although he had never been to our house. But, one day after work, my dad drove him to our house and he ate dinner with us. After dinner, I sat around the dining table with Louie and learned a few tricks, like how to bend nails with my bare hands. I was simply amazed. Here I was, a skinny twelve-year-old kid and here was this longhaired, sallow-faced sort of vagrant alcoholic teaching me how to use mind over matter.

"You see, Michael, here's how you do it," said Louie. "You take that long nail and you put it between your hands. You put both thumbs up against the center point of the nail and, with your other fingers, pull down toward you. Now concentrate," he said to me, "on the center of that nail. Don't break your concentration. Push those thumbs straight at that center point of the nail. Never for one second lose your focus."

"You will soon feel the nail heating up," he told me. "Right at the center point where you are concentrating and applying the pressure. This means the molecules in the nail are starting to move because of the pressure you're applying. That's the point at which you drive forward with your thumbs and pull down with your hands a little more forcefully. At that point, the nail will begin to bend."

Let me tell you something. It was truly amazing for me to learn how to bend nails with my bare hands from a man like Louie. He wasn't particularly strong. He wasn't exceptionally gifted. But he knew the secret of inner power. And, if I could learn how to bend nails, anybody could.

Likewise, while it appears the ACLU, the National Lawyers Guild, and other extremist left-wing groups are hard as nails and unable to be bent, if all of us freedom- and justice-loving Americans were to unite our energies and apply the proper pressures, I'm sure we could bend them like a two-penny nail.

THREE

HEALTH-CARE:
WHO POISONED THE SYSTEM?

When I was a kid, I worked in a drug store. It was one of those mom-and-pop stores in Queens, New York, long before there was a chain store on every corner. I'll never forget Doc, the pharmacist. He was a large, old-style Italian man with a short leg. I remember he used to wear a large shoe with something like an 8-inch heel. The story was he fell off a train. Maybe he was born that way. Doesn't matter. I looked at it once. That was it.

I still remember the smell in Doc's drug store. It was incredibly euphoric, like a mixture of Old Spice and a freshly scrubbed kitchen washed down with lab alcohol. I can't describe it any better than that. I'd like to bottle that stuff and sell it. I'd call it "Pharmacy Smell." You know, maybe spray it around my bathroom.

Anyway, I have great memories of working in his pharmacy. I was fourteen and couldn't wait to work in the store. Doc paid me 75 cents an hour. I didn't know he was exploiting me to save a half a buck an hour.

He gave me a job. I didn't care the minimum wage was $1.25. I would have worked for 50 cents an hour, just to have an after-school job.

At lunch, his wife would bring him veal parmigiana or some other succulent dish in a big porcelain tray with a top. He would sit at his desk and polish off whatever she sent him. He'd eat that meal for a good hour. While he was eating, Doc made me the pharmacist. I'd fill out prescriptions. How hard was it?

I would look at the paper that read "Penicillin, 250 mg." I could hardly see the counter, but I'd look for the big jar that said "Penicillin." I would get it down, pour it out, count twelve pills, and that was it. You didn't need a degree. It only got tricky when some crackpot doctor wanted something ground up. You know, I'm supposed to get 2 mg. of sulfur powder and put in the breast of a tsetse fly. I felt like I was mixing a potion for a Mesopotamian cult.

So anyway, I'm counting pills. I'm not bothering anyone. The doctor is quietly eating and passing gas over at his desk, lifting the leg. Into the pharmacy walks a guy wearing a suit. Picture Mickey Rooney in an early movie if you want an image. I didn't know who he was. He peers over the counter at me. I'm this little kid with freckles filling prescriptions. He says, "Hi, how are you, son?"

How was I to know he was a liberal bureaucrat?

I said, "Fine. Can I help you, Mister?"

He said, "No, no, just looking." A minute later he goes over to Doc with a sad, long face like a Basset hound. Doc, digesting the last of the Veal Parmigiana, wipes his mouth. The guy starts with, "Uh, I got bad news for you, Doc." He pulls out his official ID. Turns out the guy was a New York City inspector.

Doc got fined, and I lost my job that day.

Medicine and health-care in America have come a long way since then, as you well know. Most of the changes have been for the better. Just look at the advances in medicine. The miraculous medical procedures. The laser eye surgery. The life-saving emergency care. American doctors are routinely doing things in hospitals today kings of years past couldn't begin to dream of.

On the other hand, mom-and-pop drug stores and family doctors have vanished. They've been replaced by giant, faceless pharmacies, PPOs, and HMOs. We've lost the personal touch, sense of individualism, and personal dignity we once enjoyed.

We're just cattle with a number.

Gone, too, is that wonderful pharmacy smell.

But something else is at work in the field of medicine. Listen carefully, especially those of you abusing medical marijuana. The entire American health-care system as we've known it is slipping into a sinkhole from which we may never recover. If you think we have health-care problems now, just wait. If something drastic doesn't change—and soon—I give us ten, maybe twenty years and our hospitals will be like they are in Havana, Toronto, and London.

Why is this happening?

Two reasons. First, because the culture has been under attack for thirty straight years by the radical Left who fight for the rights of the parasites. As you'll see, the Ingrates, the Inmates, and the Illegals have infected our system of health-care.

These parasites are devouring the host and must be stopped.

Secondly, the Enemy Within has set America on a slow creep toward universal health-care—which is really socialized medicine. Never mind the fact socialized medicine is a flop. Everywhere it's been tried, it's been a complete failure. It's Third World medicine. Hear me. This neo-Marxist practice is the surest way to bankrupt the economy and destroy America.

PICK YOUR POISON

The first step toward universal health-care is the relentless push for prescription drug benefits for seniors. For years, we've heard Hillary, Gephardt, Daschle, Lieberman, and Gore prescribing free drugs. We're hearing it again as candidates eye the presidential election of 2004. On the surface, it sounds very noble. Who wants grandma eating Alpo so she can pay for her medication?

But don't be fooled. Even after George Bush doled out a drug plan more generous than Gore promised during his failed presidential bid, the Dems screamed for more. These insatiable politicians won't stop with free drugs. They are intoxicated with the idea of prescribing universal health-care, their ultimate goal, for all Americans.

What's wrong with that?

Everything.

Universal health-care is a carrion call for the bottom-feeders out there who think I owe them a living. They think I owe them health-care, housing, a car, a chicken in every pot, and pot for every chicken! What gives them the right to reach into my pocket for a handout? I owe you nothing. I don't owe you housing, I don't owe you a job, and I don't owe you health-care. That is what Marxists have promised from the beginning of the Bolshevik Revolution.

Sure, I might see a needy guy struggling to make it and choose to help him. But that's *my* decision.

These are the facts: While there was universal health-care in Russia, it was a poor system for the average Soviet citizen. While there was universal housing in Russia, it was sub-standard, often without heat. While there were universal jobs provided in Russia, you wouldn't want one. That is why we must stick to the free market system.

The entire Democrat machine is geared toward Marxism in one form or another, or communism if you want, Stalinism if you like. You think I'm making this up? Just listen to Dick Gephardt. He announced: "I want to get everybody covered with health insurance."[1]

What's this?

Is Dick offering to write a check to cover the tab from his personal account? Leave it to Dr. Savage to help you decode Gephardt's grandiloquence. When he says "I," he really means "you." Sheeple, he is saying, "*You* must pay to make sure *everybody* has health insurance (including people who refuse to work and illegal aliens)."

But we have heard this all before. Al Gore admitted his long-term strategy was to use the kids first to reach his utopian universal health-care nirvana. He said, "We will move toward universal health coverage, step by step, starting with all children. Let's get all children covered by the year 2004."[2]

Leading the carrion call for universal health-care is Madam Clinton. She's been at it ever since she chaired the subversive Task Force on National Health Care Reform behind closed doors in 1993. Since then, she has admitted, "We need to take step-by-step progress toward providing [health] insurance for every American."[3]

Every American? Who's going to pay for that?

You and me, that's who.

Evidently, Gephardt, Gore, and Hillary are not happy with America as it is. They would like to see it look more like Cuba, Canada, or England. Of course, illegal aliens and welfare bums rejoice whenever Hillary (who they see as Martha Washington when she's really more like Eva Peron) pushes "free" health-care. These freeloaders really expect to get something for nothing.

Here's why that's shortsighted.

GONE TO THE DOGS

What is it I oppose about universal health-care?

In a word, it will bankrupt America. There is a limit to how much you can provide a society. Where do you think the cost to pay for universal health-care comes from? It comes from the hard-working taxpayer, not the government.

This means you must pay more taxes to pay for someone else's misfortune. It means robbing Peter to pay Paul. It means small and large businesses will have to put their companies at risk in order to give everyone—including inmates and illegal aliens—a gold-plated medical care system.

There's another reason.

Universal health-care destroys the medical system.

In every country where it has been implemented, people suffer.

Witness Canada—where health-care is "free," but access to it is largely unavailable. Canada's socialist, government-run system is one of the worst. With an extreme shortage of doctors, nurses, and hospital beds, the wait for basic treatment is horrendous.

Like geese, Canadians in need of health-care flock to America by the thousands. Which explains why hospitals in New York and Washington place billboards advertising their services to Canadians who, by law, are not permitted to pay for private health-care in Canada.

Need an MRI?

If you're in Canada, forget about it. The wait is at least eight months. Unless, of course, you're a dog. When it comes to MRI machines, veterinary services, which are privately funded, are better equipped than most Canadian hospitals. Several years ago, *The Washington Post* reported the true story of a man with a brain tumor who desperately needed an MRI. Rather than wait for months and months, he scheduled an appointment with a local vet by registering under the name Fido. He paid cash.[4]

Tell me that isn't madness.

Britain's system of socialized medicine, where citizens are brought up to believe they will receive the best care in the world, is another example of why we should avoid universal health-care like the plague. According to the World Health Organization, 25,000 people will die unnecessarily of cancer every year in Britain. Why? Because experts have found Britain has "third world cancer care."[5]

I'm talking about Britain here, not Bangladesh.

This is what we're going to do to our system if we embrace national health-care. Open your eyes. Pay attention. Learn from those countries around you. Socialized medicine is an abject failure. As I've said, we will bankrupt not only the medical system but also the whole economy. Those proposing universal health-care ought to get their heads examined.

Yet, such evidence doesn't stop Hillary and the gang on the Left from announcing plans to provide what amounts to socialized medicine in the USA. They present a multi-billion dollar national health-care program as though it were the latest and greatest thing in the world. They're putting one over on the American people because many of us don't understand what's at stake when we hear the phrase "universal health-care."

Their promises sound oh-so-shiny and new. And we sheeple reach for them like a child, as though they are toys dangling over our crib. In reality, their idea is really nothing more than dead man's pants.

It's beyond me how anybody can think a socialist-based approach to medicine is an improvement to what we have in America. Show me one country where it's a better system.

Show me where it's superior.

Show me where waits are shorter.

Show me where there's greater freedom of choice.

Show me where the doctors and surgeons are better.

Show me where the medicines are more sophisticated.

Show me where people have faster access to treatment.

You can't, because such a country doesn't exist.

If the care is so wonderful in nations with socialized medicine, then go to Cuba for your next cardiac bypass. Fly down there. I'm sure Dr. Castro will be happy to perform surgery with his dirty smock. Dr. Castro went to medical school for maybe two years and did his internship operating on donkeys. Go ahead; take your hemorrhoids to Cuba. You'll find tenth-rated doctors with no medication on their shelves, long waiting lines, inferior surgical capabilities, and inferior diagnostic tools.

That's what universal health-care brings.

You see, leftists like Hillary are predictable. They appeal to the sick, injured, downtrodden, and the losers with their hands out, for one reason.

Getting the vote.

I say: Beware of an enemy bearing gifts. It's a shell game. Sometimes, instead of taking away your freedom, the Enemy Within appears to be giving you a gift. In reality, the gift comes with strings attached. They "give" you "free" health-care, then enslave you with a tax burden so heavy you go into cardiac arrest from the load.

STRONG MEDICINE

Here's a personal story of how a family can survive without universal health-care. I was a junior in college. My father, as you know, owned his own little store. He worked as hard as any man I ever knew. One day while we were in the Catskill Mountains in upstate New York, he had a heart attack. It was traumatic. A real tragedy. It struck me like a bolt of lightning out of heaven.

Out of hell, frankly.

For the first time in my life, I see a strong man, who I always looked up to, lying in an oxygen tent. He was completely helpless. As we waited for the doctor's report, Mom and I wondered where would we get the money for Dad's treatment. We had no other income. He was the sole provider. In those days, moms didn't work outside of the home. And, we had no health-care because there was no health-care insurance in those days.

After what felt like an eternity, the doctor came into the waiting room. I'll never forget it as long as I live. He says to the family, "Well, his heart is like a tire with a flat. It's like a tire that's got a hole in it. We think we've plugged it. But any minute the tire could blow up in your face and your father could be dead."

I was stunned.

But he wasn't through. The doctor explained, "In the interim, while I take care of him, it will cost you $100 a week." Now, $100 a week then was maybe equivalent to between $1,000-$2,000 a week now. It was more than the entire income of our family, I suspect.

The first thing we had to do was go directly into our savings. Which we did. Then, I had to go into the store, which I did. So what? It was tough on all of us. But we got through it. Why should anyone else pay for my father's illness? I don't think society owed us free medical care. Where does it say you have to pay for my dad's health-care? I don't understand that logic.

To this day I don't understand why my misfortune is your misfortune.

In that sense, I'm a libertarian. You can call me a mean SOB for saying, "I don't want to give you free health-care." I'm not a mean SOB. It's just that your misfortune is not my misfortune. Plain and simple.

Moreover, if you abuse your body, I don't want to pick up the tab for your negligence. Let's say you make the decision to go to the clubs every night and screw ten people a week. Tell me, why should I pay for your STD? If you put a nose ring in or pierce your navel or put a genital ring on your body which becomes infected, you're telling me I have to pay for that—just because you are a self-mutilator?

No, I don't think so.

Am *I* liable to pay for your reconstructive plastic surgery because *you* fell asleep smoking in bed? If you stick a needle in your arm, do you think I'm supposed to pay for your addiction? No. No. No. I can't carry you on my back. Nor should you be forced to carry me.

Now, for the sake of argument, if I were to say, "Yes, I'll pay for your self-inflicted problems and your health-care," tell me, where does it stop? Answer: It will not stop until we have provided health-care to the ends of the earth.

First, the Left convinces us we need to provide health-care for everybody in America, starting with senior citizens and kids. Then, out of some twisted notion of fairness, they'll propose we provide health-care for the world.

We are already seeing the dawn of that day with George W. Bush's $15 billion handout to fight AIDS in Africa. Team Bush flies halfway around the world with a fat check in hand to announce, "The American people care deeply about the pandemic that sweeps across this continent."[6]

Don't get me wrong; I care about human suffering.

But I would like to know when the United States annexed Africa. What other African relief problems will our government volunteer to underwrite tomorrow? Housing? Cars? Dental work? Psychologists?

It's one thing for the Red Cross, the Salvation Army, church and synagogue groups, or Bill Gates' philanthropic foundation to use private funds to address health-care needs overseas. It's a very different thing for this or any president to grab money from my wallet by increasing my tax burden and then pass that money out to cover the latest world health crisis.

MEDICAL MUTILATION

I asked a very important question: Where does this drive by the liberals for universal tax-funded medical treatment stop? That depends on two things:

1. How militant you are at politicizing your "illness."
2. Whether you claim your malady is a civil rights issue.

Need proof? Take the new perk regarding sex change operations. Better hold on to your pacemaker. This might shock those of you living outside of the San Fran-Freako area. Since I live in this epicenter of insanity, I'll give it to you straight from the horse's behind.

The governing Board of Stupid-visors voted in favor of funding sex change operations for city employees.[7] Which means if you are a male psychopath and you want to remove your male organ or you are a female nutcase and you want to add a male organ, the city of Saint Francis will pay up to $50,000 for the "sex reassignment."

One of the stupid-visors, Mark Leno, claimed, "This is very much a civil rights issue."[8] A civil rights issue? Where did he find that in the Constitution? I'm telling you, the liberals in this provincial little burg think they're the tip of the staff. They think they are so *progressssive* and *compasssssionate* because they think cross-dressers, transvestites, transsexuals, and she-males have a civil rights basis for medical mutilation.

What they really are is, well, the rear end of the world. So if a psychopath wants to remove his male organ, the city of San Fran (which really means you, the taxpayer) is now forced to pick up the tab for this abomination.

This is not a civil rights issue.

This is a case of the insane running the asylum.

It strikes me that anyone who says "I want to take my penis and have it cut off" is mentally ill. They should immediately be put in the hospital, put on fluroxene, put in a straitjacket, given therapy, and let back on the street when they become normal again. This is self-mutilation. This is insanity.

But in San Freaky, they give "it" a health benefit.

Now, typically speaking, it costs $37,000 if a male cuts his penis off. The cost for a less to become a more runs about $77k. I would say, look, if you are going to pay for this out of public funds, can't we at least do some cost saving?

For example, can't we take the male appendage that's cut off some of the sickos and put it on dry ice and save it for less-o's who want to become more-o's? Couldn't we bring down costs from $77k to maybe $37k if we used the cut-off member from a psycho who had his penis removed?

Why throw out a good penis?

A penis is hard to come by.

While they're at it, the city stupid-visors could start a public awareness campaign to contain costs. They could erect giant billboards around the city or even plaster this slogan on the trolley cars: *A used penis is a good penis.* Or, *Recycle your penis here!*

Granted, there are people who have sexual confusion. That's a given. That's part of the human race. No one is arguing with that. We also know there are people who choose to be homosexuals. But to remove a male organ and become a female is insanity. Doctors who promote this should be put into a mental hospital with those they encourage to do this.

Come to think of it, not only is this a civil rights issue, it is also a racial issue. You've got to match a black penis to a black lesbian and you've got to match a Hispanic penis to a Hispanic lesbian, right? Let's say a black transsexual, trans-gender, whatever, goes to claim her health benefits. But the hospital is experiencing a shortage, so they only offer her an Asian penis. That's grounds for a lawsuit. A Red Diaper Doper lawyer from the ACLU would take that case in two seconds.

This is so beyond the pale of reality that it's actually a pleasure to live here. The same liberals who said there's a lack of dollars for prescription drugs miraculously find money for this medical mutilation. How many times have I said ultra-liberalism is a mental disorder?

THE REPROBATE INGRATES

Set aside the question of socialized medicine for a moment. Even without that monster threatening to devour all that is good about the health of America's patient care, there is another threat. Our system is on a fast track to bankruptcy. Why? Because of the *Ingrates*, the *Inmates*, and the *Illegals*. These blood-sucking leaches have affixed themselves to the host and are rapidly draining the health-care system.

I'll break it down to the brass tacks.

The Ingrates in my book are those sanctimonious plebeians behind the AIDS racket. We Americans, through funding by the Centers for Disease Control and Prevention (CDC), spend a fortune on HIV and AIDS research and development. I'm talking almost *two billion* dollars each year on what is, largely, a preventable disease.

Did you know that the CDC dedicates more money to AIDS *than to any other disease*? Just less than 30% of the CDC's $7 billion budget is ear-marked for HIV and AIDS. As much as I would like to find a cure for this terrible disease, AIDS is not the leading cause of death in this country.

Did you know that?

Here is the difficult truth: *Cardiovascular disease is the leading killer of men and women from all races.*[9] Not AIDS. Not even close. In fact, more American adults, ages 25-44, die from heart disease, cancer, and suicide than from AIDS.[10] But the media does not tell you that, do they?

What's more, look at these figures from 2000: 710,760 people died from a cardiovascular-related disease, another 553,091 died from cancer while AIDS-related deaths totaled just 14,270.[11] And yet, funding for AIDS eclipses every other disease.

Why? Because HIV infection is the only politically driven disease.

The numbers in the following chart are the *actual* dollars spent by the CDC in 2002 on several diseases. As you well know, right behind lung cancer, breast cancer is the second leading cause of cancer-related death for women. An estimated 41,000 women died of breast cancer in 2000.[12] But the budget dedicated to fighting that deadly disease is a mere pittance when compared to the dollars spent on AIDS.

See for yourself.

DISEASE	ACTUAL CDC BUDGET 2002
ARTHRITIS	$ 13,808,000
BREAST AND CERVICAL CANCER	$ 191,965,000
DIABETES	$ 61,683,000
HEPATITIS C	$ 21,930,000
HIV/AIDS – RESEARCH & DOMESTIC	$ 787,421,000
HIV/AIDS – GLOBAL (CDC-WIDE)	$ 143,720,000
HIV/AIDS – (CDC-WIDE)	$ 931,141,000
TOTAL AIDS/HIV:	$ 1,862,282,000
PROSTATE CANCER	$ 14,062,000
SKIN CANCER	$ 1,647,000
DATA from the CDC Budget Request Summary FY 2004	

Instead of being thankful for the outpouring of compassion and the national commitment to fight AIDS, GLAAD, ACT-UP, and their hordes spew hatred and anger as they clamor for *more, more, more!* These Ingrates have the nerve to launch a "Stop the war on HIV prevention" campaign when more is being done for their lascivious lifestyle than for providing vaccines for children.

What makes me ill is the flagrant abuse of these hard-earned tax dollars by those claiming to be engaged in AIDS prevention. Here in San Fran-Freako, the CDC dishes out $600,000 annually in federal funds to the Stop AIDS Project.

What are we getting for that investment?

How about workshops like "Flirt, Date, Score" held on August 13, 2003. The promotion, which targeted gay, bi, tri, and trans guys, said, "Want to flirt with greater finesse and date with more confidence? Who doesn't? Share your expertise and hear how others are successful in meeting guys and staying safe today."[13] Other workshops like "Bootylicious" offered insight and advice on topics such as sex with male prostitutes, as well as oral and anal intercourse.[14] That's your tax dollars at work.

Thankfully, I'm not the only one who says this stinks. Julie Gerberding, a Bush appointee to head the CDC, questioned such workshops and threatened to withhold funding. As well she should. The more than half a billion dollars handed to the Stop AIDS Project by the CDC was supposed to be used for *prevention*—not the promotion of a deadly lifestyle.

When word of her inquiry reached the Stop AIDS Project, the damaged and deranged powerbrokers on the Left marshaled their forces. They, along with 150 HIV/AIDS likeminded groups, dashed off a letter to George Bush thrashing the CDC. As you might expect, Gerberding had to back down.

Listen to these Ingrates.

In their letter to Bush, they claimed, "The HIV epidemic is growing every day while federal resources to fight it are not keeping pace." Hold on. Not keeping pace? We are already spending one in every four dollars on a disease that could virtually be stopped dead in its tracks if the pagans just kept their flies zipped.

The Ingrates go on with this threat: "If the government does not fully fund federal AIDS programs, there is only one sure result: The American taxpayer will see both the costs of treatment and the death toll rise dramatically."[15] There you have it.

If AIDS numbers increase, it's because *you* didn't do enough.

Talk about spin control. *They* promote risky behavior, but *you're* the problem. Admittedly, it's natural to put the best spin on things—especially when you're caught with your pants down. But you and I must see through their smoke screen. Let me say it like it is: gay activists have infiltrated most health organizations. No wonder there is a massive coverup when the spotlight threatens to expose their exploits.

Americans have a right and duty to hold the CDC accountable for such squandering of public funds.

MUPPETS AND MARKETING HIV

I know a thing or two about marketing. Some of my earliest lessons were learned back at Doc's drug store in Queens. As Christmas approached, Doc asked me to dust the Old Spice display. I think he sold a total of six bottles during the holidays. I could tell he lived for this. He would say, "Christmastime is coming, Michael. We're going to be selling a lot of men's toiletries. Go in there and clean it up." I had to pull the yellow boxes out from the window display. Some of the stuff had turned green. Looked like they were leftovers from World War II.

Or maybe from Egyptian times (if you remember those wonderful Parke-Davis color drawings of "Pharmacy through the Ages").

So I'm cleaning the Old Spice boxes. I'm dusting and I'm thinking, how does Doc convince people to buy an old Old Spice box? He decided to put the boxes in a certain trick position with plastic holiday wrap over the shelf to make it look like a different color. If somebody ordered one, he'd quickly throw it in a brown bag and sell it to them.

In a way, what he was doing back then—his innocent effort to market men's cologne—is a metaphor for what liberals are doing to children today. You see, these sickos have a tough sell. They want to sell the idea that HIV infection is perfectly normal.

They want to candy-coat the reality.

To change the appearance.

To popularize the acceptance of the disease.

How are they doing this?

In South Africa, these wackos on the Left have introduced Kami, an HIV puppet on *Sesame Street*. Gloria Britain, the project manager who launched Kami's debut in September 2002, said, "by getting [young children] used to the idea of having an HIV-positive friend around, we hope the stigma associated with the virus in South Africa can be removed."[16]

Remove the stigma?

It's called common sense.

If a little child is afraid to be around a kid with AIDS or a kid who's HIV-positive, that's because the child has been properly educated. They've learned if an HIV-positive child scratches you or transfers any bodily fluids to you, there's a good likelihood you'll get infected—and might die. That's not a stigma. That's common sense. But the demented liars are twisting common sense into a stigma while trying to make you into a "homophobe" or "racist" if you tell your child not to hang around a kid with AIDS.

This is beyond the pale.

While Kami isn't coming to America, yet, I think we should at least create a tuberculosis puppet for *Sesame Street*. Maybe call him "Tommy TB." After all, America is getting flooded with uninspected Chinese who come with TB. Yes, and uninspected Mexicans who come to America with TB. I say it's time we create a TB Muppet for *Sesame Street* so your child can put aside the stigma associated with a TB-infected child.

Of course, in doing so, your child might become TB positive. But that's not as important as not hurting the feelings of the child with TB.

You gotta remember what's important here.

What's important to the politically insane crowd is that no feelings get hurt. And that sick people become integrated into the healthy community. Even if they distort the facts to do so. Case in point.

When the five-year-old Kami made her African *Sesame Street* debut, she told the thumb-suckers, "My mom told me before she died that I was born with the virus. But please hug me because I'm very lovable and I can't make you sick, although I wish there were no more HIV and AIDS and I wish everyone was happy and kind."[17]

Let me go back to that sentence; it's rich with lies. Did you catch it? Kami said, "I can't make you sick." That is outrageous! It is a flagrant misrepresentation of reality and a deadly lie. Not to mention that Kami's audience is the three– to seven-year-old crowd.

I say, instead of brainwashing children to embrace HIV and AIDS as part of life, it's time we played hard ball with the Ingrates who are milking the system. If you're spreading a disease, it should be a felony. They should lock you up. If you have syphilis or AIDS and knowingly spread it to somebody, you should go to jail for life.

That's my opinion. I realize the times and the rules are changing, largely due to the way the Left has successfully proselytized sympathizers to embrace their agenda.

For example, in my day, when you got married, you had to take a Wasserman test. I don't know who Wasserman was. I never even liked the name. Gave me the creeps. "Did you get your Wasserman test?" Creepy. The Wasserman test was for syphilis. If you had syphilis you could not get married. End of story.

Then, along came the "sexual revolution" of the sixties. Out with the Wasserman test, in with free love and pot smoking. Everywhere you turned, liberated sex addicts sang, "Why don't we do it in the road?" Now, for those of you born after Reagan was president, the attitude of the sixties was: "It's my right to spread disease wherever I want to, and you're not going to tell me what I can do. If I want to sleep with a hundred people, that's it. I'm going to spread disease, you mean old guy, and you're not going to stop me."

That was the new America.

That's the genesis of the sexual anarchy we're seeing today. Gutless politicians and health officials refuse to stand up to these maniacs and put a stop to the insanity once and for all. Especially when they target kids. Like I said, the ingrate parasites are devouring the host—with a little help from their friends, the Inmates and the Illegals.

CRIMINAL IMPLICATIONS

Talk about living in an *Alice in Wonderland* world, where up is down, down is up, and all things forward are backwards. What I'm about to tell you is not a fantasy. It's a bizarre reality.

Horacio Alberto Reyes-Camarena, a death row inmate in Oregon, was convicted of brutally and repeatedly stabbing 18– and 32-year-old sisters. The younger died. The older lived and was able to testify against her assailant. But before the state of Oregon gets around to executing him, they've got to figure out how to keep him alive!

You see, Horacio has two failing kidneys, and, by law, the state is required to provide basic health-care for all prisoners. What is it costing to keep him alive until his turn in the chair?

His three weekly dialysis treatments cost $121,025 per year; that's all.[18] But wait. In this mixed-up world, doctors suggest that he's a good candidate for a kidney transplant. As of this writing, Horacio's chances are excellent he'll be placed ahead of the 57,000 law-abiding citizens in the country who are praying for a desperately needed kidney transplant.

And Horacio, the death row felon, has the nerve to complain about the lack of a TV while he gets his treatment. What's he going to demand next?

Pedicures for prisoners?

Horacio is not an isolated case of the health-care system held hostage by the Inmates. Take the jailed felon in California who received a heart transplant. Cost to taxpayers? One million dollars. Another Californian inmate secured a kidney transplant costing taxpayers $120,000. A convicted murderer in Georgia had heart bypass surgery to the tune of $70,000.[19]

Now, in principle, it would be nice if everyone—even prisoners— could go and have anything they wanted from any doctor at any time. But as we know, that is prohibitive. We can't afford it. It's insane when prisoners are afforded better health-care than most law-abiding people receive in the free world. As it is, the state of Oregon spent $60 million on health-care in 2003—and that's just for prisoners.

If we don't put a stop to criminal abuse of the system, the phrase "Crime pays" will take on new meaning.

ALIEN ATTACK

Mainstream Republicans hold a position identical to Democrats when it comes to the single biggest issue threatening the viability of our health-care system: the invasion of the Illegals. But no one will say it. Not one politician will talk about the cost of caring for illegal immigrants, how they are bankrupting our hospitals and raping our medical system.

The states hardest hit are those where human castaways are arriving in the greatest numbers: Texas, California, Arizona, and New York. These uninvited, unwelcome sneaks steal their way across the border and then demand first-class medical treatment. They head for the emergency room like it's their personal doctor. They haven't put a dime into the system, and they want better health-care than you, the natives, get.

Not one politician will dare tell it like it is. Why?

They want the illegal Hispanic vote.

If you want to fix the medical crisis in this country, there's a quick way to do it. Stop giving free medical care to the Illegals. Got it? Ask anyone who runs a hospital in New York City, Chicago, Los Angeles, or border states like Texas. Ask them about their budget crisis. Every last one of the business managers is screaming for help, but relief doesn't come.

Witness the plea by Arizona's state Medicaid provider. The manager of the Arizona Health Care Cost Containment System (AHCCCS) was rebuffed in his attempts to curtail primary care for the Illegals, currently pegged at $75 to $80 million annually.[20] In August of 2003, the fiscally suicidal members of the Arizona Supreme Court ruled AHCCCS has an obligation to meet the health-care needs of illegal aliens.

Or take the case of Proposition 187 in California: a member of the Stench from the Bench blocked the will of the people. In 1994 the voters of California overwhelmingly voted to deny health-care, welfare, and education benefits to the Illegals. But mad dog ACLU lawyers filed a lawsuit to kill Proposition 187. There you have it. The Enemy Within, aided and abetted by Mariana Pfaelzer, a U.S. district court judge, voided the will of the people and overturned this very popular ballot initiative.

I say, tell the ten-to-twelve million Illegals to get health-care in the country of their origin. It's time Americans stopped paying upwards of $2 billion annually to pay for the health-care of illegal immigrants.[21]

Does that sound harsh?

Let me tell you something. Most good medicines are harsh. I don't sugarcoat my words with fairy dust to make them sound something other than what they are. Good medicines are sometimes very harsh. Reality is very harsh. The truth can be harsh, but it can also be very healing.

We must close the doors to our emergency rooms immediately because hospitals are going bankrupt. Maybe you didn't know illegal aliens have access to our hospitals. Maybe you can't imagine that happening. But it is. Every day. Right now.

Have you been in a hospital lately? Have you ever cut your hand on the weekend and gone to an emergency room? It looks like the Tower of Babel. Do you know why? Because the Illegals come here and the first thing they get is a pamphlet printed in many languages alerting them of their "rights."

"Me migrant, you racist, I sue. Go, ACLU."

They slip across the border, and there's a nice ACLU RDDB waiting for them with a survival kit: condoms, a health-care card, and phone numbers for a lawyer, doctor, and Indian chief—whatever they may need. And who pays for it? You, the sheeple. Because you let people who ravage our health-care industry take over the country.

Instead of fighting back, politicians in the nearly bankrupt state of California spend their time debating a bill requiring businesses to hire transvestites and drag queens or face a $150,000 fine.[22] I'm not making this up.

You talk about stupidity?

It doesn't get any worse.

RITALIN: DRUGGING THE KIDDIES

In addition to the Ingrates, Inmates, and Illegals, I must address a final, outrageous abuse of the health-care system in America: the drugging of our children. I wrote about this at length in *The Savage Nation*. However, the trend of medicating kids has shown no sign of abatement. There's no excuse for what's being done to youngsters today. At the first sign of rambunctiousness, creativity, or inventiveness, the schools drug them.

We are so used to the medicalization of everything, we miss our own double message. On one hand, we tell kids not to use drugs. Then we put them on drugs to modify their behavior. Especially boys.

Boys are not allowed to be boys anymore.

The education czarinas want them to shut up, sit down in the front row, and quietly knit Cuban flags.

No question, if I was a kid in school today, let's say in the sixth grade, I'd be on every drug imaginable. The mean-faced, clipped-haired women would say, "That little Savage, he has shining eyes, and he talks too much. Put him on Ritalin. Put him on Prozac. Put him in a straitjacket. He shows all the classic signs of maleness. We must kill it. Kill it. Crush it!"

You mothers don't even know what your poor boys go through in school, do you?

When I was a young boy, my mother bought me a pair of cufflinks. They were a set of thespian masks, you know, one was a sad face and one was a happy face. I loved those cufflinks. I'd look at them when I was bored in class. On my right sleeve I had the happy face. On the left I had the sad face. Some days I'd switch them around and would put the happy face on the left and the sad face on the right.

Many days I was so bored I didn't know what to do. I'd look at the cuf- flinks for hours while the teacher talked on and on about George Washington and the Delaware River. I didn't care what she was talking about. I had learned it already in kindergarten.

I learned George crossed the Delaware, he saved the country in Trenton, and he overthrew the British. I got that the first second of kinder- garten. They're still teaching it to me in the fourth grade. In the fifth grade, I learned what a peninsula was. In the sixth grade, it took them a year to teach me what an island was. I couldn't take it.

So I stared at the cufflinks.

The happy face, the sad face.

When I got bored with the cufflinks, I'd start pulling hair out of the skin on my arms. Today, they would have me on Ritalin or put in a nut house. They'd call my lack of attention a disease. It wasn't. It was called boredom. I inflicted pain on myself rather than listen to the teacher one more boring second.

Rather than improve the curriculum, teachers today might say, "Oh, your son has something wrong with him, Mrs. Savage. We found he looks at cufflinks instead of listening to the teacher talk about how evil George Bush is and why white males need to be put in the pillory. He's pulling hair out of his arm, and we suggest you put him on a moderate dose, just a moderate dose, of Ritalin."

That's for starters. Then, soon, the teacher might say, "Let's put him on Prozac." And we wonder why America is rapidly become an overmedicated society.

THE SAVAGE PRESCRIPTION

I raised two children, and it wasn't easy. I did it because I love them. Frankly, I wanted children instead of a cherry-red Porsche with a bib on it. I mean, it was a conscious decision I made many years ago. You know, whether to have a Porsche with a bib, housed in a heated garage, or to raise children. I chose the latter. Based on my priorities, I decided it was better to raise children than to raise a Porsche.

Back then, in order to have proper health-care coverage for my family, we had to pay for it *ourselves*. All parents wonder how they'll pay for health-care for their kids, especially when they're young parents or, God forbid, injured in an accident which could wipe out a young family.

We learned about a plan in California, sponsored by a hospital, called Kaiser Health Care. Mrs. Savage and I paid for it every month—instead of paying for a Porsche with a bib. It was a lot of money, but it took care of our needs.

There is a caveat to what I am saying.

I treated the children for minor complaints myself. I was trained in diet, nutrition, and herbal medicine. I didn't run to a doctor every time they had a runny nose. The point I'm making is this: Today we are a nation of crybabies, whiners, and losers. We run to a doctor and demand treatment for every little hiccup. That's the problem with a socialized medical system.

I have to give my mom, who is nearly ninety years old, the credit. When I was young and moaned about a bruise, she would say, "Michael, don't you think I have aches and pains? Sure I do. You just never hear me talking about them." She stopped me in my tracks from becoming a complainer.

Mom raised me to understand everyone will have aches and pains throughout their life. Little ones here and there. Maybe it's a headache, or stomachache. Or gas, or a cracked toenail. But you don't run to a doctor for every little thing.

If America is going to start talking about universal health-care, we had better start talking about *universal self-care*, Mr. Dick Gephardt and Hillary Clinton. Learn what the hell you're talking about. Teach people how to take care of *themselves* before you teach them how to take advantage of the social services in this country.

Teach people to take care of their own headaches.

Make them pay something when they visit the doctor.

Make these worrywarts pay fifty bucks every time they go in with a complaint. I don't care if they are from Russia or Pakistan. I don't care if they are from Krapistan or Afghanistan. Make them pay every time they see a doctor. That would immediately cut down costs and abuses.

What am I, the only one in the country who can see that? When you give something for nothing, someone's going to take advantage of it. Put out sugar, and see the ants come.

And another thing.

I ask you, why is the United States' health-care system the envy of the world? One word: capitalism. Our free market system stimulates the pursuit of specialization, innovation, new equipment, technological advances, miracle drugs, and medical breakthroughs. Capitalism encourages private ownership and invention and gives businessmen and women a profit motive to do more with less, to be smarter and more efficient.

Americans are the winners as a result. We are living longer and are enjoying greater mobility and freedom from ailments that used to be crippling. Take away profit motive, and you take away incentive to do more than the very minimum.

Think Russia. Think Cuba.

But the libs hate our free market approach to life. They hate the thought of rewarding an entrepreneur for finding the cure to cancer. They hate the fact that a brain surgeon makes more than a leaf-blower. They hate the idea that the government doesn't control the treatment of every last scratched knee. That's precisely why the Enemy Within pushes for socialism—which will ultimately be the death of health-care in America.

That, my friend, should make you sick.

FOUR

MILITARY:
THE WAR ON THE WAR

Whether you know it or not, America is engaged in the fight of her life. Frankly, the tragic events on 9/11 were just a wakeup call. Militant forces have painted a bull's-eye on the forehead of Lady Liberty. They spend every waking hour plotting how and where to strike once more.

Thankfully, our commander-in-chief, President George W. Bush, responded swiftly by proclaiming a war on terrorism. If it were not for a number of unpopular but necessary measures to strengthen our homeland security, I am convinced we might have already been hit again.

The threat to our safety remains real to this day.

As America fights the war against terrorism, the single most effective way to stop our effort dead in its tracks might surprise you. It has nothing to do with enemy aircraft, tanks, guns, bombs, booby traps, or the use of biological or conventional arms against our boys. As weapons go, this lethal device can do more damage than a thousand dirty bombs. Worse, it's not deployed on the battlefield. It is unleashed right here on our own soil.

What is this weapon of mass destruction?

The tongue.

The ultra-leftist traitors within our borders have unleashed a relentless barrage of words against the war on terrorism with their subversive tongues. These turncoats and their sympathizers spew a web of lies and anti-American hatred with unquenchable zeal. Their goal? Sabotage President George W. Bush's effort to fight terrorism, that's number one. Beyond that, they desire to put a Democrat-socialist in power.

Like Hillary Clinton or Howard Dean.

These modern-day descendants of Benedict Arnold are openly anti-American. They have no shame. As I will demonstrate, you will find them boldly waging a war on the war in five primary places: our colleges, Hollywood, the media, and politics, and you'll even find some of the fiercest attacks coming from the ranks of the retired military community.

Even while our troops were taking fire, these shameless malcontents were intent on destroying everything America stands for. They oppose everything that makes us great with one incessant voice. And they do so by wagging their tongues in scorn, in hate, and in unison. While I cherish freedom of speech and rely upon it in my daily radio broadcasts, I also understand the difference between dissent and subversion.

For instance, on April 10, 2003, Gary Kamiya, the executive director of *Salon*, said, "I have a confession. I have at times, as the war has unfolded, secretly wished for things to go wrong. Wished for the Iraqis to be more nationalistic, to resist longer. Wished for the Arab world to rise up in rage. Wished for all the things we feared would happen."[1]

Take this gem from actor David Clennon who stars in CBS's *The Agency*. He said, "I'm not comparing Bush to Adolf Hitler—because George Bush, for one thing, is not as smart as Adolf Hitler. And secondly, George Bush has much more power than Adolf Hitler ever had."[2] Tell me that isn't hate speech designed to divide the country.

Clennon's venom is echoed by comedian Robin Williams who likened Bush to a dictator. He said, "We have a president for whom English is a second language. He's like 'We have to get rid of dictators,' but he's pretty much one himself."[3] This is unbelievable to me. At a time of war, they bash the president and spit on the flag.

Producer and director Robert Altman said, "When I see an American flag flying, it's a joke."[4] Our flag is more than a joke to actress Janeane Garofalo. She said, "When I see the American flag, I go, 'Oh my God, you're *insulting* me.'"[5]

While much more will be said about these divisive Hollywood Idiots in the next chapter, the undercurrent of leftist, anti-U.S. sentiment runs deep. I won't argue that they don't have a right to dissent. They do. When actor Woody Harrelson claims, "The war against terrorism is terrorism. The whole thing is just bullsh—,"[6] that's his opinion. He has no obligation to be patriotic.

But there's a fine line between dissent and sedition.

Between commentary *on* terrorism, and *advocacy* of it.

For instance, we all know the unprovoked 9/11 attack against America was the worst act of terrorism in our history. The smoldering Twin Towers crystallized a new reality: We live in a world where a network of murderous thugs will stop at nothing to destroy this great country. Norman Mailer, however, sees things differently. He sympathized with the terrorists, saying, "Americans can't admit that you need *courage* to do such a thing."[7]

Aging rock star Chrissie Hynde of The Pretenders went a step further. Standing before a crowd in San Francisco she shouted, "Let's get rid of all the economic [expletive] this country represents! Bring it on, I hope the Muslims win!"[8]

Not to be upstaged, Eddie Vedder, lead whiner for Pearl Jam, the burned-out 1990s grunge-rock band, dramatized his anti-war feelings before an audience at Denver's Pepsi Center, April 1, 2003. Vedder took the stage and unleashed a barrage of anti-war jabs against President Bush. He then impaled a mask with the image of George Bush on his microphone stand. Vedder proceeded to ram the president's likeness into the floor and then stomped on it repeatedly.[9]

Do you understand how twisted this climate of public discourse has become? The Enemy Within has made it so if you love America, if you love our flag, if you love the family, God, and freedom, *you* are the traitor. These deceivers have turned nationalism and patriotism into treason.

Ironically, our war to remove the brutal, terrorizing dictator of Iraq has been one of the most brilliantly executed military efforts in American history. What the media refuses to tell you is this: Apart from nation-building expenses that follow every war, this engagement and the Gulf War *combined* cost less in loss of life and dollars than any other military action.

Hard to believe?

See for yourself.

CONFLICT	DEATHS/US SOLDIERS	COST ADJ./INFLATION
WORLD WAR 1	53,513	$ 196,500,000,000
WORLD WAR 2	292,131	$ 2,091,300,000,000
KOREAN WAR	33,651	$ 263,900,000,000
VIETNAM WAR	47,369	$ 346,700,000,000
GULF WAR	148	$ 61,100,000,000
IRAQ WAR	126[10]	$ 58,000,000,000[11]

Compiled by the United States Civil War Center except where noted.

Rather than applaud the Bush administration for a job well-done, lefties want you to believe the war in Iraq, as Sen. Ted Kennedy bellyached, "was a fraud."[12] There were no torture chambers. There were no mass graves. There were no links to other terrorist groups. Saddam Hussein was simply a strong Arab leader, or so he must want us to think.

Ted Kennedy's own son disagrees with him. Congressman Patrick Kennedy said of Saddam Hussein, "If he didn't have [the weapons of mass destruction], then how come he gassed all his people with them?"[13] Excellent question. When it comes to human rights violations and evading inspectors of WMD, Patrick maintains Hussein had "the worst track record of any international leader in the history of the U.N."[14]

Like Ted Kennedy, rather than applaud the troops for putting their lives on the line, Hillary Clinton used the second 9/11 anniversary to vent. She griped on national TV that Bush squandered "the trust and credibility of our government at a time when we have to trust and rely on what they tell us."[15]

And there's nothing like a Hollywood Idiot to add insult to injury. Speaking of post-war casualties, actor Harrison Ford told an audience in Spain, "I don't think military intervention is the correct solution. I regret what we as a country have done so far."[16] Does he mean that overthrowing a brutal dictatorship is evil?

Tell me the Left hasn't declared a war on the war.

THE BODY COUNT

Why does the media insist on providing a daily body count months after the major conflict has ended? Why the every-hour-on-the-hour death totals? With long, somber faces the networks report, "Today, two more soldiers were ambushed and died in Iraq." What are the sheeple supposed to do with that information?

Think about it.

Why don't these journalists give us a daily body count resulting from car crashes? Did you know the number of deaths on American highways *far exceeds* the number of deaths related to the defense of our nation? In 2002, 42,815 Americans died in auto related crashes.[17] That's 117 deaths *every day*. Which means virtually the same number of people die each day on our highways as have died in the *entire period of active combat in Iraq*.

When was the last time Peter Jennings or Dan Blather announced, "Today, 117 people died on the highways"? Seems to me it would be a much bigger story, right? Two deaths versus 117. Don't get me wrong. I hate seeing our boys getting shot in the back by those terrorist cowards. Still, you have to ask what the purpose is of this daily body count by the leftist-media complex.

I'll tell you.

It is to demoralize the resolve of the people and our troops. It is to erode American support for the president in his war on terrorism. Period. The agenda of the Enemy Within is to demoralize the president, the troops, and the sheeple. You see, the Enemy Within tried to stop us from going to war, and then they tried to break our resolve in the midst of war in hopes we would be unsuccessful. Having failed on both counts, they are attempting to reverse the impact of our victory. And do not for one second think this daily body count isn't having the desired brainwashing effect.

It *is* working.

Democrat Congressman Jim Marshall went to Iraq to see our progress for himself and returned angered by the way the media has been distorting the news. Contrary to most reports, he found our troops to be encouraged, energized, and making amazing strides in restoring order and rebuilding infrastructure.

Marshall said, "I'm afraid the news media are hurting our chances. They are dwelling upon the mistakes, the ambushes, the soldiers killed, the wounded . . . The falsely bleak picture weakens our national resolve, discourages Iraqi cooperation and emboldens our enemy."[18]

Thanks to this warped picture of reality by the media, the polls have shown a remarkable post-war drop in support for the president. Not to mention just about anywhere I go, I hear the nightly war news parroted by unthinking neophytes who obviously take their cues from the pancake-faced leg-crossers in the media.

For example, the other night I was working late in the studio after hosting my nationally syndicated radio show *The Savage Nation*. About eight o'clock, I wrapped things up and caught up with my family who was finishing dinner at an Indian restaurant in Rat Boy County, California. Although the place was technically closed, the owners let me in just to have a piece of naan. I should point out this restaurant is located in one of the most liberal counties in America.

I pulled up a chair and sat down, glad to be done with the business of the day. I mean, there's only so much of this culture war a person can take.

I'm starting to unwind, having a glass of beer and being with my wife and daughter. Just as I'm feeling the pressures of the day melt away, I hear a voice, a loud, obnoxious, self-important sounding windbag.

It was then I noticed the place was not completely empty. There was another table of patrons in the corner. An older guy with a little ponytail and his wife sat across from a younger couple. I glanced at them and tried not to listen, but I couldn't help myself.

The guy with the ponytail starts on a rant. His big mouth thunders away about how Bush stole the election so he and his buddies could go to war with Iraq for more oil. He says America would be better off with Al Gore. He's using every rehashed liberal platitude in the book. He goes on about how America is *inseeensitive* to the plight of oppressed people in other countries.

In between comments he is stuffing his mouth with lamb, curry, chicken, and the best of everything. He's eating off the top of the food chain, but he's lambasting America. He had more baloney coming out of his mouth than there was food on his plate. He kept putting down the war with Iraq. How Bush is acting worse than Saddam Hussein. That Bush is acting like a cowboy. That Bush actually *knew* about 9/11 before it happened but didn't do anything to prevent it.

Lies, lies, and more ignorant lies.

Somehow his wife managed to chime in with a 1930s shibboleth: "Well, you know, it is the munitions industry that is profiting from this militarism."

Munitions industry?

We heard that accusation going back to WWII.

Now, picture me. I didn't say a word, but I started to turn white. I stopped eating. It was as though I was bracing for an epileptic attack about to come over me. The edges of my ears were burning as I listened to this blowhard ape the news from National Public Radio or some other distorted liberal media outlet.

He was clearly the kind of guy who couldn't be bothered with facts, especially about blaming George Bush for 9/11. He was so full of himself

I was about to burst. I was tempted to go over to his table and straighten him out.

You see, prior to 9/11 there were specific security measures in place at our airports that would have triggered the automatic detention of certain individuals. If a passenger was of a certain ethnic extraction, if they showed up at the last minute without luggage, and if they purchased first-class tickets with cash, three security alarms would have sounded. Such an individual would not have been allowed on the plane, at least not without further inspection.

However, about a year before 9/11, a radical, Red Diaper Doper Baby lawyer sued the airlines claiming such policies were *raaacist* and discriminatory. One day I'll name this lawyer; he's still in America. Anyway, when two of the 9/11 hijackers came through the airport in Portland, Maine, to board planes for Boston, they set off every alarm bell known to the airlines.

The airlines, in turn, wanted to detain them. Under the old guidelines, the airlines would have prevented their traveling to Logan International in Boston. But they were intimidated and hamstrung by the Red Diaper Doper Baby lawyers who changed the profiling rules. As a result, those hijackers got on the planes, and the rest is history. If anybody is to blame, it is the ultra-liberal RDDB lawyers, not George Bush.

That loudmouth across the room was both factually wrong and completely clueless. The self-righteous phony from Rat Boy County was done. He launched into the next tirade. He says, "It's clear to me that we are not living in a sustainable society," as he stuffs his face with more chicken curry, lamb, and rice.

Finally, the punch line comes. Dabbing at the corners of his mouth with a cloth napkin, he says, "Do you realize that we in America should be living like the Europeans? No way can we continue to live in this non-sustainable economy of ours, especially with Bush's unrestrained military spending."

Now I'm steaming. He's one of the brainwashed sheeple I lambast every day. I leaned toward my daughter and said, "I'm going to say something. I can't take this anymore."

She grabbed my forearm and looked me in the eyes. She said, "Dad, I'll leave the restaurant if you do."

No matter what age they are, children don't like an outspoken father. They would rather have peace. I don't blame them. I said, "Okay, I'll go for a walk." So I stepped outside to blow off some steam. Frankly, I was just glad to get away from that mouth. Guys like that don't understand a thing about what they're saying, yet they say it with such conviction. Usually in restaurants.

Guess what? Minutes later the blowhard with the ponytail leaves the restaurant and gets into a brand-new luxury SUV that gets maybe twelve miles to the gallon. What a fraud. He regurgitates the liberal lies of the media over dinner and doesn't even see the contradiction in his own lifestyle. Worse, he, like many other sheeple, has unknowingly joined the ranks of the radical libs as a foot soldier in their effort to undermine the war and the nation.

HOMEWORK ASSIGNMENT: NO MORE WAR

While presidential hopeful Al Sharpton compared Bush to a "gang leader"[19] and Dick Gephardt blasted Bush saying, "This president is a miserable failure,"[20] you'll never believe what a radical mad dog professor was doing at Citrus College in Glendora, California. Rosalyn Kahn forced her Speech 106 class to send *anti*-war letters to President Bush—that is, if they wanted extra credit.

Pro-war letters did not count, as Gina Cantagallo, a student in Ms. Kahn's class, found out. "She said we could receive extra credit if we wrote a letter to President Bush in regards to the war," Gina explained. "So I went home, did the assignment, and I came back, and I had a letter that said I supported Bush, I supported our country, I supported our troops."[21]

Gina turned in her assignment the next day. Her teacher "looked at the letter and said, 'This is unacceptable.' I said, 'What's wrong? You said write a letter on the potential war.' And she said, 'Absolutely not, I wanted you to write a letter stating you were against war and against us overriding the U.N.'"[22]

This is the Left's idea of tolerance and diversity.

Classmate Chris Stevens experienced the same treatment. He said, "There was no room for dissenting remarks. You just had to follow her beliefs." Needing the extra credit, Stevens played along with the unreasonable request of his teacher. He did the assignment as required by Ms. Kahn. When he turned it in, "she said the letter had to be *mailed* if I wanted credit. I said, 'No, that's not OK,' and I took the letter back."[23]

When complaints of these abuses reached the dean of students, action was taken. While not fired for her militant intolerance, Ms. Kahn was put on administrative leave. Further investigation revealed she actively encouraged her students to visit the anti-war website hosted by the radical MoveOn.org gang and would spend the first ten minutes of her *speech* class lecturing students on her left-wing agenda.

This is not an isolated example of an attempt by a professor to manipulate or squelch patriotism and patriotic speech on a college campus. I wish it were. I wish we could turn back the clock to a time when the robust exchange of ideas was the norm in college. However, such flagrant anti-American hostility as what I have described has dramatically spiked in the wake of the 9/11 attacks.

A report conducted by the American Council of Trustees and Alumni in February of 2002 found anti-war rallies protesting our involvement in Afghanistan were hosted on more than 140 college campuses in some thirty-six states. The report concluded "many professors and administrators are quick to clamp down on acts of patriotism, such as flying the American flag, and look down on students who question professors' 'politically correct' ideas in class."[24]

Of course, anti-war rallies have been around for decades. Remember the Kent State University tragedy in 1970 in which four students were shot and killed by National Guardsmen? What is different today is the overall celebration of anti-American ideas on many campuses. Neo-socialist professors have created a climate that inhibits the free expression of pro-American ideals and conservative thinking. Not to mention there is a new crop of far-Left elective courses. For example, the class description of

"Terrorism and the Politics of Knowledge," a course offered by UCLA, says students will examine "America's record of imperialistic adventurism."[25]

There the libs go again.

Blame America for the terrorist attacks.

And get college credit.

As you well know, the University of California at Berkeley boasts some of our most illiberal professors. So I am not surprised both "The Star Spangled Banner" and "God Bless America" were not considered appropriate songs to be played at their September 11th memorial service in 2002. Why? President of the graduate assembly, Jessica Quindel, explained, "Patriotic songs may exclude and offend people because there are so many people who don't agree with the songs."[26]

Professors and college administrators who vilify America and squash contrary views are, in my opinion, morally and politically bankrupt. Such people are a clear and present danger to the survival of the United States. You see, for these liberal professors it's not enough we were attacked on 9/11. It's not enough thousands died on American soil.

It's not real to them.

They're living in a fantasy world.

It is inconceivable any informed, intelligent professor can believe the Islamo-Fascists, including their sleeper cells in this country, intend us no harm.

The contingent of re-educators who dominate the prime professorship positions think it's the sixties all over again. They think they're going to have their potency returned. The smell of patchouli oil permeates their brains. They think young girls will put flowers in gun barrels and the Beatles will come back from the dead to sing, "All You Need Is Love."

But they are totally disconnected from reality. Even after Saddam Hussein was toppled and the Iraqi people were dancing in the streets for the first time in thirty-five years, these professors would argue the war was unjustified.

Just listen to the Iraqis speak for themselves.

After the fall of Saddam's Baath party, a 21-year-old Iraqi by the name of Baha Kerou reflected, "We used to chant 'We will sacrifice our blood and souls for you Saddam' and sing songs calling him our father. You *had* to go to these demonstrations or else they would threaten to fail you in your exams—"

Hold it right there.

Sounds like that speech class at Citrus College.

He concludes, "—or throw you in jail for a few days, so we all went. Thank God they are gone."[27] Fadil Amin, an unemployed translator, shares his euphoria saying, "This is the best July 17th I've seen so far because there is no Saddam and no Baath. We're better off without them, even if we don't have any electrical power or water and security is abysmal."[28]

These stories in praise of liberation by the United States are not the kind of truths illiberal professors will have students discuss. Why? Far too often the only stories worthy of extra credit are those painting President Bush as the world's bully.

The truth is, they would rather steer classroom discussion towards the likes of French journalist Mathieu Lindon who, in a recent column, explained the mood of his peers. He said, "We are very interested in American deaths in Iraq . . . We will never admit it, [but] every American soldier killed in Iraq causes, if not happiness, at least a certain satisfaction."[29]

Indeed, today, when students aspire to win the approval of their professors, they had better concur with the likes of author and professor Jonathan Schell. In Schell's twisted view, the better course of military action would be for America to *lose* the war!

Schell wrote, "[Democratic Senator Joe] Biden says we must win the war. This is precisely wrong. The United States must learn to lose this war—a harder task, in many ways, than winning, for it requires admitting mistakes and relinquishing attractive fantasies. This is the true moral mission of our time."[30]

Schell's anti-America position is echoed in comments made by columnist Maureen Dowd who called Donald Rumsfeld "the man who trashed two countries, spent hundreds of billions, exhausted our troops, but still hasn't found Osama, Saddam, or WMD."[31]

Tell that to Jassem Mohammed, a money-changer in Iraq, who said, "The whole Iraqi people were against Saddam. He oppressed us . . . and now we've been liberated."[32]

EX-MILITARY EXPERTS

Perhaps the most troubling aspect of this war on the war comes from ex-warriors. Bored with playing Bingo, a posse of retired military generals, analysts, and former intelligence officers have joined hands to create VIPS: *Veteran Intelligence Professionals for Sanity*. This highly partisan group of lefties loves to dress up in their old military uniforms and appear on the TV talk shows as "authorities" on our military situation in Iraq and beyond.

Richard Beske, William Christison, Kathleen McGrath Christison, Ray Close, Patrick Eddingon, David MacMichael, and Raymond McGovern make up their steering committee. I didn't know we had so many anti-war generals and intelligence personnel. No wonder our military stank under Clinton.

In the wake of war with Iraq, this band of conspiracy-theory naysayers sent a letter to President Bush. In it, they called for their favorite whipping boy Dick Cheney to resign.[33] You get the picture. This is a cozy club of soft-socialists, by my analysis.

Frankly, I don't know why anybody in the media takes them seriously. But they do. Half the time I would be watching the war coverage on cable, one of these ex-military types would be trotted out supposedly because of his or her alleged deep "inside scoop."

What gets me is how the leg-crossing reporter would be so easily deceived by these talking heads. As if these out-to-pasture infidels would know more about the Afghanistan or Iraqi conflict than, say, Secretary of Defense Rumsfeld.

I can see right through these fakes.

Let me tell you what happens with these guys off-camera. These guys are knocking around the garage, dying for the phone to ring. They long for the day when their opinion matters again to somebody other than the paperboy. The retired general, that great war hero, lives for the chance to put on the pancake makeup and be on television.

Then the phone rings at last. He clears his throat and tries to sound as if he were in the thick of negotiating a Middle East peace settlement for the West Bank. He answers crisply, "Yes? Hello?"

On the other end of the line, a producer from ABC, CBS, NBC, CNN, MSNBC, or FOX inquires, "General, we're doing a piece on the Iraq conflict. Would you have time to speak with us today about your worldview?"

He stalls for a moment so as not to sound too available. "Yes, I think I can make time. What time would that be?" He listens. After another hesitation, he says, "Yes, I believe I can squeeze that in." He hangs up the phone, claps his hands, and tells his wife Millie the good news. "And make sure you run the videotape," he announces as if commanding the Ninth Fleet.

Over on the TV set, as the lights come up, his chest swells with pride. He's about to be asked a question.

Imagine the thrill.

Then the moment of truth comes. The general gets to express himself. He says nothing new. Nothing that has not been said a thousand times during the day. Instead, he goes on about how it's a terrible thing to go to war. War is awful . . . he never wanted to fight, he didn't believe in fighting although he wore the uniform . . . and yes, he was a hero and has many medals even though he never *actually* fought . . . no, he never thought America would end up this way . . . Absolutely not. War is not the answer . . . Yes, make love not war . . . no, we shouldn't kill, we should join hands and sing "Give Peace a Chance."

After two or three minutes of this, he savors hearing those final words uttered by the host, "Thank you for your time, retired General So-and-So." With that said, the lights go off, and he is ushered out. All the general wants to do at that point is drown himself in a bottle of Scotch. Instead, he goes home to Millie. She's asleep by the time he gets there. So he turns the tape on to watch himself on television. For a fleeting second, he feels like a human being again.

Then he waits three months for the phone to ring again.

The real tragedy is this: I don't mind if a retired military person disagrees with the war, although I totally think they're wrong. However, I do believe using their position at a time when our men are facing life-and-death decisions is irresponsible. Their anti-war comments both undermine our troops' morale and encourage our enemies by creating a picture of a divided front.

The ill-informed comments of these camera-craving, ex-military types, in their attempt to prop-up a sagging self-esteem, do extensive damage to the war on terror and our military.

TOLERANCE FOR TERRORISTS

If Shirley MacLaine were in charge of the war against terrorism, her approach would be to "Melt their weapons, melt their hearts, melt their anger with love."[34] If Ms. MacLame were to climb down from her ivory tower, she might find she has a kindred spirit in Richard Gere. This whackjob says, "If you can see [the terrorists] as a relative who's dangerously sick and we have to give them medicine, and the medicine is love and compassion."[35]

You see, part of the war on the war is the Left's effort to change the argument. To make the terrorists *victims* who are worthy of our sympathy and *understaaanding*, while making the American people the enemy. The way this blame game is played is to find the reasons why we deserved the rage of the Third World street thugs.

Singer Kevin Richardson, member of the Backstreet Boys and apparently a part-time foreign policy expert, wondered, "What has our government done to provoke this action that we don't know about?"[36] Norman Mailer does not have to wonder. He *knows* why we're responsible for the attack. Listen to his breathtaking ignorance:

The WTC was not just an architectural monstrosity, but also terrible for people who didn't work there, for it said to all those people: "If you can't work up here, boy, you're out of it." That's why I'm sure that if those towers had been destroyed without loss of life, a lot of people would have cheered. Everything wrong with America led to the point where the country built that tower of Babel, which consequently had to be destroyed.[37]

I can't fathom the depth of such gibberish.

Nor will I try. He and filmmaker Oliver Stoned must have been twins separated at birth. According to Stone, "Six companies have control of the world." In his small mind, those businesses are "the new world order. . . . And I think the revolt of September 11th was about 'F— you. F— your order.'"[38]

Let's see. It's our big businesses, big buildings, big egos, and our insensitive foreign policies that have provoked the madmen in dirty headscarves to attack us, right? And, according to Ms. MacLame, if only we held hands and loved them, the terrorists' anti-American rage would melt away.

I find it stunning these Caesars of Hollywood fail to do any self-examination as they look for an American boogyman to blame. You see, it's not our foreign policy the Arabic world hates. It's our *social pollution* Muslim terrorists are rebelling against.

They do not want their daughters to become harlots.

They do not want their wives to become Jezebels.

They do not want their sons to become gangsta rappers.

They do not want their nephews to become nieces.

Hear me. It is the filth and pollution of our entertainment industry wafting across the world they despise. It's not McDonald's. It's the porno, violence, and decadence exported by Hollywood that enrages them.

If you were a leader or an intellectual in the Muslim world and you saw the debauchery promulgated by the West, whether it be from the U.S., France, Sweden, or Germany, and you saw your young people gravitating toward the filth pumped out over your airwaves, what would you do? Frankly, you would support al-Qaida or any organization that would want to stop that flood of pollution from entering your country.

Why else do you think Barbie dolls have been banned in Saudia Arabia for ten years? In a culture where women must be covered from head to toe, Barbie is a threat to morality. That's the naked truth.

Sheik Abdulla al-Merdas, a preacher at a mosque in Riyadh, Saudia Arabia, is concerned about Barbie's "developed body" and her "revealing clothes." He explained, "It is no problem that little girls play with dolls. But these . . . revealing clothes will be imprinted in their minds and they will refuse to wear the clothes we are used to as Muslims."[39]

If you want to understand the war between Islam and Western civilization and why we are so hated, I believe it almost boils down to one word: sex. You see, for a traditional Arab like Osama bin Laden, this jihad is as much a battle about sexual license as it is anything else.

Consider the facts.

Islam has very strict rules about sex. Look how women in traditional Islamic countries are required to dress: the burqa, the head covering, and, in the most extreme cases, the face covering. Why? Because they know the power of a woman's beauty and the power of a woman's hair. Which is the same reason Orthodox Jews wear wigs. I don't know if you know that. To this day, modern Orthodox Jewish women wear wigs because they're not to show their hair to anyone but their husband.

The traditional Arab goes to great extremes to control issues of sex, seduction, and modesty. That's why he has his woman locked-up tight inside a burqa. If you were him, you would't want her to put on a pair of jeans and come home with a belly button ring, looking like a harlot from the Bible. He does not want a painted woman walking around the house with a STD that she's hiding from him.

The same is true about his daughter. She's dressed, clothed, hidden. He wants her to be married and have a family. He doesn't want her to become a disco slut. He doesn't want her to become a club hound. He sure doesn't want her to become a clipped-haired, mean-faced lesbian and, in so doing, bring dishonor to the family name.

Do you think that's far-fetched?

Then you don't understand the Muslim mind.

Recently, Abdalla Yones, a Kurdish Muslim living in London, admitted slitting the throat of Heshu, his own 16-year-old daughter, and stabbing her eleven times. Why? According to the prosecutor, John McGuinness, Heshu's father, "did not approve of her Western lifestyle. She wanted to be with her friends and use a mobile phone quite often."[40] Heshu had become too Westernized.

Using a cell phone?

Putting on makeup when Dad wasn't looking?

Dating a non-Muslim boy?

Those reasons prompted Abdalla to engage in an "honor killing," a practice employed by Muslims to bring justice when they believe a disgrace has been brought upon the family.

This is a religion of peace?

I ask you, if the Muslim tradition of "honor killing" permits a father to slice his daughter's throat with a kitchen knife; two brothers to hack their sisters to death with an ax because one left home to marry a man without permission and the other sister joined her;[41] and a mother to hold down the legs of her daughter while her son strangled his sister to death because she was pregnant out-of-wedlock,[42] why would Muslims be any less enraged and determined to attack America for marketing such permissiveness, decadence, and immorality in the first place?

You had better read that again.

You see, after the 9/11 attacks, the quacks on the Left blamed the Muslim's hatred on our foreign policy. And guys like billionaire George Soros completely missed the point, blaming Bush's "extremist" White House policies and "false ideology" as threats to world stability. Soros went so far as to call for Bush's removal. He said, "It is only possible if you have a regime change in the United States—in other words if President Bush is voted out of power."[43]

He and the Left can blame Bush all they want. But they're wrong. World terrorism is not primarily about our economics and policies. In addition to whatever misguided twelfth-century thinking the terrorists may have, their angst is fueled by the number one American exports:

pornography, lewdness, perverted music, and a way of life that is an insult to virtually any family man on the planet. That is why they are willing to kill.

They want to protect what they believe in.

It's not our social policy.

It's the trash from Hollywood.

Which explains why the Caesars of Hollywood have waged war against the president. They are trying to defend their turf by shifting attention away from themselves. Their ultimate aim? Thwart a second Bush term at all costs and find an internationalist leader who shares their values.

LYING ABOUT SPYING

Only time will tell what damage has been done to the strength of our military and the integrity of our war on terrorism since the Pentagon's move toward religious pluralism. Looking closely, I have found a disturbing pattern of lies and deceit that led to an act of espionage in the chaplaincy.

Let me break it down for you.

During the mid-nineties when Clinton was president, the Pentagon authorized the Norfolk naval base in Virginia to open the first on-base mosque for Muslims.⁴⁴ Since that time, a dozen Muslim chaplains have been picked and trained to serve within the U.S. military.

How were these men selected?

Abdul Rahman Alamoudi, an American Muslim activist and founder of both the American Muslim Council and the American Muslim Foundation, was authorized by the Pentagon to nominate and help train these Muslim chaplains. Alamoudi's involvement deeply concerned Arizona Sen. Jon Kyl who said, "It is remarkable that people who have known connections to terrorism are the only people to approve these chaplains."⁴⁵

Naturally, Alamoudi dismisses such concerns.

Keep in mind, Alamoudi is the same guy who, in October of 2000, participated in an anti-Israel protest outside the White House and declared, "Hear that, [then-President] Bill Clinton? We are all supporters of Hamas. I wish they added that I am also a supporter of Hezbollah."[46] He has since attempted to backpedal on his remark, although his activities over the following years have revealed where his true loyalties lie.

On September 28, 2003, Alamoudi was arrested for making ten secret trips, using a Yemeni passport, to Libya, a country to which travel has been banned by our government for years. Several weeks before his arrest, Alamoudi was caught by British customs agents carrying $340,000 of sequentially numbered $100 bills, which he hoped to smuggle from London to Syria, in his suitcase.[47] He confessed the cash dealings were connected to Moammar Khadafy's rogue nation, Libya.[48]

Here's where the plot thickens.

Halfway around the world, military police arrested one of the chaplains trained *by* Alamoudi, Army Capt. James J. Yee. Stationed at the high-security prison on Guantanamo Bay, Yee's job was to counsel al-Qaeda and Taliban detainees—a dubious practice indeed. Why in the world is our military providing spiritual *commmmmfort* to prisoners? I thought military chaplains were supposed to be servicing our troops—not the enemy. Yee had "unlimited access to prisoners"[49] who desired prayers and spiritual counsel.

In any case, Yee was arrested for allegedly doing much more than offering spiritual guidance. Published reports indicated Yee possessed classified documents and "diagrams of the cells and the facilities at Guantanamo"[50] as well as lists of the detainees and their interrogators. What possible reason would a chaplain have for pilfering such information?

Especially troubling, Yee, who graduated from West Point in 1990, spent four subsequent years in Syria, of all places, to study Arabic and Islam. You've got to wonder why a terrorist-sponsoring nation would welcome one of our boys—a West Point graduate at that—to live amongst them. And you've got to wonder why our military didn't do a better job screening Yee upon his return with a Syrian bride in tow.

There is one little detail you must know about this unholy web of subversives. All twelve of the Muslim chaplains working in our military are adherents to the Sunni sect of Islam known as Wahhabism. This eighteenth-century hard-line variety of the Muslim faith "stresses literal belief in the Koran and *seeks the creation of Muslim states based on Islamic law*."[51]

So we should not be surprised when our soldiers and military personnel were encouraged to explore a website that, according to a story in the *Washington Post*, "promotes material from radical Muslim jihadists, including two Saudis who have been identified as Osama bin Laden's spiritual advisers."[52]

How did our armed forces fall for this Trojan horse? Retired Army General James Hutchens points to that dreadful decision made years ago to be more *incluuuusive* and pluralistic. In his view, "The Pentagon's uncritical commitment to multiculturalism has led to this problem."[53] The Enemy Within has seized and capitalized upon this misguided and dangerous attempt by our military to open the door to all varieties of chaplains.

What does all of this boil down to?

Acting in the spirit of inclusion under Bill Clinton, our military expanded the chaplaincy program to include Muslim clerics. Alamoudi, a radical Muslim activist (with terrorist sympathies), was empowered with the task of selecting and training a dozen Muslim chaplains. He picked all twelve from the radical Wahhabi Islamic sect. Yee, one of these "holy men" who just happened to spend four years training in Syria, was caught red-handed with classified documents pertaining to enemy combatants in Guantanamo Bay.

What about the other eleven Muslim chaplains?

Where do their loyalties lie?

Are they, too, waiting for their turn to undermine our war effort? That seems to be a reasonable question to ask. Which leaves me mystified since Donald Rumsfeld quickly dismissed the value of profiling those with Arab or Muslim ethnicity or religion. When pushed by the press, Rumsfeld said, "Raising the question you did about profiling is not a useful thing to do. The fact of the matter is that there are a variety of vetting procedures, and people who happen to be of one religion—I don't think one has to assume that they have a monopoly on this type of activity."[54]

I'm sure he means well. But in my opinion we cannot afford to be naïve or worried about tolerance when our national security is on the line. When America is at war with radicals in Islam, they *are* worthy of special scrutiny. That includes those who may be hiding behind their holy robes.

GIVE PEACE A CHANCE

I mentioned most Americans don't have the foggiest clue what it's like living under the thumb of a dictator. Nor do they have the slightest inkling of what a tyrant will do to keep the peasants in line. We're so spoiled by freedom, we can't imagine the depths of depravity and the breadth of barbaric brutality evil men will employ against their own countrymen.

This explains the simplistic solutions and naïve thinking by peaceniks and pop stars alike. Singer Shakira says, "I just feel that there are always pacifist solutions" and the people "have the obligation to demand to our leaders to give us the pacifist solutions."[55] Maybe she should first try to understand the nature of the beast.

For years, Saddam Hussein's son Uday tortured athletes who didn't play up to par. Uday, you see, in addition to being a sadistic animal, was the head of Iraq's Olympic Committee. It was said players had their feet scalded and toenails ripped off if they failed to win a soccer match. Since his dad controlled all of the media in his country, few outside sources could investigate the truth.

Thanks to our military effort to liberate Iraq, such evidence of his torturing has been uncovered, literally, in the pile of dead leaves. A mummy-shaped metal coffin large enough to house a grown man was discovered just sixty feet from the building housing the Iraqi football association—in plain view of Uday's office.

Commonly used in medieval times, this iron maiden was equipped with long sharp spikes mounted on the door. When the door closed, the victim would be impaled. And Uday would be able to listen to every last pathetic scream. According to *Time* magazine, the "one found in Baghdad was clearly worn from use, its nails having lost some of their sharpness."[56] This apparently does not bother any of the leftist peace-lovers.

If this is evil we could see, imagine the evil we couldn't see . . . the evil plans cloaked behind a web of lies and deceit . . . the evil conducted in secret chambers and behind closed doors.

No, the Dems and libs would have you trust the integrity of a raping, torturing, murderous monster like Saddam, rather than put your trust in a man of faith, whose most flagrant "sin" is encouraging Bible studies for staff members on their own time. They want to convince you that life in Saddam's world was nothing more dangerous than a stroll through Mr. Rogers' Neighborhood.

Someone should explain to the peaceniks, the Hollywood Idiots, the good Democrats, and the Malibu mansion-dwellers that this iron maiden is a torture device, not the eighties rock band.

In light of the misguided peace movement and verbal assault from the Left, columnist Bret Stephens is concerned about the future of our war on terrorism. He dares to ask the question of the year: "After Iraq, will the media ever again allow a democracy to topple a Fascist dictatorship?"[57]

You see, the media paints the peaceniks as the good guys wearing white hats while they plant a black hat on Bush. Stephens puts it this way: "One day, perhaps, we'll get a satisfactory explanation as to why a president whose chief sin seems to be that he was born to an influential family, isn't articulate, and piously believes in Christ should be treated as the Great Satan. In the meantime, we must bend every effort to prevent our media jihadis from doing to Western public perception what the Middle East's jihadis are trying to do to Iraqi infrastructure: Destroying the foundations upon which a more hopeful future may arise."[58]

In spite of evidence to the contrary, dimwits like Democrat Dennis Kucinich are convinced we can join hands across America and love our way out of conflicts with world dictators. Maybe they would change their minds if they had spent one minute inside Uday's private playground. In the spring of 2003, Kucinich introduced a bill to create a cabinet-level, so-called Department of Peace. He intends this hopeless waste of dollars to use "mediation" and "nonviolent intervention" to make the world a better place. Kucinich's spokesbabe Denise Hughes believes "we have the unique opportunity to confront the root cause of these evils and the ability as a society to build a safer world."[59] Is that so?

While Kucinich dances around with flowers in his hair, Dianne Feinstein is dancing around the issue of our military's strategic need to constantly improve its weapons. She worked overtime to halt research on a new generation of low-yield nuclear bunker bombs capable of penetrating reinforced hideaways hundreds of feet in the ground. She went so far as to blast the Senate, saying, "If we let this happen, I think there's a moral degradation that's spread over this whole body."[60]

Ted Kennedy, another ludicrous pacifist, said, "This issue is as clear as any issue ever gets. You're either for nuclear war or you're not."[61] Seems to me the issue is you're either for the survival and defense of America or you're not, Mr. Kennedy.

Why do Feinstein and Kennedy oppose the development of such weapons? I believe it's because they don't understand this simple fact: Whoever holds the most technologically advanced weapon usually takes control of the battlefield. Just look at history. The guy with the bow and arrow beat the guy with the sticks and stones.

The rifle beats the arrow.

The tank beats the rifle.

The B-52 bomber beats the tank.

World War II proves those with the best weapons win, with one notable twist. Hitler had the jet, the Messerschmitt. More than 1,400 of them. His jet flew so fast and was so superior to our planes that our pilots could barely see them. They certainly could not shoot them if they did spot them.

However, Hitler's mistake was he got greedy. He wanted to convert the jet into a bomber rather than rely on its speed to shoot down our warplanes. If he had left well enough alone, he could have knocked everyone else out of the sky. Instead, the conversion of the Messerschmitt to bombers took precious time he did not have. Not to mention he had difficulty fielding enough trained pilots.

In the end, we bombed his fleet as it sat on the tarmac and took away his advantage. After the war, we captured several of his German engineers as well as the plans for the Messerschmitt, which lead to the development of our jet technology today.

Another interesting lesson about military preparedness can be learned from history. Napoleon instructed his cooks to always have a chicken roasting on the stick. Why? Because they never knew when he would come home, and he wanted them to be ready—even if it was the middle of the night. Likewise, our military must constantly have a new weapon in the fire, because we do not know what our enemies may be doing.

PICK YOUR BATTLES

Just days before the Iraq war, I received this one-page letter of invitation to participate on an anti-war panel:

Dear Michael:

On behalf of the board of directors of the Creative Coalition we are delighted to invite you to be a distinguished panelist at the Creative Coalition Forum on *Freedom of the Press During Wartime*. Other invited panelists include Sean Penn, Norman Lear, Mayor Willie Brown, Maria Shriver, and U.S. Senator Dianne Feinstein. The audience will include leaders from the media, entertainment, and the arts . . . and we're going to talk about the war. The Coalition was started over a decade ago by industry activists Susan Sarandon, Christopher Reeve, Alec Baldwin, Ron Silver, and Steven Collins.

They invited me to be the token conservative! Isn't this amazing? I looked at the letterhead; it listed William Baldwin as president. Members of the advisory board included Tony Goldwin, Alec Baldwin, Harvey Keitel, and other foreign policy experts including Robin Williams who, in between his imitation of a chicken with a fat behind, I imagine is an expert on international affairs.

Here's the response I faxed back:

"Shall I bring my own horns and tail?"

I'm not making this up. This is the absolute truth. How could they have been serious? Did they honestly think I would go to an event funded by these people? This was unbelievable to me. The invitation said: "This is a premier, non-profit, non-partisan social and public advocacy organization of the arts and entertainment industry. Our mission is to educate and mobilize leaders in the arts community on the issues of public importance, specifically in the areas of First Amendment rights."

These are the same people behind the gutter groups who are trying to drive me off of the radio. So much for First Amendment rights. These illiberal would-be intellectuals don't believe in the First Amendment. What audacity to send me such a snare. Oh, and here's the good part: They were planning a private VIP dinner after the program.

I'm wondering if they planned to provide me with a food taster.

My point? You have to pick your battles. There will be times when you will want to stand up for America in the classroom. You will want to defend your president at the beauty parlor. You will want to publicly show support for our military as they fight the war against terrorism. Yes, times when you want to lock horns with the libs. But a word of caution is in order: Sometimes you might be walking into an ambush.

So watch your back.

The Enemy Within is playing for keeps. Don't be seduced by their seductive increase-the-peace rhetoric. Don't be intimidated by their anti-America trash talk. Don't be fooled by their lies about our mission. And whatever you do, don't let them extinguish your passion to defend your country. Why?

One dirty bomb can ruin your whole day.

FIVE

MEDIA:
THE HOLLYWOOD IDIOTS

When I was a kid, I used to watch TV until my eyes hurt. I remember sitting in front of the television with a bowl of ice cream waiting for the TV to warm up—remember those days? As the Philco flickered on, Walter Cronkite filled the screen. He was the voice of America.

I trusted him.

Now I see that Walter Cronkite, Dan Rather, and Peter Jennings are not the trusted father figures I grew up believing them to be. To me, back then, they were Mount Rushmore. They were the truth-sayers. The best in their field.

Today, I have found out the granite that I thought they were made of was really nothing but feldspar. Never in my lifetime have I witnessed such a breakdown in journalistic integrity. Take Dan Rather.

As you well know, this useful idiot flew to Iraq to interview that Hitler in a headscarf, Saddam Hussein. Dannyboy tossed the genocidal dictator a few softball questions that nobody cared about, questions like this brilliant gem: "Mr. President, do you intend to destroy the Al Samoud missiles that the United Nations prohibits?"[1]

What's Saddam Hitler going to say?

"Uh, you got me cornered with that one, Dannyboy. I'll confess everything. I'm a thug, it's true. I rape and murder my own citizens. Here. Let me show you where we've hidden the bombs. I'll show you the mass graves. Just promise me one thing, Danny. All I ask is a chance to tell my side on *Larry King Live*."

Did Rather lose his mind?

What did he expect Saddam to say?

Saddam, who slaughtered tens of thousands of his own men, women, and children, is obviously going to paint himself as a benevolent leader. A real champion of the people.

Even a freshman flunky taking a course in Journalism 101 can grasp that. But not Dannyboy. Evidently he was more concerned with the PR value and a chance to boost his sagging ratings than the fact his visit bestowed a level of credibility on a mass murderer.

If Dan Blather was living during Hitler's rise to power, I suppose he would have been the first one in line vying for an exclusive interview with *der Führer*. I can see it now. Hitler, wearing a suit and a little felt cap with a feather on his head, would sit at a long table surrounded by security.

Dannyboy takes a seat and lobs him a question about the death camps. "Are the rumors true, Mr. Hitler, that the Jews are being *mistreated* in death camps?"

Hitler forces a smile. "Death camps? What death camps? What are you talking about? I know nothing of which you speak. The Jews are happy in the camps. They're all sewing. They're making nice little shoes. I assure you they're happy. Everybody is happy."

Dannyboy feigns surprise, while secretly hoping his pancake makeup covers the wrinkles. "Oh, so you're saying there are no death camps."

Hitler shifts in his seat. "What are you talking about? We've relocated the Jewish people . . . for their own safety. All is well."

Tell me that's not propaganda.

Tell me that Rather's interview of Saddam Hussein wasn't a travesty. Tell me that CBS shouldn't have fired him on the spot. Tell me he didn't disgrace his profession. Tell me he didn't dishonor his country. Tell me he didn't mislead the American people.

If you don't agree with me, you're crazy.

You don't know history.

You don't understand journalism.

You are a useful idiot, too.

You see, you can't be neutral in these times. Your life is involved in a sweep of history and either you're resolved to save yourself and your country or you're not. I've dedicated my life at this point to saving my family and my country as best I can.

And another thing. Don't dare think the media circus surrounding the war with Iraq over Saddam's barbaric regime is "old news."

History is instructive.

History is a great teacher.

History reveals the lessons we as a nation must learn. What's the lesson here? We, the American sheeple, need to keep Stalin's propaganda ministry in mind when watching CBS, a network that hires people like Comrade Rather.

Or Peter Arnett.

Or Peter Jennings.

Why? We're still seeing the same kind of coverage and the same kind of treatment of dictatorships in Cuba, Burma, and Syria. These so-called journalists of today are about as reliable as the former Iraqi information minister, Baghdad Bob.

HOLLYWOOD'S USEFUL IDIOTS

Actors in Hollywood have elevated America-bashing into an art form. I wouldn't be surprised if Ed Asner didn't one day host The Stalin Awards Show. A panel of like-minded leftists would pass out little bronze statues of Stalin to actors who best vilified America.

Who would be among the top contenders?

There are plenty to choose from. How about Danny Glover calling

Bush a racist?[2] Or Julia Roberts? She said of President Bush, "The man's embarrassing. He's not my president, and he never will be, either."[3] Or Cher, who said, "I don't like Bush. I don't trust him. He's stupid; he's lazy."[4]

Take Jessica Lange spouting off in Spain. She told a crowd how embarrassed she was to be an American, and, just to be entirely clear about her angst, she said, "I hate Bush. I despise him and his entire administration."[5] Nice touch. Especially when your country is at war. She and Natalie Maines of the Ditzy Chicks, who blasted Bush while touring in Germany, can duke it out for first place.

Toward the top of the Stalin Awards list of hopefuls would be Michael Moore for his tantrum during the Oscars. This pompous, dirty-faced, ne'er-do-well belched, "We live in a time where we have a man sending us to war for fictitious reasons . . . shame on you, Mr. Bush, shame on you."[6] Is he nuts? Tens of thousands buried in mass graves, the torture chambers, the mobile weapons labs.

Fictitious reasons?

And who could forget the anti-war posturing by Tim Robbins? Or Susan Saran Wrap? Brabra Streisand? Richard Gere? Dustin Hoffman? George Clooney? Sean Penn? Alec Baldwin? Martin Sheen? Or how about this leftist loon, comedienne Janeane Garofalo? She was asked, "Is George W. Bush more of a danger to this world than Saddam?" Her answer?

"Equal, in a different way."[7]

It wasn't always this way.

When I was a kid, almost without exception, all Hollywood actors were patriotic. They were red, white, and blue Americans. Just look at Jimmy Stewart. Talk about a gifted actor. I bet you didn't know he was a colonel in the Army Air corps, did you? Stewart was a certified bomber pilot in World War II.

Unlike the cardboard script-readers of today, Jimmy Stewart put his life on the line when his country needed him. He flew numerous missions against the Germans for which he was awarded two medals: the Distinguished Flying Cross and the Air Medal. If he were alive today, I bet he'd tell this crop of lefty commu-soc actors to "take this flag pole and shove it."

Then again, he would probably be too polite to do so.

Clark Gable is on the distinguished list of actors who loved and faithfully served their country. Clark, as you well know, made it big as Rhett Butler in *Gone with the Wind*. This 1939 classic grossed what today would be something like 900 million dollars, making it one of the top grossing films of all time.

For those of you too young to remember, Clark was one of the hottest properties in Hollywood. By 1940 he starred in more than forty films. The guy was a living legend. A real American icon. His razor-thin moustache and his slicked-back, Brylcreemed hair made an entire generation of women swoon for him.

Life was good. The whole world was his stage.

But the world changed on December 7, 1941, with the attack of the Japanese on Pearl Harbor. When Franklin Delano Roosevelt declared war on Japan, Clark Gable had a choice to make. He could have built a house in Malibu from which to protest the war. He could have spouted off in front of the cameras denouncing FDR's call to arms.

Instead, at age forty-one, when most actors were playing golf, signing autographs, or chasing sex, Clark sent FDR a telegram requesting permission to join the army. Can you imagine that? The guy was way past the age of military service.

Roosevelt is reported as saying, "Stay where you are."

That didn't stop Clark from enlisting as a private.

Like a true blue, hard working American, Clark Gable worked his way up the ladder. He made first lieutenant. Then captain. Then major. Clark flew air raids with the 351st Bomb Group at Polebrook, England as well as in a B-17 bomber with the 91st Bomb Group. At one point, the Nazis put a reward on Clark's head because of his bombing campaigns.

I'd like to know what happened to such men of conviction and action. I'd like to know why there aren't more actors today willing to put their lives on the line.

For the love of their country.

For something that really matters.

For the sake of their precious freedoms.

You think Jimmy Stewart and Clark Gable are the exceptions? Think again. Ronald Reagan was a captain in the U.S. Army Air Corps. Henry Fonda served in the Navy. He got a Bronze Star for Valor. James Arness was awarded the Purple Heart and the Bronze Star from the Army. Charles Durning had three Purple Hearts and the Silver Star.

Need I go on?

Take Alan Ladd, Jack Palance, Glenn Ford, Van Heflin, George Montgomery, Don Adams, Jackie Coogan, Lee Marvin, and Arthur Kennedy.

Actors, yes. Soldiers, yes. True American heroes, yes.

Every last one of them.

They, unlike the empty suits of today, fought shoulder-to-shoulder alongside America's finest young boys. The farmers. The steelworkers. The taxi drivers.

The people who made this country great.

THE ACADEMY OF DUNCES

Martin Sheen will never be president. I think we can all agree on that. But the mere fact that he plays one on TV causes him to actually believe his opinion is more informed, more valid, and more worthy than that of President Bush. Actors these days are delusional—along with the blathering goon squad of Hollywood reporters who cover their every scripted move.

Actors build their lives around playing somebody they're not, and that's supposed to give them the moral authority to lecture the rest of us sheeple. Why would anybody take them seriously? I don't.

Think about it. Actors act.

Actors read scripts written by others. If the script says "look angry," the actor looks angry. If it says "cry," then they manufacture fake tears and cry for the camera. If the script says "jump," they jump, or "be nice," they force a happy face. Actors are nothing more than good-looking puppets.

Flesh-marionettes, all of them.

Now, are you ready for the Savage truth?

Many have no formal college education. Yet these hollow souls come before the microphones to lecture us over issues that they don't know the first thing about. And we're supposed to take them seriously? All that's missing when they speak is the laugh track.

We've all heard the shameful America-bashing from these Enlightened Ones—the actors and actresses who think they walk on water. I'd like to know why the media elite have given these tiny minds a pass when they blast the president and his cabinet with adjectives such as "ignorant," "moronic," and "stupid."

A simple fact check would show otherwise.

President Bush's formal education includes graduating from Yale and then completing a master's of business administration from Harvard's business school. He's been certified as a F-102 pilot and has flown with the Texas Air National Guard.

Some dummy.

Our vice president, Dick Cheney, is also a learned man. He holds both a BA and MA in political science. Secretary of State Colin Powell went to George Washington University where he earned an MBA. Not to mention his collection of distinguished military awards. Condoleezza Rice, who serves as the national security advisor, graduated cum laude from the University of Denver. She furthered her education at the University of Notre Dame, earning a master's degree. She went on to earn a Ph.D. in international studies.

Stooges. All of them, right?

Now, what about the Enlightened Ones who walk among us? You know, the actors who know more than the dunces in leadership. As I understand it, Barbra Streisand, unlike Cher,[8] managed to finish high school. I say, "Way to go, Babs." God bless her. Maybe Barbra could help Cher complete her GED. Better yet, Julia Roberts who also made it as far as high school, could pitch in to coach Cher.

We don't want to leave any actor behind.

Sean Penn, Ed Asner, Jennifer Anniston, Sarah Jessica Parker all finished high school. That, of course, in the world of affirmative action, puts them on equal footing with the president and his cabinet in terms of collective smarts. A virtual brain trust, no doubt.

Of course, a few of these American-bashing libs tried their hand at college. Let's see, Martin Sheen flunked the entrance exam to the University of Dayton (as in Ohio).[9] Big school, no doubt. Kind of tough, I'm sure.

Jessica Lange actually made it to college but dropped out after a few months as a freshman.[10] She probably thought she had learned all there was to know. At least Alec Baldwin had an excuse for dropping out of George Washington University: he was embroiled in a personal scandal. Other college dropouts: George Clooney, Michael Moore, Janeane Garofelo.[11] You get the picture.

It's utterly unbelievable.

Don't get me wrong. I'm all for holding a high school diploma, especially when you work for it.

Here's the irony.

You have any number of stars who amassed fortunes playing tough guys with guns, who freely shot, killed, and stabbed their way to the top in their *movies*. But when a real war is brewing, they claim to be peaceniks.

They go to Baghdad or some other hotbed of world tension, with sunglasses to cover up their high, and pretend to know more than our government.

Take George Clooney.

Clooney played a doctor on *ER*, but he doesn't know the first thing about being a doctor other than what is scripted for him. That doesn't stop him from prescribing his anti-American sentiments. He had the audacity to refer to America's war with Saddam as "senseless."[12] Clooney the Looney. So he played a soldier in *Three Kings*. Big deal. He played a brawny lieutenant colonel in *The Peacemaker*. Does that mean he's qualified to speak on issues of war?

Acting doesn't a soldier make.

So when Clooney spouts off against the war, he expects us to swoon like schoolgirls with a crush. What does he think we are? A bunch of flunkies? These leftist actors presume to know what's in the best interest of America.

Don't get me wrong. I fully support freedom of speech. You're entitled to your view. I have mine. That's the beautiful thing about America. Nobody will cut out your tongue and feed it to your dog if you refuse to tow the company line.

Freedom of speech is one of our most cherished liberties. Brave men and women paid the ultimate sacrifice for that freedom by spilling their own blood. Why? To ensure that you, your children, and one day your grandchildren will *still* have that right.

Make no mistake. It's one thing to express your opinion as a *private citizen* engaged in a healthy debate about various topics. It's entirely another thing to pass yourself off as an objective media spokesmouth and then lecture us with a leftist slant on mom and apple pie. And, I might add, in turn, endanger the lives of the men and woman who are fighting for your very freedom.

While Hollywood Idiots certainly have a right to air their contempt for America, they also have to understand that people have a right *not* to go to their movies. Indeed, the Bill of Rights does not require us to *listen* or *agree* whenever the Enlightened Ones speak.

In other words, there are consequences to dissent. We don't have to worship the Enlightened Ones and throw money at them as they continue to assault everything we believe in. That goes with the territory. Only a sadist would continue to embrace those who kick Lady Liberty in the teeth.

If they want to stand up and spout off, they should just be prepared for the consequences.

I face it every day on the radio with boycotts from the brown shorts.

FROM BROWN SHIRTS TO BROWN SHORTS

And now we've come from actors who were all patriots, and for whom "patriotic" wasn't a dirty word, to actors who, almost without exception, are America-haters.

How did this happen?

It's the same thing that has happened to our schools, our courts, and all other aspects of our society: a takeover by the Red Diaper Doper Babies.

This shift in attitude has been fostered by a combination of the RDDBs' communist ideology foisted on the sheeple through the liberal educational system, along with the intense use of drugs. I believe these factors explain the perverse twisting in the mindset of this country. The liberal media has aided and abetted this disaster.

These RDDBs have turned an entire generation of actors into subversives, who hate the country that gave them fame and fortune. Even to the detriment of their own careers, they continue to hate America. They're losing audiences across the country, but they continue to sabotage the nation. Which shows you what an insular world they really live in.

Don't get me wrong. Not all actors are peacenik potheads. Robert Duvall, commenting on political activism by Hollywood Idiots, said, "They should keep their mouths shut."[13] Actor Jason Priestley, who made his bucks on *Beverly Hills 90210*, concurs.

Still, the question arises as to why many more actors beyond this handful, who might be inclined toward patriotism and loving this great country, are afraid to speak out?

Answer: Because in this day of ultra-tolerance there now ironically exists a redlist in Hollywood.

Remember in the 1950s when people with communist affiliations and such were blacklisted from working in Hollywood? We've all been told over and over again about actors being blacklisted and the "horrors" of the McCarthy hearings and investigations.

Today, we've come full circle.

In the 50s, the question was, "Are you now, or have you ever been a member of the Communist party?" Even if you said "No," you were condemned before you answered. You were blacklisted from working in Hollywood if you had any association whatsoever with left-leaning groups.

Today, there is a redlist. Here's how it works in the age of "tolerance."

Unless you're on the redlist and a fellow traveler of the likes of the Ed Asners and the other power brokers of Hollywood, you do not work in "their" town.

So, the question today is, "Are you now, or have you ever been *racist*, or *homophobic*, or *intolerant of alternative lifestyles?*"

If you answer "Yes" to any of these questions, you do not work in Hollywood. Period. End of story.

You think I'm making this up? I happen to be going through it right now. I've been redlisted throughout the media. That I survive and thrive is a miracle of a few brave souls within.

The brown shorts of today have targeted me because I do not kowtow to their agenda. What is perplexing to me is that in the media and on the air I rarely mention homosexual issues at all.

I am probably a libertarian when it comes to sexuality for both political and personal reasons. I do not want the government to intervene in anyone's sexual behavior unless such behavior can be proven to be bad social policy (that's why there are laws against rape, molestation, and incest), or, if children are affected.

In those cases, I'm adamantly in support of the children. Particularly the straight children, such as the Boy Scouts. I back the Scouts 100 percent. I do not back the perverts who are trying to destroy this fine organization by imposing their twisted agenda on boys who are trying to lead the straight and narrow life.

However, in the media, I rarely talk about these subjects. And so what if I did? This is America. This is the land that is supposed to entertain the free exchange of ideas. Or did the brown shorts forget that piece of history? Maybe if they spent less time in the bathhouses and more time in the schoolhouses they'd learn a thing or two about the principles upon which this country was founded.

The vendetta against me is complete.

Now, I've used the pointedly sarcastic term called "brown shorts" to describe those who have targeted me as their enemy. This should be put in context.

Who better than Dr. Savage to provide you with the history lesson you should have been taught in high school while your hat was on backwards? I realize you may need to pause occasionally during the lesson for a hydration break or to catch a smoke. Just stick with me. Why?

The future of your freedom of speech is on the line.

In the early 1930s, while Hitler was terrorizing his way to power in Germany, he used thugs who dressed in brown shirts to conduct terror campaigns in the streets of Germany. These hooligans were members of the SA, short for the *Stürm Abteilung*, better known as the storm troopers.

The SA was run by Ernst Roehm, a notoriously aggressive homosexual. The SA leadership was largely a cult of violent homosexuals who, like Hitler, bullied people into submission thereby opening up Germany for Hitler's takeover.

Shortly after Hitler's rise to total power, Hitler unleashed his SS (the *Schutzstaffel*, which means the "Protective Echelon") on the leadership of the SA in the infamous "Night of the Long Knives."

By the way, when the brown shirts wanted to eliminate the Jews, they didn't start with concentration camps. They started with economic boycotts.

No one starts with a death camp.

They start with trumped up moral outrage.

Then boycotts.

The brown shirts would paint *Juden* on the stores of Jewish-owned businesses. That was to tell the Germans not to shop there because the owners supposedly weren't good, loyal Germans who followed the Nazi party line.

Instead of that today, we have the *brown shorts* painting the equivalent of the word *Juden* on the window of anybody they want to destroy. And when they gain total power, I see a dire end to the conservatives in this country.

This is the central battle for the future survival of this country.

The invasion of the brown shorts is one of the hottest flash points in the culture war of values. I'm telling you, whether or not we preserve our rights to freely and openly express our opinions depends on our ability to keep the brown shorts at bay. And, if you are a conservative actor, your ability to maintain your livelihood is on the line.

Even some mainstream actors have joked that there is a gay mafia running Hollywood. I'm here to say the Velvet Mafia is no joke. It's a reality. It's a sick, dark reality, worse than any horror movie Hollywood could dream up.

It's no secret that some of the richest power brokers are overtly homosexuals. David Geffen. Barry Diller. Sandy Gallin, *et al.* They are out-and-proud "gays." Their position is either you follow their views or you don't work. Period.

And while they like to think of themselves as munificent, their generosity ends if you cross them. It's well known within the artistic community that Geffen can end a career with a phone call. Just ask Michael Ovitz, the former head of Creative Artists Agency whose career was sabotaged[14] by what he calls the "Gay Mafia."

I don't really care what these power brokers can do with their phones. As long as I have breath in my lungs, I will expose these modern Pied Pipers for the frauds they are before they seduce America into total ruin.

You see, the reason the homosexual radicals in GLAAD targeted me on TV is not so much that they hated *me* but that they were trying to use me as a *pawn* in their bigger game. For starters, they wanted to get a meeting with the president of NBC, the parent company of MSNBC, so that they could get their teeth into General Electric, which owns NBC.

Then, in turn, the homosexual radicals wanted a meeting with the president of GE to negotiate domestic partnership rights. They wanted more gay-friendly programming and more gay actors on NBC. Again, they're not stupid. They understand that the best way to sell America on their radical agenda is to take the message into every living room in the Corn Belt.

Familiarity breeds indifference.

Frankly, militant homosexuals won't be happy until they have completed the homosexualization of America with the legitimization of homosexual marriage, adoption, scouting, teaching, preaching, and the like.

That, my friend, is the ultimate goal.

Thus far, they have been very successful.

By the way, this is not to say all Hollywood Idiots are gay. That's not the point. But there *is* a connection between deviant sexual behavior and a negative view of the overall society. That deviant sexual behavior seems to trigger a rejection of structure, of authority, of monogamy, and of family. The two worldviews cannot coexist.

And this deviance is reflected in an overall anti-America disgust.

I want to take this further.

This is why we should pay close attention to the Bible's prohibition against this kind of behavior. God was warning us that there is something about the practice of homosexuality that seems to short circuit the moral circuits of a man or a woman, and it turns the individual both against himself and society as a whole.

Witness the attack on the Boy Scouts.

Can you imagine in your father's generation that homosexuals would be presented as morally superior to Boy Scouts? That judges in San Francisco would refuse to serve as Scout leaders of the Boy Scouts because the Scouts were not kowtowing to the homosexual agenda? United Way stopped giving to Boy Scouts across the country because they would not bend over for the radical homosexual agenda.

I ask you again: Can you imagine any of this happening in your father's generation?

WHO LOVES YA, BABY?

What is it with these Hollywood actors today? They go overseas just to stab us in the back. Take Woody Allen. This over-the-hill nebbish hasn't had a hit in years. Probably because he insists on casting himself as a leading man opposite sexy young actresses who have to pretend they find him attractive.

Sam, my paternal grandfather, the "astronaut" of the family. Manhattan, 1920s.

Rebecca, my maternal grandmother, and little "Speedy" Savage. Bronx, early 1940s.

Janet, my Muse and inspiration for all these years.

With Mom in her kitchen.
Queens, New York, 1980s.

Dad and Tippy the Chow.
Spring Glen, New York,
1953.

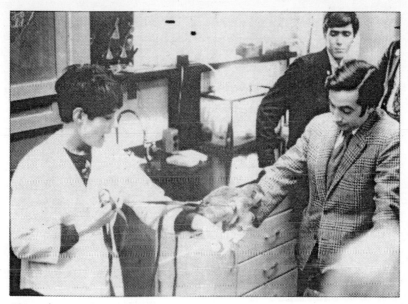

Bio teacher. Manhattan, 1967.

In search of the durian. Hawaii, 1980s.

Pioneering ethnobotanist. Viti Levu, Fiji, 1969.

River crossing. Waidina River, Fiji, 1971.

Many years in the wilderness of corporate consulting. Pittsburgh, 1994.

Snowy, the angel with fur.

Rebecca, my guide through the natural world. Stinson Beach.

With Russ, who kicked off The Paul Revere Society and is now a giant of commerce.

One of many "Compassionate Conservative" Conventions, long before the Republicans used it.

Too real for TV.

At last, a station (KNEW) in my city that understands what talent is. San Francisco, 2003.

My ship has come in. (But where will I steer her?)

That's about as believable as my being elected mayor of San Fransicko.

While our boys were dying in Iraq, Woody flew to France where people still think he's talented. So much for the notion that the French have good taste. Why does Woody Allen love the French even when they stab us in the back? Because they find him funny. It's worth asking *why* the French find him funny. Could it be they like to laugh at Jews who act like stereotypical weaklings?

Whatever the reason, this self-appointed spokesman for the sheeple said he wanted Americans to put their differences with the French to rest. Why? Was it because the French had apologized for their obstructionist role in the war with Iraq? Was it because the French finally decided to send troops to keep the peace?

Hardly. Woody wanted America to mend fences because he is tired of calling the thin strips of potatoes boiled in grease "Freedom Fries." I guess he's forgotten the price we pay for freedom in this country. A price, I might add, the French weren't willing to pay. I say, *Au revoir*, Woody.

Joining the ranks of the Hollywood Idiots is Dustin Hoffman. He's another genius. So he got lucky with Mrs. Robinson. Big deal. That makes him a scholar on world politics? So he played a sleaze ball producer who manufactured a bogus war in *Wag the Dog*. Does that mean he's an expert on warfare?

I'll let you in on a little secret. I'll tell you exactly why the Ratso Hoffman voiced his opposition to war. But first, think about this. Where did he give his speech attacking America? In what country did the Ratso Rizzo Hoffman put a knife in our flag? I'll tell you where. Ratso Hoffman spoke out after receiving a lifetime achievement accolade at the Empire Film Awards in London. How come? Why did he go over to old Vic to give us the old stick?

Because he feels safe there.

Because he wants their affirmation.

Because he lives for their applause.

He jets halfway around the world just to say essentially this: "Gee, folks, I really hate my country. Although they made me rich beyond my wildest dreams, although I realize I don't really deserve the money and fame I have because I'm really only a marionette, I hate America. I'm like you; I hate America. I really do. Do you love me now? Do you love me now?"

Richard Gere is no different.

Gere traveled to the 53rd Berlin Film Festival to peddle his new wares. While the American sheeple were busy watching sports and golf and things of that nature, Gere expressed his anti-war sentiments to the Germans, saying, "the Bush administration's plans for war are a bizarre bad dream."[15]

Gere exclaimed, "There doesn't appear to be any sort of basis for any of this."[16] He was speaking of the war, not his movie, of course. Gere was skeptical of Bush's motives. "I have a feeling that something hidden is at work here that will someday see the light of day."[17]

He went on to claim that "America has never paid any attention to other people, so it's absurd for Bush to say that it's all in the best interest of the Iraqi people."[18]

Hold on Richard.

America has never paid any attention to other people? Richard, what are you smoking? Have you heard of the Nazis? The Japanese "factories of death"? Of the Stalinist death camps? Of Pol Pot's mountain of human skulls? Of the North Vietnamese slaughter of one million South Vietnamese *after* the U.S. withdrew?

What really gets me is the outright hypocrisy of many of these dullards. Their motto is "Do as I say, not as I do." Case in point: Brabra Streisand. She fashions herself as an "environmentalist" and a "conservationist." If you mean she lives in a heavily guarded "environment" where she's "conserving" several prime acres of Malibu coastline for her own personal enjoyment, then she's right.

Meanwhile, her website offers inspirational messages to her fans urging them to wash their clothes in cold water and then line dry them. Does Babs do this on her own Malibu estate? If she sets herself up as a conservationist, she should lead by example. Unless, of course, she's just another Hollywood hypocrite. While we're at it, I'd like to know where her electric car is. Her windmill generator. I wonder what it costs to air condition her eight bedrooms and eleven bathrooms? Or is the song "Evergreen" really about her bank account?

As I've said before, liberalism is a mental disease.

That certainly explains part of their disorder. And yet, there's something deeper at work here. For the longest time I was stumped. Then, one day reading the paper, it dawned on me like the morning sun rising above the fog. I discovered there's actually a latent behavioral pattern here affecting both men and women actors.

For instance, the women actors who once had good behinds are typically neutral about their politics as long as their gluteus maximi are still high on their legs. But the lower their gluteus maximi, the higher their liberal quotient. The L.Q. goes up as the B.Q. (butt quotient) goes down.

And so it is with the men.

Dustin Hoffman and Richard Gere are over-the-hill. They, as well as most of the "famous" men who are attacking America on foreign soil, are fundamentally Viagra cases.

Let me connect the dots.

It comes down to one word: acceptance. These actors thrive on acceptance. On applause. They're affirmation junkies. They'll travel half way around the world, stab America in the back, all to get another fix. Without applause, they emotionally die. Period.

Take the Oscars.

The Oscars are a bore; they're just a trade show. You know, every year the producers come up with new "inventive" categories. Soon they'll be schlepping out awards for the "Best Neck Job," the "Best Botox Smile," the most "Original Breast Implants," the "Best Hidden Junkie."

You get the picture.

I'm telling you, that's the level on which they operate. They have to find a way to massage all of the star-studded egos. You know, in this day of liberalism where everybody has to feel good about themselves, producers have to manufacture creative ways to pat all of the Hollywood Idiots on the back. It's just an orgy of self-importance.

Of course, the day after the Oscars, half of the audience of actors are back in the rehab wards. Imagine what they feel afterwards when they don't win anything. All night long they sat there with their fake smiles plastered on their faces, clapping their hands together with about as much enthusiasm as watching a golf match.

Then, when they walk away empty-handed, they rush to their limo to score a horse tranquilizer. Especially the women. I imagine they have to get illegal Quaaludes from Mexico to control the women when they lose.

No wonder they run off to other countries to trash-talk America. Like I said, they're affirmation junkies in search of a fix. There's another reason. Fundamentally, many actors are searching for significance. They mope around hoping their lives really, *really* matter. They long to make a difference, so they join any number of misguided, liberal feel-good causes.

Save the trees. Save the whales. Save the snails.

Abort the babies, no problem. Just hate America if you want to work in Los Angeles's film world.

As you'll see in a moment, that's why I think dimwits like Sean Penn intentionally jeopardized our war effort in search of his personal self-actualization.

POTEMKIN VILLAGE, THE SEQUEL

When the far-leftist, anti-America actor Sean Penn traveled to Baghdad to protest the war, it was like Potemkin village all over again. Let me explain.

Sean Pencilhead's hatred of conservativism and of President Bush is well-documented. This failed actor, a stooge of the radical Left, traveled to Baghdad for a three-day visit. Mind you, he is a man who never went to college. He is just an actor. He only reads scripts.

He has no background in history.

No background in diplomacy.

No background in the rules of engagement in war.

What was his destination? A hospital.

Tell me. What could Pencilhead learn about the situation in Baghdad from visiting a hospital? Why, nothing, that's what. At best, he might have seen hospital beds without sheets and hear the same tired stories that they lack medicine. It's the same lie that the radical Left was putting out for years to cover up the truth about Iraq.

The answer is, of course, simple.

If the Iraqi doctors and nurses did not have medicine, then the dictator needed to stop building palaces and aggrandizing himself with his mistresses and spend the money instead on medication. Moreover, Pencilhead could have donated a few million bucks for medicines with his Hollywood lefty friends instead of wasting money on international airplane trips, expensive hotels, and meetings.

His experience is nothing but a carbon copy of Potemkin village. In 1930, Stalin was the absolute ruler of Russia. He was also a mass murderer. Millions who would not go along with the Communist program were being slaughtered. Millions who would not sufficiently kowtow to the political correctness that swept through Russia were being re-educated in slave camps.

We in the West knew Stalin was an evil man. He was as evil as Hitler. But the radical liberals of the time, the socialists, the Left, and the Communist sympathizers sent a contingent of visitors to the Soviet Union to see what conditions were like. It was a whitewash.

Stalin built a village paradise called Potemkin Village. Everything was just perfect. It was the original Disneyland. Happy little village people strolled through the well-lit streets. There was ample food. The people were well-dressed.

For their part, the stooge actors of the Left came back all smiles. Impressed, they glowed as they offered their report: "We have just come back from Mother Russia, and we are thrilled that the people are very happy and very well cared for. What a wonderful place."

That was Potemkin Village.

Pencilhead's meddling in the affairs of state just three weeks before America went to war was both irresponsible and, in essence, a rerun of the Potemkin Village experience. It's a sad day in America when, thanks to a failed educational system, few understand the dynamics of this lesson. Must we repeat history?

As the Spanish philosopher George Santyana said, those who do not know their history are condemned to repeat it. And if you liberals don't know your history, you will be condemned to repeat it along with the rest of us.

I don't understand how this can go on, how uneducated puppets like this can engage in politics and be taken seriously. It's beyond comprehension.

Here is a man who built his film career by shooting people, stabbing them, or punching them violently on screen—or acting like a complete dimwit. He claims he's a pacifist—who has punched his share of photographers, including one knockdown that landed him a month in jail.[19] Why would you take him seriously?

The answer is because the media is so leftist they put him on an equal footing with the president of the United States. I'm sorry; Pencilhead did what the radical leftists did in the 1930s with Potemkin Village.

SOME PEOPLE JUST DON'T GET IT

Affirmation. Self-actualization. Significance.

Whatever the reasons motivating this crop of Hollywood actors and their Siamese-twin accomplices in the news media to badmouth their country, I'm encouraged by the backlash. Yes, we're witnessing the first stirrings amongst the sheeple. It's a search and a hunger for the truth.

Is it any wonder my last book, *The Savage Nation*, spent the better part of three months atop the *New York Times'* bestseller list?

The fact that the book you are holding will also be on numerous bestseller lists is a reflection that this is a changing of the guard; it's a changing of the tides in America. Trust me, the world is a different place. Of course, the last people to tell you about it are those who are still pushing the worn-out, failed liberal messages.

I say it's about time. We are on the verge of losing this country. We have been teetering on the edge of no return. But the scales are starting to tip back towards thoughtful American ideals, especially with the help of unfiltered news sources. No longer must we rely on the Big Three networks or CNN for our information.

Yes, the murky, liberal haze that has blinded and held this nation hostage is losing its audience share. Time after time, the overt efforts to propagate the liberal agenda in the media fail miserably.

Just look at Phil Donahue.

Once the king of daytime TV, Donahue's latest TV show was comatose. It was DOA. Watching it was less interesting than a visit to the morgue. His was an old, sad story by an old, sad man. The leftist powerbrokers thought they could shuffle him out and he would sell big.

He didn't sell. Why not?

Because the American people have moved beyond the social engineering ushered in by the sixties movement. Let me put it this way. This trend toward conservative thinking is similar to what happened to the silent movies.

In the early days of film, the stars acted but couldn't be heard. With the introduction of the "talkies"—movies with both sight and sound—the industry was forever changed. Naturally, the silent movie stars resisted this change. They said, "Ah, come on, no one's gonna listen to them talkies. They want silent movies with organ music."

They were wrong. Silent movies became obsolete. The talkies took over.

We in the conservative media are the talkies. The libs are the silent movie stars of yesterday. But they don't just give up. The liberals in the media will do anything to preserve a place in front of the masses. They will lie to you, they will manipulate the truth, they will tell you up is down and down is up. They will tell you sin is in.

I say that message no longer resonates with *thinking* people. As an independent conservative, my message is about family values; it's about patriotism; it's about supporting the police and the military.

I believe in the traditional family. I believe we must close our nation's borders to those who would sneak or cheat their way in, or who wish to come and do us harm. I support English as our only national language, and I especially support our common culture.

Borders, language, culture—that's my motto.

Whether a you're a journalist or an actor, you can't have it both ways. You can't pretend that, for example, as a liberal, you care about the traditional family and then celebrate leather bars or celebrate homosexual marriage or celebrate the explosion of lesbian propaganda on television and the popular media. It doesn't work that way.

You can't say you're a patriot and then turn around and attack the military. Or interview our sworn enemy for the sake of a scoop. You can't say you support the police and then call for the abolition of the death penalty. Many of the bums on death row are there for killing police.

You can't have it both ways. Nor are people that stupid. Most of the libs underestimate the American people. I don't. While the elite of the mainstream media believe that you're a bunch of imbeciles and that you need to be spoon-fed, I see you as the sleeping giant who is finally getting your hands around the truth.

WHY LIBERALS FAIL IN TALK RADIO

When it comes to talk radio, liberals flop (unless they resort to shock and schlock) and the conservatives win, hands down. It's the one place where liberalism constantly misfires. Why?

Here it is.

Conservative talk radio has exploded because it is an alternative to the prevailing leftist doctrine hammered day and night by the press and television. And, while conservative talk show hosts are likeable, thoughtful communicators, ultimately it is the message that we project that keeps the listeners coming back. What message is that?

Americans want to uphold our family values.

Americans are hungry for our passion and patriotism.

Americans want to support the police.

Americans understand the vital role of the military.

That's why conservative talk radio is a winner. There is no Lib-O-Meter filter coming between the listener and the host, distorting his value system. What's more, listeners spend five to fifteen hours a week with us. They get to know us. There is no makeup. There are no lights. They live with us, and they have to come to like us to become regular listeners.

I began in the ultra-liberal bay area of San Francisco on a single AM station. I now have more than six to eight million listeners a week and can be heard on over three hundred radio stations nationwide.

I received my Ph.D. from the University of California at Berkeley in nutrition and epidemiology. I wrote eighteen books in the field of alternative medicine prior to beginning my career in talk radio. I searched the rainforests of the South Pacific for well over twenty years, searching for cures as a leader in the field of alternative medicine.

Do I fit the stereotype of the guy driving a pickup truck and carrying a shotgun that the mainstream media projects as representing conservatives? Am I just a disc jockey who got lucky?

I don't think so.

I and other conservative talk show hosts are passionate about saving America. We are passionate about protecting our borders, preserving the English language, and preserving the common cultural values that built America.

Liberals, by contrast, support the Tower of Babel called multiculturalism, ultra-tolerance, and multilingualism. Liberals attack every significant aspect of our culture that has made America great, while conservatives continue to support the values inherent in the common culture.

Liberals, by the way, who have failed on talk radio, all have had the same flaws. They were too strident and sounded like junior Lenins. This has forced many networks and radio stations to cancel liberal shows, including those of Jerry Brown, Mario Cuomo, Jim Hightower, Alan Dershowitz, and Ed Koch. Radio stations didn't cancel these hosts for political reasons. They're in business to make a profit, plain and simple. Profits require an audience. But the listeners were never there.

No wonder these losers bash the country.

Or play the victim card.

I know many of you liberals are offended by this analysis. Many of you are offended more by me than by Osama bin Laden. Many of you are so bent in your mind that you think that my free speech should be banned by the brown shorts while the speech of bin Laden should be broadcast live from al Jazeera television—or CBS for that matter.

Many of you are so twisted in your mind that you trust our enemies more than you do President Bush. This, of course, is what liberalism is. It is Trojan horse fascism without the jackboots. But I've got your number. You don't fool me. And you're not going to keep fooling the American people. *You* are the Enemy Within.

Now, for those of you in the middle, I say turn your hat around and learn to think for yourself. When the Enlightened Ones speak, test their liberal ideals. It is then and only then that you'll see what an abject failure liberalism really is. Maybe then you will join me as I work to make America a better place.

You think that's sentimental?

Then join hands with Pencilhead, Dannyboy, and the Ditzy Chicks while the culture bombs drop on your family; while the growing population of illegal immigrants who refuse to adopt to American ways or speak our language slowly become an internal threat to our national survival; while the radical Islamic hordes sweep across the globe.

SIX

FAITH:

THE DOGS OF HATE

The Dogs of Hate have been tearing at people of faith since the cultural revolution of the 1960s. They've torn apart our courts and schools and are now ripping apart the military and police. Snarling with utter viciousness against our houses of worship, the Dogs of Hate have been unleashed by the radical Left. And like the rabid canines that they are, this angry pack won't back down until they've sunk their teeth into every believing person to make them distrust the teachings of God.

The anti-religious radical left-wingers have ratcheted up their attacks upon the moral underpinnings of American society—our religious institutions and sacred symbols. At no time in our history has their hatred for people of faith been more vicious or more blatant.

Do you think I'm making this up?

I'll prove it to you in this chapter.

But first you should know that, from my perspective, I really don't care if you choose to worship God, Buddha, Allah, the moon, or nothing at all. That's your business. But hear this: Your constitutionally protected right to worship as you wish, especially if you are Jewish or Christian, is in jeopardy. If the intolerant Dogs of Hate have their way, you will lose your right to speak about your faith in any meaningful way—unless, of course, you're a Muslim.

I'll explain why Muslims get a pass in the next chapter.

What's even more outrageous is how the irreligious Left has tricked you into *paying* for their attack on *your* faith. Yes, religion is under siege, and thanks to the co-opting of tax dollars, you're funding your own crucifixion. As you'll see, the self-righteous phony high priests of ultra-liberalism are relentless in their efforts to drive the Church out of public life once and for all. How?

By altering or eliminating religion from history textbooks.

By censoring the public display of the Ten Commandments.

By inflaming hostilities toward people of faith.

By invading the leadership of faith-based groups.

By seeking to remove God from the Pledge of Allegiance.

By insulting, smearing, and desecrating religion and religious symbols in the name of art.

By rewriting religious restrictions on homosexual activity.

I can only pray that the American sheeple wake up to that reality before it's too late.

Whether or not you are a religious person, any rational thinker will recognize that the free exercise of religion is both a necessary and valuable institution for maintaining the health of this nation. Our Founding Fathers understood this, contrary to what the irreligious Left would have you believe.

ENTER THE GAY BISHOP

The most insidious attack by these mad dogs has been their ambush of the clergy. How? By rewriting religious restrictions on homosexual activity and by convincing the sheeple that God has recently changed His mind on the subject.

On August 6, 2003, the irreligious Left within the Episcopal Church voted to make "Reverend" Gene Robinson, a loud and proud gay clergyman, the next bishop of New Hampshire. As news of the vote surfaced, Episcopal churches across the country—and around the world—braced themselves for the worst—and got it. The vote sent shockwaves from Chicago to Canterbury.

Within minutes of the final tally, the Anglican community watched helplessly as their denomination headed for a split. The conservative leadership, at least those who didn't resign in disgust, immediately called upon the Archbishop of Canterbury, Rowan Williams, to intervene.

No other decision in recent history has caused such a schism amongst the faithful. It's not just that Gene Robinson's sexuality is a violation of all the teachings of the Bible. That's the least of the problem. It's the man's egomania, which approaches that of a psychopath. To selfishly elevate himself above the Church, to risk the split of his own denomination, and to say that his sexuality is something that God is doing as "a new thing," is indicative of a pathological personality.

Listen to what this egomaniac said after his confirmation:

> The whole notion of sexual orientation is quite a new one. It's only about a hundred years old, and we can't take a modern day concept and plug it back into an ancient text and pretend that's what those people knew and meant when they wrote it. At the time of the writing of those scriptures, everyone was presumed to be heterosexual, so to act in any other way was against their nature. So what I would say is that Scripture simply does not address what we're addressing today, which is faithful, monogamous, life-long intentioned relationships between people of the same gender.[1]

Let's look at his credibility as a student of history and of the Bible.

First, to suggest that the "concept" of sexual orientation is only a hundred years old is nuts. Where did he get that? What about the rampant homosexuality in Greece? In Rome? Or back in the days of Sodom and Gomorrah?

Second, to say "those people" presumed everyone to be heterosexual doesn't jibe with reality. Where did he get his theology degree? What Bible is he talking about? While he's at it, why doesn't he just get a bottle of white-out and change other parts of the sacred text he doesn't think are contemporary enough?

Do you see what's happening? This egomaniac is actually saying he is greater than God and Abraham. This lost soul, and those who defend him, have pushed God aside and inserted themselves in the role of the Almighty.

Third, I believe he's delusional. Robinson claims he was chosen for this roll. He said, "It's been a long time in coming, it's not so much a dream as a calling from God."[2] He actually thinks God felt it necessary for *him* to reinterpret the scriptures. This crackpot sees himself as a new Luther of the sexual organ. He's attempting to create a new sexual reformation of the Church.

That's why he went on to say, "I believe God is doing a new thing in terms of its [sic] inclusion of gay and lesbian people in the church." Which makes perfect sense if your "god" is located three inches below your belt buckle.

What's Gene's ultimate goal? He told Diane Sawyer, "I suspect that before too very long, other denominations will follow and welcome openly gay and lesbian people into leadership positions. That's certainly my prayer."[3] In other words, he's the pioneer. He's the Anointed One designated to stimulate gay leadership worldwide.

This goes to show you how demented he is. He suffers from a mental disease. As I've said, extreme liberalism is not a philosophy; it is a mental disorder. At any other time in history, this man would have been put into a mental institution for these statements. Of course, instead of locking him up, the leftist-run media puts him on the silver screen to gain a few pieces of gold.

America's favorite liberal Archbishop, Dezi Tutu, can't understand what "all the fuss" is about. This fake thinks the gay bishop debate is no big deal. Dezi said, "For us that doesn't make a difference, the sexual orientation."⁴ Could that be why he's named Tutu? Or does his name describe his garment?

BEHIND CLOSED DOORS

While Tutu and others like him can't understand what the fuss over the gay bishop is, let me explain it this way. I host *The Savage Nation* from a studio in a high-rise building overlooking the San Fransicko Bay. It's got three elevators. A lot of old people live in the same building. Here's my problem. The elevators have no ventilation. None whatsoever.

Why is that an issue, you ask?

Because the old folks pass gas in the elevator. They get out, you get in. I've got to go up twenty-five stories, and some days my eyes are smarting so bad I've got to put a scarf on my face. Here's the connection to the gay bishop story.

Gene Robinson and his ilk would argue that what happens "behind closed doors" is none of our business. Out of sight, out of mind. What's the big deal if the Church welcomes gays into leadership positions with open arms? After all, gay sex done out of view doesn't affect us, so why should we care what two consenting people want to do?

That's where they're wrong.

Bowel gas released behind closed doors lingers in the air, poisoning those who come along later. In the same way, the reckless "private" sexual practices of homosexuals behind closed doors ultimately affects every one of us.

You think this illustration is a stretch? I don't know how else to help you understand the nature of the lie that's at work here.

I ask you, how many *billions* of our tax dollars have been spent to deal with the AIDS mess over the last decade? How many millions of our tax dollars are being spent right now for supposed AIDS awareness and prevention? Don't tell me that sexual activity of a certain kind doesn't affect all of us. It does.

On April 18, 2003, the *Washington Blade*, a radical homosexual newspaper, ran a full-page ad promoting what was supposed to be about prevention but was nothing more than a gay dating service. The ad asked, "Tired of the bar scene? Tired of phonies? Want to go beyond type? COME AND MEET REAL MEN."

Do you know who paid for the ad?

You did. That's your tax dollars at work. The Washington DC Department of Health used tax dollars to run and promote the seminar which was billed as a "social workshop" for bisexual and gay men to learn how to "deepen intimacy with fun exercises."[5] That's nothing more than a payoff to the lobby of the suicidal militant pro-promiscuity crowd. Period. And we're surprised that the number of gay and bisexual men diagnosed with HIV has risen three years in a row? According to the Centers for Disease Control, this "private activity" has created a 17.7 percent jump in new HIV cases since 1999 among gay/bi/tri men.[6]

As cases of infection go up, so will your taxes, in order to deal with the fallout. That's a fact. That's not being homophobic. That's the scientific reality. I don't care if the culture of death wants to "get it on" behind closed doors. Their stench, like a black fog, is lingering in the air, and we, as a nation, are gagging on the fumes.

Now, Gene Robinson, this psychopathic clergyman hiding behind his holy robes, wants the Church to add its blessing. I'm telling you, the Dogs of Hate are using every trick in the book to paganize our churches and rewrite our history.

FROM PLYMOUTH ROCK TO PLYMOUTH CROCK

One of the favorite ploys of the irreligious Left is to write God out of the history books. They, with the aid of their co-conspirators in education, seek to eliminate any and all references to our religious heritage. Even though historical evidences of our Judeo-Christian heritage, and the celebration of the Bible as a basis for American law, abound. Here's one your history teacher left out of class.

Back when Rhode Island was a colony, instead of the inbreeding ground for liberalism as it is today, their citizenry crafted the Charter of 1683, which defined the worship of God as one of their core values.

Imagine trying to teach kids that God is a part of American history in a public school where transgender studies in "Your Mommy Used To Be a Daddy" are the rave. The liberal education establishment doesn't want your kids to know that the "absolute laws" found in Scripture as referred to in the Charter of 1683 became the basis for our Declaration of Independence.

I'll give you another one.

Eighteen years after the Pilgrims set foot on Plymouth Rock, they saw a need to train pastors for future generations and decided to found the first American college. Harvard College to be exact.

I'm sure the idea of training God's teachers would give fits to the trust-fund babies running Harvard today. Harvard's "Rules and Precepts" adopted in 1646 required that "Every one shall so exercise himself in reading the Scriptures twice a day that they be ready to give an account of their proficiency therein."

These days, any student openly reading a Bible on Harvard's campus would be ridiculed and ostracized.

As I said, the signs of our Judeo-Christian national heritage are etched in concrete—for now. Next time you visit the nation's capital, see for yourself. Stop by the Washington Monument, the Jefferson Memorial, the Lincoln Memorial. Read the inscriptions. They're replete with references to God and the Bible.

Or stop and see the Supremes in the Supreme Court building. There you'll find a copy of the Ten Commandments hanging above the head of the chief justice and a statue of Moses on the east front section. I'd suggest you plan that trip to Washington DC before the Dogs of Hate have these national symbols expunged.

Does this seem redundant? I must counter the years of leftist brainwashing that has programmed you to believe America does not have deep religious roots.

But the clipped-haired, hard-Left czarinas of the National Education

Association suppress such knowledge in favor of *sensitiiiivity* training for gender-obsessed adolescents. If Abraham Lincoln, John Quincy Adams, and Calvin Coolidge were alive today, the Christophobic NEA would ram Ritalin down their throats and march them off to reeducation camp.

Just a few short decades after the founding of America, Daniel Webster, a real statesman and America's foremost advocate of nationalism during his day, felt compelled to remind his contemporaries, "Our ancestors established their system of government on morality and religious sentiment. Moral habits, they believed, cannot safely be trusted on any other foundation than religious principle, nor any government be secure which is not supported by moral habits."[7]

Webster refused to lose sight of our moral bearings. He was a far better man than the hollow statesmen of today, like Sen. John Kerry. Kerry, bursting with all the charisma of a mortician, is a very liberal Catholic. Kerry had the nerve to lecture Pope John Paul II over the Church's stance on gay marriage, arguing the pontiff "crossed the line"[8] when the Vatican called on American politicians to thwart the legalization of homosexual marriage.

Rather than stand with Webster on the side of God and country and our religious heritage, Kerry failed to exercise the good sense to support the views of his own church. Kerry chafed, "It is important not to have the church instructing politicians."[9] Why not offer the same caution, Mr. Kerry, about not having radical homosexual and lesbian groups instructing politicians?

Let's not get sidetracked by the arguments from the lefties who like to muddy the waters by suggesting the Founders were not truly pious. That's not the point. What matters is this: Our Founders placed a premium on preserving the right for Americans to practice their own faith. Freely, publicly, and without apology.

They believed so much in the Ten Commandments (of God) that they made them the cornerstone of our constitutional rights! Try teaching this to the phony proponents of tolerance who crafted the Pennsylvania Public School Code in such a way as to restrict a teacher's right to religious self-expression. The code prohibits teachers from wearing personal religious symbols (such as a cross or a Star of David) unless *hidden* from the view of the morally numb student body. On May 6, 2003, Brenda Nichol, a teacher's aid at Penns Manor Area Elementary School, learned her lesson the hard way. She dared to wear a one-inch cross and was *suspended for one year*. A second violation would bring permanent expulsion from teaching at that school.

Thankfully, a federal judge had enough sense to reverse the school's action.[10]

Make no mistake. First, the Dogs of Hate snap the crosses from off of your necklaces. Then they snap off the crosses from the war memorials of the men and women who died to preserve the freedom of religion. What's next? Maybe these unhappy pagans will decide that the Torah is too "exclusionist" and outlaw the core of Judaism.

Benjamin Franklin hit the nail on the head when he asked, "If men are so wicked with religion, what would they be without it?"[11]

I'll answer that one: They'd be exactly like what we're seeing in the bathhouses of San Fransicko. A lost and hedonistic people undistracted by a moral compass. A people who routinely engage in high risk, indiscriminate sexual practices with multiple, and often HIV-infected, anonymous partners even when they know such insane behavior is suicidal. A people so confused and so militant, they not only want the freedom to act recklessly, they demand silence from any and all who would dare question the morality or health consequences of such activity.

If you hold personal convictions about faith, these players in a real-life "satyricon" and their RDDB compadres believe it's you or them. *Your* very existence is a threat to *their* way of life. They've abandoned their sixties credo: *Live and let live*. Instead, they've twisted it to be: *We live, and your beliefs die*. Die to the notion of right and wrong, good and evil, the high road and the low road.

That's why today's anarchists of the soul have spent the better part of forty years vilifying, undermining, discrediting, marginalizing, and silencing the voices of faith. These Christophobes are rewriting American history.

The last thing they want you to know is the *truth* about our Founding Fathers—excuse me, our "Forepersons." For those readers who may have skipped history class to score a joint in the back of the parking lot, I'll show you why and how these Dogs of Hate are working overtime to systematically silence religion.

RELIGION-FREE ZONES

When I was a kid in religious school, I was more inclined to sit with my friends in the back of the classroom than in the front paying attention to the Bible. To me, at the time, religion wasn't important. It was all mumbo jumbo. I didn't take it seriously.

I have since come to understand the true presence of God and the meaning of His teachings. However, I'm afraid there are tens of millions of people in our country who are still like that kid in the back of the religious school, thinking religious studies are all a big joke.

One winter day, we were especially bored as the teacher droned on and on and on. The room was stuffy from the piped-in heat. His hot air wasn't helping matters, either. I remember we were rapidly approaching narcolepsy from the boredom. You couldn't pay me to stay awake in that class. I should mention that my best friend Joe was another jokester. He and I were always getting summoned to the front of the classroom because we wouldn't pay attention.

This particular afternoon, Jokester Joe secretly tore up tissue paper into hundreds of little pieces. As I glanced over in his direction, I couldn't figure out what he was trying to do. His hands worked like crazy under the desk, ripping the paper, while his eyes looked straight ahead.

Throughout the room there were vents with forced hot air blasting heat up from the floor. There was also one strategically located at the front of the class, just under the blackboard and beside the teacher. All of a sudden, as the teacher turned his back to write on the chalkboard, Jokester Joe took this shredded mountain of tissue paper and threw them over the hot air vent.

He shouted out, "Look teacher, it's snowing in here."

We thought it was a hysterically funny scene. The truth is, it made a mockery of the teacher. It made a mockery of authority, of structure, and of the religion class. Everything the school was holding up as sacred was dismissed in a moment of anarchy. For those few seconds, we thought we had tasted freedom.

I realize it was just a mild prank that didn't really hurt anybody. But I'm afraid we have millions of people who, like Jokester Joe, are throwing torn up sheets of tissue paper trying to obscure the Word of God. While the innocent jokesters like Joe are not a real threat, there are others today who are far more dangerous, far more malicious, far more militant.

These empty souls have a clear agenda to destroy the meaning of the word "God," our houses of worship, and the practice of true religion. For these people, it's not sufficient to obscure the Word of God with mere pranks, their goal is to obliterate it altogether.

Take Patsy Ireland, the former head of the National Organization for Women. Patsy was appointed CEO of the Young Woman's Christian Association. This bisexual, pro-abortion feminist, who managed to penetrate the YWCA, likes to pretend she's pure and holy, but in reality she's making a mockery of everything that this religious institution represented for 145 years.

For starters, today's crop of impressionable young girls might have been led to believe that bisexuality is a good thing. Why not? Top-dog Patsy Ireland has both a husband and a girlfriend. I'm sure in time she might have offered a new class on the joys of the bi-polar life. Who knows, maybe she would have ordered new YWCA stationary without the "C" and tell those who don't like it to just "get over it"—a favorite phrase she uses to deflect criticism of her bulldozer policies.

This dangerous radical was working from within to co-opt the YWCA's policies and values and, in turn, shape them with her perverted worldview. I say she "was working" because after just six months at the helm, she was asked to resign. The board of directors saw the light (or perhaps the heat) and felt the YWCA "proved to be the wrong platform for her to advocate on these issues."[12] Patsy refused. That's when they dismissed her before she could further tarnish the YWCA's once stellar legacy.

Or take the case of Teresa Becker. In 2000, Teresa enrolled in Ave Maria College, a Catholic liberal arts college in Michigan. Her freshman year she received $1,200 in state scholarship funds. Her sophomore year, the state provided $2,750 in aid and was promised the same for her junior year.

That is, until she declared her major: theology.

Once the mad Dogs of Hate noticed her choice of studies, they dashed off this note to her: "Students enrolled in a course of study leading to a degree in theology, divinity or religious education are not eligible to receive an award. Your award has changed from $2,750.00 to $0.00."[13]

She's not alone. To date, eleven other states have eliminated scholarships for students whose major of choice is theology.

You can study to be a porn star.

You can study to be an eco-terrorist.

You can study to·be an illegal alien activist.

But God forbid you chose to study theology.

Why do you think the agents of liberalism, who for the most part are aligned with the Demoncat party, view the Judeo-Christian faith as public enemy number one? Why do they ban traditional Christmas carols, which, admittedly, have a Christian message, during the "Winter Holiday" choral performance in public schools?

Contrary to the biblical notion of one God, in the worldview of ultraliberalism each person is his or her *own* God! Plain and simple. You might want to read that again.

Look at it this way.

Divide the country into the red and the blue, the Republicans and the Democrats. By and large you will find that Republicans come from a stronger relationship to the Judeo-Christian doctrine of monotheism, or one God. I'm not saying this holds across the board. But for the most part they believe in a Supreme Being to whom they are accountable.

The Dems, especially the more vocal ones like the Hollywood Idiots, are more Hellenistic. These modern day Hellenists are deluded by their popularity, by their red carpet treatment, by their reserved seating, and by virtue of the fact that they actually believe they are *more enlightened* than the American sheeple.

They are God, and there can be none other before them.

In other words, ultra-liberalism is based upon a belief system steeped in self-worship, or idolatry. Which is why most actors are Democrats. Because they're Hellenists; they think they're God. That also explains why I don't know of one Red Diaper Doper Baby in the ACLU who is a registered Republican. To them, the idea of absolute truth and being accountable to a Supreme Authority is laughable.

Occasionally you'll see an actor or lawyer with a tinge of humility, who understands his or her place in the world. Against the odds, they understand that this is one nation under God—unlike the vast majority of chronic rehab cases who think America is one nation under them.

They're demi-gods.

In true demi-god fashion, these egomaniacs proclaim that we must save the "environment" by driving a "hybrid" car while *they* are chauffeured in a limo. Anybody who doesn't bow down at the altar of their ego gets a thousand tongue-lashings. While we run around trying to placate the demi-gods among us, they're busy mocking people of true faith, ripping the Ten Commandments off the wall and censoring religious symbolism.

THE BIG TEN

In spite of the aggressive efforts by the secular humanists to de-God public schools and society at large, I believe God and religion are absolutely necessary for a child's development. At the very minimum, you've got to teach a child the Ten Commandments. You've got to show them right from wrong. You've got to instill in them a standard of civility and appropriate behavior.

This is what the Ten Commandments offer.

A standard to live by.

A moral compass to guide each generation.

This seems so obvious, yet our educational system refuses to acknowledge the need for such a standard. Instead, they argue that to teach right and wrong is "moralizing"—which it is. What's wrong with that? We could use a little moralizing.

As you well know, not all choices are equal. Some choices are better than other choices. A moral compass would help students stay on the straight and narrow. But the teachers' union and liberal establishment reject that.

What have decades of such negligence brought us?

Look no further than the brutal hazing incident at an affluent suburban Chicago high school, May 4, 2003. Remember that one? A dozen girls and three boys, all seniors who should have known better, smeared feces, garbage, and paint on each other.

They smeared feces while the cameras rolled. The whole nasty business was like a scene from *Lord of the Flies*. Several students were captured on videotape repeatedly beating a group of junior class girls. Five kids ended up in the hospital as a result of the horrible acts of brutality.

Why are we surprised? During their entire school experience, the device of the Left was to de-vice evil while turning the saints into sinners.

But that's not the worst of it.

The school officials suspended their leftist tendencies long enough to suspend the students who were responsible for the torture they inflicted on fellow students. But then, amazingly, several of the parents of the students involved filed a lawsuit to get the charges dropped. Why? They didn't want there to be a black mark on their kids' records when they applied for college.

First, the negligent parents failed to teach their kids basic decency or moral constraints at home. And they didn't insist at minimum that the school instruct students to maintain a sense of morality. Then, when their kids got caught smearing feces on their friends and pummeling them, they've got the nerve to sue for damages.

Only in Hellenistic America.

To be perfectly redundant, liberalism is a mental disorder. This is a classic example of what intolerance for the Ten Commandments brings. This crop of delinquents were caught on tape committing a crime. They ought to take the punishment. End of story.

Now, I realize there are those of you who don't believe in God. What if we took out the first commandment which says, "I am the Lord your God . . . you shall have no other gods before me" (Exodus 20:2-3). Tell me, which of the other nine commandments do you find unacceptable? "Honor your father and your mother"? How about "You shall not murder," "You shall not steal," or "You shall not give false testimony against your neighbor"? Which one of them do you think would *not* be a good guideline for a child?

I don't know which one it is.

Let's say for the sake of argument that you want to throw the whole thing out. Answer this. What gives you, your children, and our society a basis for the concepts of right and wrong? The law? Wake up, my friend. American law is based on the principles of the Ten Commandments. That's why a copy hangs over the heads of the Supreme Court justices— not that they've noticed recently.

And another thing.

As I've studied the teachings in the Bible, I've come up with only one conclusion: God is a conservative. Think about it. This is why liberals tend to deny His existence. Don't you understand the logic of what I just said to you? God is a conservative by definition because everything that is of a conservative nature or value emanates fundamentally from God's laws as presented in the Bible.

The radical irreligious Left not only dismisses God's laws as unworthy of mankind; they claim God doesn't exist. Their egocentric position suggests the Bible is a collection of myths, and so, in turn, they embrace the religion of secular humanism where man replaces God and the State replaces the Church. Which is actually nothing more than the rebirth of Marxism, communism, or Leninism, depending on the likes of the leftist.

Are you beginning to understand how they operate?

SO HELP ME, GOD

Of course, once the libs toss the Big Ten out the window, they've effectively canned truth as the basis for law and order. Which creates a problem for the courts. Truth, as we learned from eight torturous years under Bill Clinton, is in the eye of the beholder. How else could that egomaniac place his hand on a Bible and swear to tell the truth?

That's what you get after the Dogs of Hate have gnawed away the very foundation of justice. A man's testimony can no longer be trusted. Yes, the time is rapidly approaching when our courts may have to resort to an old tribal custom in order to validate the testimony of a witness.

Now, you should know that I'm a man who loves to study the genesis of words. This will astonish you. Take the origin of the word "testimony." If you break it down, "testimony" goes back to the word "testify" which, in turn, has at its Latin root the word "testis."

What other English word derives its meaning from testis?

Testicle. The reproductive gland of a male.

Here's where it gets fascinating. When I was collecting medicinal plants in the South Pacific (1969-1989), I met a professor who went into the mountains of New Guinea in 1948 to do anti-malaria research. When he arrived, he learned about a peculiar custom that the primitive tribe embraced. When you approached them to speak, their leader would cup your testicles in his hand!

That's just the way the men greeted each other. When they talked, they would put their hands on the other guy's testicles. This is not a lewd tale. The fact of the matter is they did this to see if the man was lying or not. Because, apparently, if a man lies, something happens down there. Know what I'm saying?

I guess the family jewels would shrink up if he was being untruthful. I don't know exactly how it worked. But it worked. Naturally, my friend didn't want anyone touching his privates. When he first experienced this treatment, he wondered if they were nuts. But he had to go along with the program.

So that's where the word "testimony" comes from. I say that's where we are headed if the libs succeed in killing the Commandments. Come to think of it in this era of secular humanism, maybe we'd be better off if, in a court of law, instead of putting your hand on the Bible, we did it the old fashioned way.

These days, we'd probably get more truth out of people.

INSIDE JOB

While the public schools hang leper bells around the neck of religion, there's an enemy lurking within our houses of worship co-opting the very core of faith. I'll give you two prominent examples.

Take the sad state of liberal Judaism. I'm just calling it as I see it. What else would you say when a leftist rabbi goes and joins a lawsuit to ban the public display of the Ten Commandments?

This so-called rabbi, a phony in holy robes who will remain nameless, joined the rabid mad dogs of the ACLU and five demented, antireligious "Christian" slime bags to knock off the Ten Commandments from the state capitol grounds in Frankfort, Kentucky. They claimed that the display of the decades-old granite monument was unconstitutional.

I say shame on you, Rabbi Pinhead.

Why on earth would you fight for the removal of a piece of your own history? Thanks in part to the coercive efforts by this enemy of the faith, a federal judge prohibited the placement of the Ten Commandments. On appeal, the U.S. Supreme Court rejected the request to hear the case to reverse the lower court's decision.[14]

Big surprise there.

In other words, the U.S. Supreme Court has now said, "Drop dead, Ten Commandments." And a rabbi, playing the part of Judas, wasted no time betraying his own religious text. This rabbi should be defrocked. While we're at it, the Supremes who ruled against the Big Ten should be exposed for the judicial tyrants they are.

I ask you, why is it permissible for a copy of the Commandments to hang in the halls of the high court in Washington DC but barred from the state capitol of Kentucky?

Whoever said "Justice is blind" sure got it right.

The Supremes are so blind, I must remind them that *the author of the First Amendment,* James Madison, argued vigorously *on behalf of the Commandments.*

Madison said, "We have staked the whole future of all of our political institutions . . . upon the capacity of each and all of us to govern ourselves, to control ourselves, to sustain ourselves, according to the Ten Commandments of God."[15] Did you get that? The Establishment and Free Exercise Clause does not require the obliteration of all our religious traditions.

It's a sad day in America when a rabbi betrays his high calling and tramples on the Ten Commandments in his race to be perceived as *tolerant* by the neo-pagan Left.

The other outrageous heartbreaker comes from Georgetown University, once a great Jesuit school of higher learning. Leftists of the middle order of deceit have invaded those once sacred halls and unleashed the mad Dogs of Hate.

Case in point.

Cardinal Francis Arinze is a well-respected Catholic cleric from Nigeria. Some suggest he's a possible successor to the pope. He was invited by this Catholic institution to address the seniors at their spring 2003 graduation ceremony. I'm sure the dean of students figured having an African-African would show sensitivity to cross-cultural, international solidarity. He's a good man.

Now, had the Right Reverend Jessie Hi-Jackson been invited to speak, you'd expect a tirade about rape-R-nations, affirmative racism, and multi-culti-transgender equality. Maybe they figured Cardinal Arinze would deliver the same kind of canned speech.

Within minutes of his opening comments, the faculty found out how mistaken they had been. I can only imagine the looks of shock, embarrassment, and rage on the faces of the faculty members responsible for giving him the platform as he barbequed more than a few of their sacred cows.

It's amazing they didn't unplug his microphone.

His message? Cardinal Arinze, a devout *conservative* Catholic who isn't trying to score points with the liberal establishment, gave them the ultimate tongue-lashing. He said, "In many parts of the world, the family is under siege. It is scorned and banalized by pornography, desecrated by fornication and adultery, mocked by homosexuality, sabotaged by irregular unions, and cut in two by divorce."[16]

At that point in his passionate address, a female theology prof, who has no business teaching at a Catholic university, stomped off stage. Her radical secularist feathers were ruffled by a dose of genuine Catholic doctrine. This snake wasn't alone. A cadre of other equally offended dunces slithered out.

In the aftermath, Jane McAuliffe, dean of the College of Arts and Sciences, dashed off a letter of apology to placate the school's sizable gay contingent known as GU Pride. Let me get this straight. A Catholic priest states the fundamental truths found in any Catholic catechism and the Enemy Within a Catholic university walks out? And the dimwitted dean apologizes?

At the beginning of this chapter I told you that the high priests of ultra-liberalism are relentless in their efforts to drive the Church out of the public square. The truth is, I didn't go far enough.

They're driving God out of the Church.

Do you see what's happening?

If this trend keeps up at so-called religious institutions, watch out. One day you'll send your daughter (that little darling you used to put into snow pajamas) off to Georgetown U., and a year later she'll come home with a nipple ring and a butch cut. Perhaps, to experience her inner-self, she'll have slept with the entire sorority!

This just shows you what we're facing in America. The mental disease of liberalism is invading our churches†, our liberal synagogues‡, and, to a large extent, our faith-based colleges. Priests and pastors are afraid to mention the word "God." How often do you hear God's name anymore in liberal religious colleges and houses of worship? They're afraid to mention His name. It's like a pornographic phrase to speak the name of God. Why?

Thanks to the relentless attack of the Dogs of Hate, our houses of worship are no longer about God. They're about saving chickens—not babies—and they're about social work, gay rights, anti-war movements, and sending SUVs to the crusher.

WHERE THE SHROUD OF TURIN
MEETS THE ROAD

Do you remember the "What Would Jesus Drive?" ad campaign co-sponsored by the ultra-far-Left National Council of Churches? This socialist front group launched a misguided attempt to steer you away from owning a SUV.

Talk about a bogus non-issue.

Get this. The NCC opposed the liberation of Iraqis from torture chambers and mass rape, but they sure got up in arms over the gas consumption of SUVs! The anti-SUV drive revved into high gear when these liberal phonies tried to link your choice of vehicle to world terrorism.[17]

---

† In the late 1990s, a move by liberals within the religious publishing industry worked to create a "gender neutral" edition of the popular New International Version of the Bible—arguably the most widely used version of Scripture in churches today. After an overwhelming backlash by religious leaders in 1997, the International Bible Society and Zondervan Publishers inked an agreement with leading evangelicals to placate the concerns about a politically corrected edition. However, Zondervan disregarded their commitment and, in the spring of 2002, released a politically sensitive, gender inclusive New Testament called Today's NIV. The complete alteration of the Old Testament is expected in 2005. The move triggered alarms by conservatives in the Church who contend this is nothing more than a bow to the agenda of feminism.

‡ In Orthodox synagogues, religious Jews continue to read the Torah without alteration. How long will it be until the radical Left seeks to alter Torah scrolls?

Forget about Saddam's slaughter of innocent men, women, and children. Forget about the torture chambers. The Rev. Dr. Robert Edgar, general secretary of the National Council of Churches wants you to believe it's *your* SUV that's really killing people and, by God, the leftist loonies at the Council want *you* stopped.

This insanity is what happens when God takes a backseat to fashionable liberal causes. Instead of addressing the poor, the needy, the homeless, the widows, and the orphans, the Council spends its time and vast sums of money to ban SUVs.

The ignorance of this misguided campaign is astounding. Jesus was a carpenter, right? It stands to reason if Jesus were living in America today, he'd drive a 4x4 Chevy Avalanche pickup truck. Then again, with twelve disciples to cart around, he'd need *two* Suburbans—or two Hummers.

In the wake of this idiotic effort by the NCC, and in the interest of being multi-cultural, a cartoonist in Florida raised the question which the NCC failed to ask: "What Would *Mohammed* Drive?" His answer?

A Ryder truck.

SEVEN

MORALITY:
THE BIBLE BELT VS.
THE LIBEL BELT

One of my earliest memories of a great religious service took place in Harlem, New York. That's where Brother Billy, a white preacher from the Deep South and, I should mention, a real Bible thumper, led a little church in a Harlem storefront. You know the kind of place. Nothing fancy. Curtains in the window. No parking lot. Makeshift sign over the door, I think it was some Abyssinian church.

Brother Billy was one of those street preachers who'd stand on a busy corner preaching to everyone passing by. Me? I was a young man in my early twenties just out for a walk, you know, savoring life in the big city. So I'm walking along, and I see this guy in the street stirring the crowds up. I hung around to listen, probably because he had such a compelling voice.

Day after day, Brother Billy would be preaching his heart out, and I'd catch him from time to time. The guy was fascinating. Over time, he and I struck up a friendship. One Sunday, I was driving him around

Manhattan, and he had me take him up to his church in Harlem. I figured why not go in and see the guy in action, right?

Once inside, the only thing more passionate than Brother Billy in the pulpit was the choir. They were singing and clapping their hands as the walls were shaking. And when Brother Billy prayed, I said to myself, "Now this is a man who knows how to talk to God." That was one of the great religious moments of my life.

Today, when you go into one of the "great" churches in America—take your pick of the many edifices—and you listen to what's going on, so much of it is liberal mumbo jumbo. Or, let's face it, many homilies and sermons have become just rote and meaningless. They don't touch anyone. I'll take that Harlem Abyssinian church any day.

I'll give you another side, the Jewish side. In the 1970s, I had some Hasidic Jewish friends who took me back to Brooklyn. We went to a synagogue on Eastern Parkway in New York. I found myself in the midst of seven thousand men wearing black suits and hats chanting together on a Friday night to usher in the Sabbath.

Out came the head rabbi. I remember he was a revered, almost saintly, figure. After listening to him speak, I'd have to say no one like him has appeared in one hundred years. He was amazing. Between the chanting and his message, I have never felt as much public human emotion.

As I've said, where and how you choose to worship is your business. That's the beautiful thing about it. The freedom to gather and to worship in your own way is one of the most cherished cornerstones of our Constitution. But if the Dogs of Hate have their way, people of faith in America will one day lose that precious right.

Do you think that's far-fetched?

Then you don't know contemporary history. Extreme religious intolerance and persecution is practiced around the globe today. If you think, "Yeah, but not here in America, right?" you'd be wrong. I'll tell you exactly what these irreligious zealots are up to today—and why the Muslims are exempted from such attacks.

JACKHAMMERING THE TEN COMMANDMENTS

The Dogs of Hate will stop at nothing to besmirch, insult, smear, and desecrate religion and religious symbols. These neo-Bolsheviks are attacking the Ten Commandments in Pennsylvania, Alabama, Kentucky, and California. And they won't relent until every last display has been expunged from public view. To them, these guidelines are worse than vile pornography.

The enemies of our religious freedom are relentless in their efforts to redefine the American way of life. The case of *Glassroth v. Moore* is a classic example of their aggression and intolerance.

In August of 2001, Roy Moore, the chief justice of the Alabama Supreme Court, installed a beautiful granite monument in the rotunda of the Alabama Judicial Building. He wanted to affirm the roots of American life, liberty, and law. As such, the monument displayed the Pledge of Allegiance, the national anthem, the national motto, the oath of all public officials, along with a copy of the Ten Commandments.

Who could have a problem with that?

Stephen Glassroth, that's who. As the plaintiff in this case and, apparently, an attorney with nothing better to do, he mounted the charge to remove a display of the Ten Commandments. Listen to this intolerant nonsense. Glassroth said, "It offends me going to work every day and coming face to face with that symbol."[1]

Is this lost soul not offended by the smut on TV? He's not offended by the slaughter of unborn children? He's not offended by Saddam's torture chambers? No. Rather than tackle real life-and-death issues, his blood starts to boil when he sees the Ten Commandments on display.

Glassroth was not alone. Three un-civil liberties groups hastened to join Glassroth in his effort to stifle the display of the Big Ten: the Red Diaper Doper Babies of the ACLU, the Southern Poverty Law Center, and Americans United for the Separation of Church and State.

We're talking about the Axis of the Irreligious-Evil here.

You need to know two things that were not reported anywhere in the media. On the home page of the Southern Poverty Law Center website, you'll find a link to their sister organization, Tolerance.org. What's this? The SPLC preaches tolerance? In bold letters they claim to "FIGHT HATE AND PROMOTE TOLERANCE." Let's see. That must mean they are tolerant unless they come in contact with the Ten Commandments. In which case, they sue and trample on *your* freedom of expression.

The arrogance and hypocrisy of these freedom-hating agitators are unmatched. They take donations to promote tolerance; they lecture the sheeple in ways to be tolerant; but then they turn around and drag those people with whom they disagree to court.

The SPLC expects everyone to practice tolerance just so long as it's a tolerance for their narrowly defined pet issues: gay, trans, bi, tri, *et al.* But the moment someone expresses a faith-based opinion, they whip out the jackhammer and blast away with all of the hatred and intolerance they supposedly preach against.

There's a second irony that defines these hypocrites.

On the SPLC web page, they proudly display a quote attributed to Martin Luther King Jr.: "*Until justice rolls down like waters and righteousness like a mighty stream.*" Of course, MLK was paraphrasing Amos 5:24 from the Old Testament. Are you getting the picture? On one hand they quote the Bible *when it suits their agenda.* On the other hand, they censor your free expression to do the same.

MONUMENTAL MISCHIEF

After listening to one week of arguments, Federal Judge Myron Thompson ruled *against* Justice Moore and *in favor* of tossing the Ten Commandments out on the streets. Thompson called Moore's tribute to American law "nothing less than an obtrusive year-round religious display."[2] Thompson's ignorance of American history and his contempt for our constitutional foundation is stunning.

Frankly, this stench on the bench is making me clench.

Constitutional scholar Dr. Alan Keyes blasted Judge Thompson, calling him "a lawless judge who is taking his opinions out of thin air, not on the basis of any law . . . [H]e has no grounds, no [legal] basis whatsoever, from which to address this issue."[3] This judicial tyranny must stop!

Do you see what Judge Thompson has done?

"What they are doing," Keyes says, "is imposing a uniform national regime of disbelief and atheism on the people of this country! They are doing exactly what the Constitution of the United States forbids."[4] Evidently, that's perfectly fine with Alabama Supreme Court Associate Justice Douglas Johnstone, who opposed Judge Moore from day one. On the heels of this federal decision, Johnstone whined, "My personal concern is the theocratic movement in Alabama and in this country."[5]

Hold on. What "theocratic movement" is this mental dwarf talking about? Johnstone droned on about his opposition to the display of the Ten Commandments, saying, "Theocracy is a real problem in the Middle East . . . and it's something we need to avoid here." Do you see what this Demoncat is doing? He's equating the Ten Commandments with Middle Eastern terrorism.

Would someone explain to me how the public exhibition of the Ten Commandments "establishes" a religion in this country? Tell me, how does it perpetuate a theocracy? Last time I checked, the Commandments were not required reading.

You are free to ignore them.

You are free to embrace them.

You are free to reject them.

You are free to celebrate them.

But you are not free to rewrite history. As I pointed out in the last chapter, James Madison, the author of the First Amendment, argued forcefully *on behalf of the Ten Commandments.* He couldn't imagine a nation that wasn't governed and "sustained" by them.

Mark my words. This battle over the Ten Commandments is a defining issue. We are at a defining moment in our history. Will you allow the vacuous vultures to devour every last vestige of religion?

You see, once they have successfully pulverized the Ten Command-ments, their next target will be to remove "under God" from the Pledge of Allegiance. In fact, the San Fransicko-based 9ᵗʰ Jerkit Court declared that the Pledge of Allegiance was unconstitutional. These ignoramuses sided with the angry atheist who sued his school district because he claimed his child "was injured" by the reciting of the Pledge as part of the daily school routine.

As of this writing, the decision has been appealed to the U.S. Supreme Court. If the Supremes rule the Pledge of Allegiance is unconstitutional, taking "In God We Trust" off of your last penny is next. And that's for starters. Beyond that, I warn you, all public displays of a religious nature, starting with the cross, will be snapped off and burned in a dumpster—as was done after the Communists took over Russia, when they burned reli-gious articles from churches and banned the Bible!

The truth is, we're already seeing this happen today.

Sun Myung Moon, leader of the Unification Church (widely consid-ered to be a religious cult), has marshaled an effort to tear down the crosses from Christian churches. How?

By labeling the cross a "symbol of oppression."

By equating the cross as a symbol of religious intolerance.

By convincing the gullible clergy *they* are the ones standing in the way of reconciliation with the Muslims.

Do you think that's far-fetched? Do you think it couldn't happen? You'd be wrong. In 2003, pastors at more than three hundred churches took down the crosses from their buildings for these very reasons.[6] It's only a matter of time when a Star of David or a Crescent will suffer the same fate.

Make no mistake about it. The Dogs of Hate are using the "I'm offended" argument to force the removal of every religious symbol from our houses of worship.

From our private schools.

From our front yards.

From around our necks.

And a host of liberal judges are pleased to facilitate these initiatives. Before you know it, you will not be free to express your religious beliefs in any meaningful way. Why? Once God has been chased out of the country, those who believe in Him are the next to go.

I, for one, don't believe we should allow the irreligious minority to dictate how the majority should live. That's one reason I founded the Paul Revere Society and wrote *The Savage Nation* and the book you're reading now: to sound the alarm that the Enemy Within is encroaching on our most sacred freedoms.

ONE-ARM FRANK

My father was an antiques dealer. He'd go to the estate sales, the outlets, and homes looking for old treasures to put into his store. Once in while, a guy we called One-Arm Frank would come around to work with my dad. I don't know how he came to have just one arm. It didn't matter. Frankly, while we didn't know a lot of people with one arm back then, we never made a big deal of it. Frank had his arm sewed up in his suit, that's all.

Before I tell you the rest of the story, I should point out that nobody tried to alter reality in those days. If you were missing an arm, that's how you got your name: "One-Arm Frank." Whatever the anomaly was, that became your name. There was no harm done. There was no malice intended. The truth is, those labels made it easier for the average person to individualize everybody.

But today, forget about it. The Left wants us to treat guys like One-Arm Frank as if he's *better* than normal. According to the Keepers of Sensitivity, he's special. Now, if you have one arm, you're better than a guy with two arms. Or if you have no arms and no legs, you're Superman in the politically altered world of today.

Anyway, One-Arm Frank was a very nice guy. Always helpful. Never made excuses about his handicap. He wasn't looking for special treatment or a government handout. He fit in like the rest of the guys and did the best he could.

But the breath on him—whew! His breath could peel wallpaper. Now, I want to tell you, there are bad breaths, there are very bad breaths, and then there are medicinal problems. Frank's condition had to be solved with a medicine that hadn't been invented yet.

Once in a while, my old man would drive One-Arm Frank home at the end of the day, and I'd get stuck in the back seat with Frank. He didn't speak much, but when One-Arm Frank would start talking, watch out. I tell you, it could be minus four degrees in New York, and we'd have to ride with all the windows open.

Did you ever know a person who, when he opened his mouth, filled the car with a noxious fume? At first, you're not sure what's going on. You wonder, did we run over a muskrat? Did something get caught in the muffler? Did I step on something? Are we going past a slaughterhouse? After a while, the realization hits you.

It's just Frank talking.

Here's the connection between noxious breath and the stench from the bench. Radical libs like Judge Myron Thompson, Stephen Glassroth, the ACLU, and the SPLC have a lot in common with One-Arm Frank. Every time one of these irreligious vampires opens their mouths to attack the Ten Commandments, I've got to roll down a window. The stench is unbelievable to me. Every last word they speak stinks like an abattoir. I'm choking on their toxic fumes. I have to wonder how anything could reek so bad.

The answer came to me the other night.

I was lying in bed and couldn't sleep when it dawned on me why everything these RDDBs say stinks. I pictured in my mind a map of America. If you were to view America as an animal, the head would be New York and Maine, the ears would be Michigan, and Florida would be the front paws of the animal. Of course, if you look at Texas, you could get very physical there. It resembles part of the male thing.

Nebraska and Kansas look like the short baby back ribs. Then, the entire West Coast, which has been taken over by the radical Left and the RDDBs, would be the hindquarters of America.† Which makes perfect sense. That's where they'd take over—you know, anything to do with the hindquarters. I'm serious.

This explains why everything these unhappy pagans say has a certain odor about it.

MOCK AROUND THE CLOCK

The single most effective tool in the arsenal of the Left is to attack our traditional Judeo-Christian values through much of today's entertainment. What's worse is how the radical fringe reaches into your pocket and swipes your tax dollars in order to fund their hate speech against you. Anybody who thinks this isn't happening or that it's no big deal is uninformed. Remember the "art" called "Piss Christ"?

A no-talent Bolshevik peed in a jar, submerged a crucifix in the urine, took a photo, and called it "art." The dullards at the National Endowment for the Arts, a sister "sleeper" government agency that should be defunded, agreed that "Piss Christ" was art and wrote a check for 15,000 of your tax dollars to pay this derelict for his efforts.[7]

How did they come up with that figure?

How much does it cost to urinate? Not only was it a crass work of "art," the tax funding of it was even more obscene. Whoever approved that scam must have had a lobotomy. Can you imagine an artist getting away with that stunt if he had urinated in a jar and then inserted a crucified Mohammed?

The rag-libs scream, "Separate Church and State!" but not when they wish to unite Church and hate.

In terms of wasting and abusing your tax dollars, the urine/crucifix fiasco is chump change when compared to what's happening in New York.

---

† After Arnold Schwarzenegger's victory in the recall election that made him the governor of California, we will have to see how much of the Kennedys' liberalism is in him.

On February 16, 2001, the Brooklyn Museum of Art in New York hosted a collection of ninety-four contemporary African-American photographers. One of the featured works was created by a femi-nasty photographer. Her hate-art was entitled "Yo Mama's Last Supper" and featured her mocking Christ, posing nude surrounded by twelve black disciples.

Another "artist" whose name is not remembered, created a collage depicting a topless woman crucified.

Of course, this mockery of Jesus and this anti-Christian attack is not new to the Brooklyn Museum of Hate-Art. In 1999, you may remember the flap that swirled around Mayor Rudy Giuliani. He blasted the museum's abuse of tax dollars to host a show called "Sensation: Young British Artists from the Saatchi Collection" in which the Virgin Mary was embellished with elephant dung and clipped pictures of vaginas from porn mags.

In a bold move, Mayor Giuliani froze the city's annual $7.2 million subsidy[8], which is about a third of the Brooklyn Museum's revenue. Mayor Giuliani went a step further and tried to have the bums evicted. The museum filed a countersuit in federal court. RDDB judge Nina Gershon, who presided over the zoo, gave Jesus the boot when she ruled in favor of the museum citing the First Amendment.

She is the perfect contemporary example of the kind of dangerous individual whom John Witherspoon, a signer of the Declaration of Independence, warned his generation about. Witherspoon said, "Whoever is an avowed enemy of God, I scruple not to call him an enemy to his country."[9]

But I'm not through with the story. It gets worse. The city was strong-armed into a settlement that required them to shell out an additional 5.8 million in tax dollars to the museum—that's money right out of your pocket if you live in New York. You see now what I mean when I say the radical left-wing conspirators control the culture.

This is what you're paying for.

When it comes to a mockery of Christ, which side of the coin do you think "Reverend" Al Sharpton was on? Listen to this windbag: "This has nothing to do with Jesus. This has something to do with censorship. If Jesus was here today, he would not be worried about art pieces at the

Brooklyn Museum."[10] What a phony. He wouldn't even stand up to defend his own faith.

Moving from New York to Hollywood, it should come as no surprise that the Left Coast demi-gods vigorously mock persons of faith in film after film. Remember, they like to think that they are God. Which means they must defend their turf by taking potshots at the One True God. The truth is, I need an entire book just to document the vast left-wing conspiracy against Christians and the Bible in the movies.

A few examples of their hostility will have to do.

• Charlie Sheen is cast as a gun-toting Christian in *Young Guns* who finds time to pray while he engages in multiple mass killings.

• The villain in *Cape Fear*, played by Robert DeWeirdo, is wallpapered with Bible verses all over his body.

• One of the most disturbing films of the nineties was *Pulp Fiction* in which John Revolta plays a brutal hit man whose partner, played by Samuel L. Jackson, quoted Scripture before pulling the trigger point blank at a victim's head.

Hold on. Let me ask you a question.

Do you think anybody in Follywood would ever make a movie in which a Muslim hit man would quote from the Qur'an before slitting the throat of a flight attendant and then ramming a plane into a building? Not in your lifetime. These traitors would call that kind of treatment of Muslims hate-propaganda. It might lead to a backlash of anti-Muslim hostility. They would never make a film with that storyline—even though it would be a true story.

Need I go on?

• *The Last Temptation of Christ*, that pathetic waste, pictured Jesus as a mentally unstable lunatic who dreams on the cross of fornicating with Mary Magdalene.

- *Carrie*, that mid-seventies horror "classic," depicts a crazed religious mother brutally torturing her child with religious symbols.

- *The Birdcage*, a celebration of the homosexual, drag queen, and transsexual lifestyle, casts Gene Hackman as an uptight, racist senator who heads up the Coalition for Moral Order.

There's one more I must bring to your attention. America will never forget the Columbine high school shooting. But the media doesn't want you to know that the two boys, Eric and Dylan, who pulled the triggers, were homosexual lovers and huge fans of *Basketball Diaries*. In the filmic version, Leonardo DeCrapia vents his rage against—you guessed it—the big, bad, Catholic school.

No other institution is more vilified than the Church in this film. It's rarely cast as anything more than a negative, oppressive, backwards force in society.

Television's attack on faith is at least as bad as if not worse than what we're seeing in the film industry. I'm not going to argue with you that two or three successful religious-oriented shows have aired in recent years. Shows like *Touched by an Angel* and *Seventh Heaven* are the exception. Not the rule.

Instead, a Christian is presented as either a self-righteous buffoon, deranged, a villain, a closet white supremacist—anything other than a person worth admiring. You think I'm exaggerating? Name one example in prime time where a character of faith is treated as a warm, colorful, funny, or smart individual.

You won't find one.

Now, you will find more than two dozen gay or lesbian characters in lead or supporting roles. In virtually every case, they're presented as witty, charming, lovable, talented, or the victim of some injustice. But never the villain. A coincidence? A double standard?

Why don't we stop mincing words.

What you're seeing is a militant and concerted effort by the vast left-wing conspiracy to attack the "quaint" values of America's Corn Belt every chance they get.

It's the Bible Belt vs. the Libel Belt.

One problem. It's a stacked deck, and the enemy holds all of the cards. Think about what I just said. The enemies of religion are the dominant force in Hollywood. They control the music and film industries and television networks. They own the production companies and dominate the distribution channels.

The enemies of religion control the studios and run the actors union. And there isn't a damn thing you can do about it—except to turn them off. Your power comes only when you take away their audience share. When you stop watching, their ratings sink. When you stop attending movies and don't rent their crap that attacks your faith, you will drive down their bottom-line.

No audience, no influence.

That's the only way to fight back.

AMERICA'S MORAL MELTDOWN

The other night, I was trying to unwind after a tough day on the radio. So I did what I like to do: eat some Italian take-out and watch some TV. I watched the *Sopranos* on HBO, which, by the way, is the only reason I originally subscribed to that channel. After the show ended, I kept watching HBO. The next thing I saw was a program based on sex outtakes from around the world. I couldn't even tell you the name of that show.

It belonged in a porno theater of the Weimar Republic!

The narrator goes, "Now we go to England where a man is tying his penis into knots. And now we go to Sweden where we did a piece on a talking anus. Now we go to Brazil where we show men . . ." All with graphic pictures of nudity. One scene was lower than the next. Each was more vile than the last.

I'm sitting there thinking, can't a guy eat his dinner without getting a face full of filth? I reached for the remote and zapped the pervs off. Mind you, I've seen everything in my life. I'm no prude or holy roller, trust me. But I'm telling you, I've never seen such disgusting sewage in my life. I wish to God I could turn the clock back and erase those pornographic images from my mind.

I wish to God that it had been illegal for HBO to pump that crap into the living rooms of America. I wish that the punishment for programmers who create such filth would be a stiff fine and imprisonment.

Again, I understand America's moral meltdown will never be reversed. Why? We don't have the political willpower to drive away the gambling, the drugs, the rampant pornography, all of which were, in my youth, illegal. Everything that was in the closet has come out of the closet.

That's what the vast left-wing conspiracy has wrought.

The libs argue America is a much better place because we have successfully shed the "old-fashioned," "outdated," and "intolerant" ideals of the Pilgrims. That America is a safer place for your children. That America is a friendlier, safer world in which your grandmother can walk to the corner store at night to get a carton of milk.

I would disagree with you.

CHICKEN FINGERS AND LEFT-WINGERS

The animal rights front group, PETA, better known as People for the Unethical Treatment of Humans, has joined the Dogs of Hate in bashing religion. These animals had the audacity to compare the plight of the Jews in Hitler's concentration camps to the way chickens are contained in slaughterhouses.

Did you get that?

These neo-socs have no regard for the value of human life. They care more for chickens than captive Jews. These bird brains launched an extensive billboard campaign with photos of Jews incarcerated at Auschwitz on the left and chickens pictured in a coop on the right—as if there is a moral equivalence between people and birds. Their slogan?

"End Today's Holocaust: Go Vegan."[11]

I ask you, where is the moral outrage from the synagogues and churches across America? Every Jew in America was offended by that, but you don't hear them talking about it in the synagogues, do you. Why not? If Jews don't defend themselves when the Dogs of Hate take the first bite, it will only be a matter of time before the Jewish people become completely devoured.

At the very least, practicing Jews should be doing a letter-writing campaign. The leadership should be telling congregants not to give ten cents to environmental groups like this. That's what should be going on in the synagogues of America.

Another warped variety of PETA's shameful tactics was an ad with the slogan, "Holocaust on Your Plate," featuring eggs and meat for breakfast.[12]

Look at the poison these hate-filled soul vampires are spewing. This, from PETA's own website: "What will you tell your grandchildren when they ask you whose side you were on during the 'animals' holocaust'? Will you be able to say that you stood up against oppression, even when doing so was considered 'radical' or 'unpopular'? Will you be able to say that you could visualize a world without violence and realized that it began at breakfast?"[13]

Matt Prescott, a PETA puppet who claims to be a Jew, says, "This is truly our generation's 'banality of evil.'" He says nothing about the human holocaust in Iraq. Why am I not surprised when he goes on to quote Princeton University im-moralist Peter Singer, who is Jewish and who we're told lost family in the Holocaust.

Singer said, "In many ways, suffering can be worse for animals in confinement because the animals may have no understanding of what is happening to them or why they are being subjected to this torment."[14] What an outrage! Tell me that's not evidence Singer belongs in a mental hospital instead of Princeton. Or is the Ivy League of today little more than ivy-covered asylums?

Prescott goes on to quote Isaac Bashevis Singer, who said, "[T]hey have convinced themselves that man, the worst transgressor of all the species, is the crown of creation. All other creatures were created merely to provide him with food, pelts, to be tormented, exterminated."[15]

It's in the Bible, Genesis 1:27. Look it up. God created man in His image.

God charged Adam and Eve to eat of animals. What's more, God was the first furrier. He dressed them in garments of animal skins (Genesis 3:21).

Now, in my opinion, every rabbi who's a real rabbi should give a sermon on how the Jews are being debased and defamed by these phony animal rights activists with this comparison of Holocaust victims to chickens in a coup. Just imagine the outcry from the Pink Community if PETA dared to picture the faces of homosexual men who died of AIDS on one side of a billboard and then featured chickens in a coop.

"HERE COMES THE (TRANSGENDER) BRIDE"

The radical leftists and the RDDBs are equally passionate about destroying religion in America. That's their number one target. They have succeeded in taking down the Ten Commandments from our schools and courts; they've succeeded at almost every turn in defaming the Church with false lawsuits and lies.

Next, their number two target has been the traditional family and normal sexuality which, as you well know, rely upon a Judeo-Christian value system. That's why they are engaged in a proactive, systematic campaign to redefine the legal status of marriage.

Case in point. Thirty-seven states have passed a Defense of Marriage Act. In Nebraska, an overwhelming majority, more than 70 percent of the adult population, ratified this state constitutional amendment. The ink was barely dry when the RDDBs of the ACLU rushed to file a lawsuit challenging the decision. Big surprise there. You see, a democratically-enacted law is not good enough for these mad dogs. Instead, they appeal to unelected judges to thwart the will of the people and to inflict their radical agenda on Nebraskans.

Wake up, sheeple!

There are heavily-financed groups like the Fund for a Feminist Majority, the Human Rights Campaign, People for the Un-American Way, and the Freedom to Marry Collaborative organizing across the country to destroy the sacred tradition of marriage. Evan Wolfson, a gay RDDB and founder of the FMC won't stop until marriage rights are extended to same-sex couples. He said, "I have boundless confidence that we will win the freedom to marry."[16]

If recent decisions by the U.S. Supreme Court are any indication, he may be right.

In June of 2003, the radicals pushing homosexual marriage got a boost from the stench on the Supreme bench. When the highest court in the land struck down a Texas sodomy law in the *Lawrence* decision, they knowingly threw open the door to gay marriage. That, according to Justice Antonin Scalia, who sharply disagreed with the majority. He came out and said what we all know, that the Supreme Court "largely signed on to the so-called homosexual agenda."[17]

Let me point out something else that you might have missed. The leftist forces have recruited a new ally: *Bride* magazine. What's the big deal with that? I'll tell you.

For this ambush on traditional values to work, the militants on the Left know they must infiltrate the high profile media outlets and then steer them to having a favorable position on gay marriage. They also know that millions of newly engaged couples have turned to *Bride* since 1934 as the bible of wedding etiquette. It's the oldest, most widely circulated publication of its kind, making it a perfect takeover target by the homosexual community.

In the fall of 2002, *Bride* turned its back on almost seven decades of monogamous reporting by running an article called "Outward Bound," a pro-gay wedding piece. A spokeschick for the Gay and Lesbian Alliance Against Defamation, who will remain nameless, gushed, "A story like this really energizes the gay and lesbian community."[18]

Hear me: This insane drive towards gay marriage isn't the last stop for the bus. It's about expanding marriage to include polygamy, polyamory, transsexual marriages, and open marriage. Perhaps bestiality will get a new image. Why not? There are also single people who want to marry themselves and, in turn, enjoy the benefits afforded married couples.

Is this hyperbole?

On May 28, 2003, Jennifer Hoes, in a bizarre ceremony in the Netherlands, stood before a Haarlem registrar decked out in a wedding gown covered in two hundred latex nipples where she pledged to love, respect, obey, and cherish herself.[19] The act of self-marriage was reported in both Dutch and German newspapers.

In the end, Jennifer Hoes and these self-loathing moral vagrants on the Left will have achieved their primary goal: to trash the traditional, faith-based marriage.

Since the beginning of time, every civilization provided special protection for the institution of marriage because, as you well know, marriage is about *procreation*. It's about raising children and ensuring the future of a society. By definition, homosexuals are incapable of bearing children. So why are they pushing for the right to marry?

It's the ultimate rubberstamp on their lifestyle.

Don't think for one minute this can't happen in America. Recent legal maneuverings in Massachusetts and Vermont by the hard-Left have come dangerously close to yielding a court-sanctioned gay marriage. If and when that day comes, a flood of homosexuals will deluge that state, get married, return to their respective home states, and then insist on recognition of their married status. If refused, they'll sue the state, which, in turn, will cause the first domino to fall in what is sure to be a prolonged, ugly fight to the finish.

This will be the mother mega-cultural battle of our time. Why? If you change the meaning of marriage, you make marriage meaningless. And you can forget about the notion of "monogamous same-sex marriages." It's a smoke screen. How so? As I've pointed out, gay marriage is just the first step in their agenda. We're already seeing examples of polyamory within our borders.

Take the 2000 Minnesota case of *La Chapelle v. Mitten*. Instead of throwing the case out the door, a court assigned parental rights status *to three adults*. In what amounts to a group marriage, the judge said it would be in the best interest of the child if custody was shared between two lesbian lovers and the sperm donor.[20]

Welcome to the world of three-parent families.

This triumvirate arrangement will increase if same-sex marriage is permitted and as lesbian couples seek to have children through sperm donors. The possibilities are endless. What happens when both women want to bear a child and they become inseminated by two different male donors? And what if a judge, based upon the precedent set by *La Chapelle*, determines that both male donors are entitled to parental rights? Marriage becomes a foursome.

Am I the only one who thinks that's utter insanity?

Imagine the psychological damage on the children when traditional marriage is replaced with psychotic three– and foursomes.

Still, there's a thread of good news. To his credit, President George Bush announced, "I believe marriage is between a man and a woman, and we ought to codify that one way or another."[21] According to a Wirthlin poll released March 4, 2003, he'd have the backing of both the Hispanics (63 percent) and African-Americans (62 percent) who overwhelmingly support an amendment to defend the traditional definition of marriage.

Likewise, Pope John Paul II and the Vatican have challenged politicians in North America and Europe to resist the legalization of same-sex marriages. The pope, speaking to one hundred thousand Catholics in Croatia, said, "God's authentic plan" for the family was based upon "the stable and faithfulness of a man and a woman, bound to each other with a bond that is publicly manifested and recognized."[22]

In the wake of Canada's move to recognize gay marriage, Cardinal Karl Lehman warned, "Now the associations of homosexuals have a potent arm to obtain further concessions on the road toward full equality with married couples, including the right to adoption."[23] He's right. And he's one of the few courageous leaders speaking out. I'm telling you, as far as this issue goes, you can hear a pin drop in most houses of worship; they're that silent. Why aren't there more religious leaders on the frontlines?

I say it's time to put on your Savage Nation hat and stand in front of this steamroller. It's time you understood we're not talking about something trivial like sports, fashion, or yesterday's game show. It's time

Americans fought for a constitutional amendment defining marriage as a union between a man and a woman.

It's time we took the fight to the Dogs of Hate.

ISLAMA-RAMA-DING-DONG

What's interesting to me is that there is only one religion that's favored by the Left. Islam gets a pass. Why? In a twisted way, it's because the Dogs of Hate hope to see Islam spread in America in order to overcome the hated Christian white male. You don't understand the psychology of these people. You haven't any idea how sick and demented and dangerous they really are.

I warn you, don't underestimate your enemy.

I want them to prove Islam is a religion of peace. I'm not going to sit here and prove that I'm not a racist. Let them prove that they're not racists. What do you call Saudi Arabia, where you're not allowed to practice Christianity except behind closed doors; where you're not allowed to wear a cross except underneath your blouse; where you're not allowed to wear your hair out because it offends these religious bigots with oil spigots?

What do you call a nation like that?

You call *that* a sensitive nation?

They have no tolerance for anyone else. None. In fact, as I write, I find it hard to dismiss this fact: Of the major religion-based conflicts on earth today, the overwhelming majority involve Islam. I'm just calling it the way it is. Count them for yourself.

There are jihads in Afghanistan, Bosnia, Chechnya, Cyprus, East Timor, Indonesia, Kashmir, Kosovo, Kurdistan, Macedonia, the Middle East, Nigeria, the Philippines, the Sudan, and Uganda. Fifteen conflicts with one common denominator. All involve Muslims who can't get along with their neighbors.

Closer to home, there is the case of Asan Akbar, a U.S. sergeant who, during the war with Iraq, allegedly rolled live grenades into the tents of his sleeping superiors. What the media didn't want you to know, what you had to read in the fine print, was that Akbar was a convert to Islam. He appears to be an enemy among us, just waiting for his turn to stab us in the back.

After his arrest, he said, "You guys are coming into our countries, and you're going to rape our women and kill our children."[24] Of course his mommy, Quran Bilal, ran to his defense citing persecution of his Muslim faith as the *real* reason for his arrest. Never mind the fact he killed his division captain and wounded more than a dozen soldiers in the process. No, according to his mother, he was a good boy arrested for being a Muslim.

Akbar seems to be just another one of the many Enemies Within. His cowardly action makes me wonder what should be done with the other Muslim converts within the armed forces. How many of them are just waiting for their turn to attack us in the name of religion while we're sleeping?

Don't for one minute think that Islam is a religion of peace. Don't be lulled into a deep sleep by the far Left. While we snooze, radical Islamic terrorists are secretly planning their next 9/11 attack. It's not a matter of "if" they will attack; it's a matter of "when and where." So says the CIA and the FBI.

Anis Shorrosh, an Arab-American convert to Christianity and author of two books, reported on a secret Islamic twenty-year plan to bring America to her knees. He writes, "The following is my analysis of an Islamic invasion of America, the agenda of Islamists and visible methods to take over America by the year 2020."[25]

I'll summarize several of his key points.

The first order of business by this Enemy Within would be to thwart America's freedom of speech through the use of so-called hate-crime legislation. We're already seeing evidence of that.

Second, they'd manipulate the likes of Jessie Hi-Jackson and Louis Farra-con to advocate Islam as the religion of choice for black Americans, while positioning Christianity as the white man's religion.

A third prong of the attack is to sway public opinion both within the institutions of education and in the public square to view Islam as just "one of the boys." You know, to suggest Islam is historically no different than Judaism or Christianity.

Fourth, they'd position Muslim sympathizers in public office in order to bring about legislation favorable to Muslim causes.

Fifth, by purchasing a controlling share of stocks they could control much of Hollywood, TV, the Internet, the press, and the radio industries.

Shorrosh, who has traveled to more than seventy-five countries, lists a host of other strategies in his astonishing book, *Islam: A Threat or a Challenge*, including:

- Through sizable grants, the Muslim invaders would create "Centers for Islamic Studies" at the major universities and colleges.

- Open "front" charities in the United States who ultimately funnel American dollars to support Islamic terror activity.

- Encourage mass immigration of Muslims, which has averaged more than a hundred thousand annually since the sixties. Then, teach them to have as many children as possible since all children automatically and irrevocably become Muslims.

- Manipulate the intelligence agencies (FBI, CIA) with false and misleading reports of terrorism to elevate the sense of vulnerability and strike fear in the hearts of Americans.

- Use all possible channels of propaganda to convince the American sheeple that terrorists have co-opted Islam when, in reality, the opposite is true. Islam has hijacked the terrorists for their purposes.

Is the fog beginning to lift? Are you seeing how the radical Left and radical Muslims are aggressively working hand-in-glove to choke the life out of this great country?

In spite of the overwhelming evidence of this worldwide modern-day "crusade" by Muslim terrorists and by old line Marxists, FBI Director

Robert Mueller is diverting resources to hold Muslim sensitivity training sessions for FBI agents!

Retired FBI special agent Don Lavey, who faithfully served for two decades on the counterterrorism team, had a few choice words for this new program. He said, "Let's just hope the director is leading the charge in this war against terrorism with an equal amount of zeal that he shows for cultural sensitivities."[26] The signs aren't promising.

The FBI held daylong sensitivity training classes near Ground Zero in New York City where they handed the microphone to Imam Feisal Abdul Rauf.[27] For the better part of two hours, he lectured our FBI on how the Islamic faith is one of peace, as well as how to be respectful when dealing with potential terrorists.

I am getting sick of all this hypocrisy. The Dogs of Hate have so twisted religion in America, they vilify the houses of worship, while suggesting we all take sensitivity lessons to embrace elements of the "religion of peace"—which has already attacked New York City and Washington DC.

So let's connect the dots. The vast left-wing conspiracy, whose only goal is to bring America to her knees, views Islam as a pawn in their crusade of personal hate and destruction. And, as I said at the outset, the Dogs of Hate view this spread of Islam in America as a means to overcome the hated heterosexual Christian white male.

Now you have the whole picture.

THE DEVIL MADE ME DO IT

I imagine there are some readers who find all of this discussion of religion quite amusing. Maybe you think it's one big joke. Or maybe you're an atheist. I happen to think the greatest trick that the devil has ever come up with is convincing many of you that he doesn't exist. Why? It's elementary. Watch closely.

If you believe the devil doesn't exist, then you can by the same token say God doesn't exist. With God out of the picture, you feel that you're a free man to do as you please. That's what the secular humanists, RDDBs, and the mad dogs on the Left do. They say, "Ha, I don't believe in the devil, and I don't believe in God. Hell, I am God. I determine the outcome of my own life."

I want you infidels to think about something.

Maybe what I am about to say will help you understand and show some level of respect to people of faith. The next time you fall off a ski and are lying in an emergency room, tell me God doesn't exist. The next time one of your children, God forbid, gets injured, and you're in that hospital listening to that heart monitor beep, tell me God does not exist. Tell me the next time one of your family whom you love is injured and dying, that God does not exist. There is only one God. And God looks over all of us— for better and for worse.

You should also know: God is a vengeful God.

This is the one thing that you people don't understand.

God is not dressed up in Mickey Mouse pajamas.

God doesn't wear pajamas with little teddy bears on it.

God is not a nice guy. That's the one thing modern Christianity tends to deemphasize. God is a vengeful God. Man, is He vengeful. He doesn't like certain things, and He lets you know about it. Sometimes quietly, sometimes loudly, sometimes immediately, sometimes later. Sometimes twenty years later you get to know it.

And, I should say, He's a silent God.

Which drives most people crazy because they want a figure to whom they can bow down. They want something that speaks to them directly so they can point and say, "There's God." You know, it's got little eyes that move up and down and smoke comes out of its ears. Jumps around the room and incense burns in its nostrils. That's called paganism. That's not God. That's called idol worship.

And good luck if you believe in that stuff, but that's not the foundation of this nation. Make no mistake. America is strong because America has experienced the blessing of God. It's up to you to fight the Dogs of Hate who want to strip you of your rich, faith-based heritage.

Who want to silence your practice of religion.

Who want to see America as one nation under black robes, tinged in red.

FEELING LIKE MOSES

Remember Moses and the burning bush?

In case you were playing hooky from Sunday School when they taught that one, here's the story. Moses was tending his sheep and minding his own business when he stumbled on a burning bush. Even though on fire, the bush didn't burn up. His curiosity consumed him. "This I got to see," Moses thought. So he wanders over for a closer look.

That's when God spoke. Of course, God was using the bush to get Moses' attention. Turns out that the Lord wanted Moses to confront Pharaoh, the king of Egypt, to release the people of Israel. Moses says, "But I got a lisp. What do you want from me? I'm happy just being a shepherd."

God said, basically, "No problem, I'll put my words in your mouth." Unconvinced, Moses says, "Look, I'm just a regular guy. How am I supposed to lead the people out of Egypt?" But no matter what Moses said, God kept saying, "I want you anyway. You're not getting out of this one."

Like I said, sometimes I feel like Moses. I'd rather be out on my boat watching the gulls. I'd like to drop anchor and watch the seals. Maybe eat a sandwich as the sun sets, watching the terns hovering over the San Francisco Bay. Some days I'd like to do anything other than wake up and fight against the advancing Dogs of Hate.

But what choice do I have?

What choice do you have?

I believe it's our God-given duty to stand for what is right. If God-fearing Americans don't stand for something, they will fall for anything. As Reverend Jerry Falwell has said, the time comes for civil disobedience whenever an act is in conflict with your core religious beliefs.

Where do we start?

The most important thing to do is take back the judiciary. Why? This assault on the Bible Belt by the Libel Belt was energized when Ruth

Ginsburg was put on the Supreme Court in 1993 by Bill Clinton. There was no objection by the asleep-at-the-switch Republicans. America is paying dearly for that negligence today. Ginsburg is possibly the most radical lawyer in the history of the United States of America!

After all, when Clinton appointed her to the highest court in the land, she was the chief counsel for the ACLU—that ultra-leftist group which believes, among other things, that virtual child porn is protected speech.[28] Surely such extremism should have triggered an immediate and vocal rejection of her nomination by the Republicans. But, no.

The silence from the Right was deafening.

And so today we have a Supreme Court that has slowly but surely come under her control. The only way to get America back is to begin at the top. The *capo di tutta capo* of the entire RDDB brigade is, in my opinion, none other than Ruth Bad-girl Ginsburg. She must be impeached.

She *can* be impeached.

Who would have thought a few years ago that the governor of the state of California, with the fifth largest economy in the world, could ever be recalled. And yet, in our democracy, there is a mechanism in place to weed out those who fail to faithfully execute their responsibilities.

Likewise, do not for one moment think that a Supreme Court justice is beyond impeachment. She can and she must be impeached. All it takes is the courage and the unwavering commitment to face the Enemy Within. If you're thinking, "But Michael, I'm just one person." Start small. Light the impeachment fires at the grassroots level. Watch it blaze as other like-minded patriots fan the flames through petitions, editorials, and phone calls.

If you don't act, who will?

If you don't act now, then when?

If not this issue, then what will it take?

EIGHT

SCHOOLS:
CONDOMS ON CUCUMBERS

Early summer is the greatest time on earth for kids. Without the ball and chain of school holding them back, they're liberated. They come alive. You can see it in their faces. You can hear it in their voices. They quickly forget the multiculturalism classes. There's no homework on transgender sensitivity and no Ritalin doses to dull their senses. Kids are free to explore the world on their own terms.

When I was a little kid, the summer had a defined rhythm to it. In June we'd play cowboys and Indians in the woods. Of course, PC linguists would have us change that to "cowpersons and Native Americans." Even as July approached, I still had forever. You know what "forever" was to a kid? Those eight hot weeks of summer when the sun didn't set until 9 P.M.

Those were such wonderful days.

At the first change of the season, somewhere around mid-August, I remember feeling the impending return of slavery. The first hint of fall was announced by thunderstorms, and I'd feel the shackles of school coming back. I knew I would soon return, dressed in corduroy pants and armed only with a meatloaf sandwich, to my horrible, mean school. I'd have to face teachers, chalk dust, and bullies in the bathroom. It was awful.

When September rolled around, I was doomed.

Let's not make any mistake about it. Personally, I hated school. I detested the testing. What do you think, that because I went all the way through the system and got two master's degrees and a Ph.D., I somehow loved it? I never did. I didn't study because I *liked* it. I did it because I wanted to learn and advance myself. Learning is hard work.

Learning is supposed to be a discipline.

It's not always going to be fun.

Unless, of course, you had a friend like Woodchuck Bill.

Bill was unlike any teacher I ever had at school. Man, could he tell stories. Woodchuck Bill was a big guy with leather skin, big hands, and a thick neck. He was as strong as a mountain lion. He lived most of his life in the outdoors with his wife and a knife. You know, the kind of guy who lived off the land.

For the record, not everyone who is homeless or lives in the backwoods is a backwards person. Just about 99 percent are. However, Woodchuck Bill was that 1 percent who was more like a cross between a vagabond and Daniel Boone. Don't confuse the homeless of today who are often drugged-out alcoholics, who defecate in mailboxes and urinate in doorways, with the vagabonds of yesteryear. Back then, unlike now, vagabonds were not bums. They just loved wide-open spaces. The truth is, vagabonds were a good part of the American tradition.

Anyway, my family used to visit a little bungalow colony in the Catskill Mountains in Spring Glen, New York. I will remember those paradisiacal days, until my last moment on earth, as the greatest times of my life. Dad was alive and Mom was young. The relatives were with us, and everything was perfect. It was so beautiful. It was the world as it should be. Everyone was happy because the men left their cares behind in the city during the weekends.

That's where I first met Woodchuck Bill and his wife. They lived on the edge of town out in the woods in a simple barn-like structure. She had the long, flowing gray hair of a beatnik woman. What few pots and pans she had were hung from the ceiling. He was a part-time handyman for the colony who survived off of game or whatever he would hunt. You might say he was a benign sort of self-reliant, nature-living guy.

Woodchuck Bill's life had been filled with so many unusual adventures. He would tell us kids stories as we sat cross-legged and captivated. To this day, I can picture him resting his hands on his huge potbelly as he spoke. He'd say, "I've been through hurricanes and tornadoes. I've seen death, and I've seen life . . ." and would proceed to tell us fascinating stories about courage, commitment, and bravery. We would sit on the floor and listen to Bill like he was Methuselah coming back from the dead.

Then one day, as if to reinforce a point, Bill said, "I'll show you kids how tough I am. Come over here and punch me in the stomach." Every one of us skinny little kids lined up and took a shot. We were like seven, eight, maybe nine. We didn't know we weren't that strong. A kid thinks he's strong at nine. So we all punched him in the stomach, and nothing happened. He didn't even flinch.

We absolutely thought he was Superman.

Hanging around Woodchuck Bill is the perfect example of the education I got *outside* of school that was just as important to me, if not more so, than what I'd get in a stuffy classroom. As odd as Bill was, he had such insight into living and enjoying life and being an independent thinker. He possessed a pioneer spirit that made us think we could tackle the world with our bare hands.

Woodchuck Bill is long gone. I only wish kids today could experience the education I got from a man with his streak of independence, imagination, and zest for life. Unfortunately, students are rarely introduced to men and women of courage, honor, inspiration, or traditional principles. Instead, the schoolhouse has become a hothouse of radical ideology. Instead of stimulating their minds, teachers are instructing students from kindergarten to graduation how to stimulate other parts of their body.

Why is this happening?

The radical national teachers' unions with their bloated leftist agendas have overrun local schools and school boards. That's number one. These powerful unions oppose most efforts to teach children independence from government and how to think for themselves. To them, educational success happens whenever activism replaces reading, writing, and arithmetic.

We've gone from the three "R's" to the three "D's": degeneracy, disorientation, and deconstruction.

Yes, I blame the teachers' unions. Leading the pack is the National Education Association (NEA), the largest and most powerful teachers' union in the United States with more than 2.7 million members. These obstructionists oppose parental choice through school vouchers and tax credits.

They oppose genuine abstinence-based sex education.

They oppose teacher competency testing.

They oppose a moment of silence at the start of the day.

They oppose "English only" initiatives for schools.

They oppose teaching Creation alongside the theory of evolution.

They oppose textbooks that accurately reflect American history and American culture.

They oppose any attempt at an ideological balance.

They oppose the creation of charter schools.

They oppose homeschooling.

What more evidence do you need before you come to grips with the fact they, too, are the Enemy Within? This renegade socialist union is doing incredible damage to our schools and our students. It's time to deconstruct the NEA, that's all.

If you're a teacher, you know exactly what I'm saying. Every time you raise your hand to object to a neo-socialist policy of the NEA, or question their push for community-operated, school-based family clinics,[1] you are ostracized. Especially if you're a conservative educator who happens to wear a cross or Star of David around your neck.

The reign of academic terror by the NEA must stop.

Number two. The teaching profession by and large has succumbed to postmodern thinking. I'm talking about the far-Left ideological rhetoric. By dismissing traditional morality, right and wrong, and truth and lies, as being quaint, or worse, intolerant, concepts, they're making a mockery of everything that has made this country great.

Think about it. Without a moral framework, without some baseline of truth, and without historically accurate facts, how can they teach students to be honorable, responsible, and productive citizens?

I've been fighting these academic crackpots for years. Make that decades. No matter how I try, I feel like I'm shoveling turd against the tide. Everywhere I turn, liberals are trampling on genuine academic inquiry. They are emasculating our schools and bastardizing our ninnyversities.

When it's all said and done, these America-hating subversive schoolmasters are risking our nation's future by rewriting her past. Now, for those of you with your hat on backwards, Dr. Savage is about to give you the most unbelievable lesson of your lifetime.

THE DEATH OF INNOCENCE

Do you remember your first day going to kindergarten? Maybe your mom or dad packed a lunch, walked you to the bus stop, and blew kisses as you headed off to school for what was probably the scariest day of your life. Or maybe they drove you to school and held your hand as they introduced you to a class of complete strangers.

Turned out it wasn't too bad. You played games. Sang about Old McDonald's farm. Played kickball. Had snack time with cookies and milk. Maybe doodled a little with crayons as the teacher read a story. The last thing you'd expect to hear about was sexual orientation and masturbation.

Of course, all that has changed.

Innocence is out. Indoctrination is in.

The radical social engineers on the ultra-Left, which includes the

NEA, have embraced a bizarre, comprehensive, lifelong sex indoctrination curriculum *beginning with kindergarteners*. The taxpayer funded Centers for Disease Control (CDC) commissioned the publication of the *Guidelines for Comprehensive Sexuality Education* by the Sexuality Information and Education Council of the United States (SIECUS).[2]

You probably don't know it, but this abominable report is considered the bible for comprehensive sex education in public schools today. The *Guidelines* are reported to be "the most widely recognized and implemented framework for comprehensive sexuality education across the country."[3] It divides a student's sex-ed experience into four levels:

> Level 1 Middle Childhood. Children ages 5 through 8.
>
> Level 2 Preadolescence. Children ages 9 through 12.
>
> Level 3 Early adolescence. Children ages 12 through 15.
>
> Level 4 Adolescence. Children ages 15 through 18.

Here's what these social engineers want to teach your children starting in kindergarten. The following excerpts are the exact verbiage taken from the SIECUS guide.

Middle Childhood (ages five through eight):

- Vaginal intercourse occurs when a man and a woman place the penis inside the vagina.[4]

- Some men and woman are homosexual, which means they will be attracted to and fall in love with someone of the same gender.[5]

- Touching and rubbing one's own genitals to feel good is called masturbation.[6]

- Some boys and girls masturbate and others do not.[7]

- Both boys and girls may discover that their bodies feel good when touched.[8]

I'd like to know what degenerate thought up those guidelines for sex education. Kids at that age need to learn about fair play on the playground—not foreplay in the backseat. They should be singing "I Want to Hold Your *Hand*" not "I Want to Hold Your *Gland*."

Things are not much better for the nine– to twelve-year-old crowd. Again, quoting from the morally bankrupt SIECUS sex manual, students are supposed to learn that:

- Sexual intercourse provides pleasure.[9]

- Homosexual love relationships can be as fulfilling as heterosexual relationships.[10]

- A legal abortion is very safe.[11]

Why does a ten-year-old need to know about abortion?

She hasn't even learned arithmetic yet.

Could it get any worse?

Sure. We're talking grade-A liberal minds at work here. These degenerates know no boundaries. To further warp your middle and high school students ages twelve through fifteen, they're supposed to be taught about bi-sexuality ("some people feel attracted to both men and women"[12]) and the general availability of condoms ("young people can buy some contraceptives in a drug store, grocery market, or convenience store without a doctor's prescription."[13])

They forgot to mention truck stop bathrooms.

In California, consistent with the bi-sexual aspects of this indoctrination campaign, the Gay, Lesbian and Straight Teachers Network distributes a "Heterosexuality Questionnaire" to stimulate more than discussion on the topic. In it, they ask students to identify:

- When and where did you first decide you were heterosexual?

- Is it possible heterosexuality is a phase you will grow out of?

- Is it possible you are heterosexual because you fear the same sex?

- If you have never slept with someone of the same sex, how do you know you wouldn't prefer that?[14]

Gay or straight, the CDC wants to make sure your kids and condoms go together like, well, hand in glove. For fourth– to ninth-graders, they offer "Focus on Kids" with its "Condom Race Activity." Picture your child playing along with this one. The teacher is supposed to "Divide youth into two teams and give everyone a condom. Have the teams stand in two lines and give the first person in each line a dildo or cucumber. Each person on the team must put the condom on the dildo or cucumber and take it off . . . the team that finishes first wins."[15]

And you thought I was exaggerating when I subtitled this chapter!

After they've stretched the Trojans or rammed the Ramseys over the end of a cucumber, they're supposed to settle into a cozy brainstorming activity. What will they be encouraged to think about? Abstinence? Right?

Wrong. Try these recommended talking points from the CDC on for size: "Ask youth to brainstorm ways to be close to a person and show you care without having sexual intercourse . . . the list may include . . . bathing together, masturbation, sensuous feeding, fantasizing, watching erotic movies, reading erotic books and magazines."[16]

Worse, seventh– to twelfth-graders are offered the "Be Proud! Be Responsible!" program by the CDC. Students as young as thirteen are to brainstorm these ideas: "[I]f they weren't mentioned by participants: Think up a sexual fantasy using condoms . . . Act sexy/sensual when putting condoms on . . . hide them on your body and ask your partner to find it . . . tease each other manually while putting on the condom."[17]

That's for starters. Once they've got condoms on their minds, students are encouraged to "go to the store together. Buy lots of different brands and colors. Plan a special day when you can experiment. Just talking about how you'll use all of those condoms can be a turn-on."[18]

And we're supposed to wonder why kids can't say "no" to sex? Why should they exercise a scintilla of restraint? They've been told to try sex ever since they shuffled into kindergarten with their Barney lunchbox. No wonder that in 2000, more than 240,000 babies were born to kids eighteen or younger.[19] Kids having kids.

Isn't liberalism great?

They've failed these children who have no earthly clue about the emotional, physical, or financial implications of what they're doing. Our negligence in looking the other way while the Enemy Within rapes the minds of our children is inexcusable. Who is going to tell these kids-who-have-kids that, all because of this liberal brainwashing and their subsequent poor choices, they're headed for long-term poverty?

That they will probably skip college.

They may never learn any advanced skills.

They will be hooked on food stamps and handouts.

Their best friend for the next few decades will be a welfare agent.

I ask you, who is going to give them the Savage truth? A study in 2003 found that teen sex puts children at greater risk for disease, depression, and suicide: "When compared to teens who *are not* sexually active, teenage boys and girls *who are* sexually active are significantly less likely to be happy and more likely to feel depressed . . . [and] more likely to attempt suicide."[20]

Who is going to get that message out?

Certainly not the teachers' union. They are hard at work within our schools attempting to "liberate" students by taking the forbidden fruit of premarital sex and shoving it down their throats. And, while they're at it, they push gay sex and homosexual marriage.

Look, I live in the middle of this liberal cesspool. I'm not blind. Everywhere I turn, these activists have turned elementary classrooms into human labs for multi-gender studies. Beneath the veneer of academic respectability, these ruthless sociopaths are wrecking society and destroying everything you believe in.

Just look at what the Novato, California, school board did in the fall of 2002. Literally in the middle of the night they approved the highly controversial homosexual agenda video, "That's A Family!" for use with their *fifth grade classes*.

The producers bill it as a "Media Resource for Kids on Family Diversity." In it, brainwashed kids extol the virtues of a variety of family arrangements for the camera. "My dads are gay, and gay means . . . two men or two women love each other" says a happy, smiling, maybe-ten-year-old girl in the video. "It's sort of like having a mom and a dad love each other, just that it is a man and a man."[21]

Really? How would she know it's the same?

Who's putting that twisted crap in her head?

Trust me, my heart goes out to her. She has no way of knowing the putrescent Left is using her. Then again, maybe I should just lighten up. I mean, if Sesame Street can have an HIV-positive Muppet, why should I be surprised this garbage is making the rounds in our elementary schools?

I maintain that *diversity is perversity*.

SAVAGE FOR CLASS PRESIDENT

When I was in elementary school, we didn't even know what a condom was. For the most part nobody talked about them. We were too busy being kids. Forget about being graded on your ability to snap a condom on a cucumber. It wouldn't happen. In my day, we were graded on things like character and behavior and cooperation.

See if you can remember this one on your report card: "Gets along well with others." I sometimes got a "U" for UNSATISFACTORY. I'm not boasting about it. The fact of the matter is, I sometimes didn't get along well with others. It's not that I was a troublemaker. I certainly did not go out of my way to bother people. But I sure wasn't a social butterfly.

Today, the teacher would go to jail if she dared tell a kid he doesn't get along well with others. It might hurt his *self-esteeeeeem*. Might even *daaaamage* him for life, they'd say. I guess by that standard, my self-esteem was damaged every step of the way. Especially after what happened when I ran for class president in the fifth grade.

One morning the teacher listed names on the chalkboard of those who were running for president. On a lark, I raised my hand. Now I'm in the race. I've got to do my campaign, you know, "Vote for Michael" and all that for the rest of the morning. Not that it was a big deal. As president, I think you got to select who would be the chalkboard monitor.

Right before lunch it was time for us to vote. Our teacher passed out little slips of paper, and we had to write down who we wanted as class president. She sat on the edge of her desk and watched us like a hawk while we scribbled away.

Then she walked up and down between the desks like a drill sergeant collecting the slips while my heart pounded so loudly I was convinced the principal could hear it down the hall. Suddenly, it felt like this was a much bigger deal, my first election and all. So she tallies the votes on the board while we're on the edge of our seats watching the drama unfold. I'll never forget the look she made each time I got a vote and she had to put that checkmark by my name. Her face got that scrunched-up look, as if she had just sucked a lemon with Tabasco sauce on it.

Don't ask me how or why, but somehow I got elected.

In the grand liberal tradition of manipulating the will of the people, just like the Ninth Jerkit Court of Appeals does with startling frequency, this teacher claimed a mistrial because *I* won. I already knew she didn't like me. But this crossed the line, and everyone knew it. My classmates protested, "Wait, that's not fair. We voted for Michael."

She said, "No, it *is* fair, because I'm the teacher." So she had us retake the vote. And I won again. That really steamed her, I could tell. At which point she put her foot down and declared, "Savage is not the president. He can't be the president. The election is over."

She was like a mini–Fidel Castro.

When the kids protested, she agreed to doing the election a *third* time but on one condition. She announced, "Savage can't even run this time." She stacked the election and got the results she wanted. Lesson learned: The teacher holds all the cards.

They're the power brokers.

Nothing happens unless *they* want it to happen.

Which, by the way, reminds me of what's happening in California these days. The votes and will of the people are often thwarted by RDDB judges who try to veto any vote they don't like.

Realistically, as kids in that classroom, what were our options? Go on a hunger strike by skipping lunch? So I sat there feeling frustrated and powerless to do anything about the situation while another kid got picked.

I learned some teachers wanted to break your will to fight, even back then. They wanted to squeeze every last ounce of spunk and soul from you. Why? Conformity and control was the name of the game. Still is. You will see just how far PC control-freaks have gone to keep kids under their left thumbs. Maybe that explains why I was so drawn to nonconformists like Woodchuck Bill.

FROM TROJANS TO TEXTBOOKS

Let's raise the discussion to matters above the belt. You see, there are two areas of study in the schools: lower and upper. The *lower studies* have to do with the Left's preoccupation on all things below the belt. That would be lessons on human sexuality, gender bending, sex, abortion, sexual orientation, condoms, oh, and did I mention sex? Basically, members of the Left are intellectuals at the crotch level.

The *upper studies* have to do with the way radicals are working to control your mind. That's Ritalin, revised textbooks, ultra-intolerance, socialist indoctrination, deconstruction of patriotism, censorship of conservative ideas, and a host of other mental gymnastics they expect students to perform until they're completely lost.

Entire books have been written on these topics. But there are several disturbing trends I must touch on beginning with textbooks. When was the last time you took a look at your kids' textbooks? If it's been a while, you'd be shocked to learn what free speech goons are doing to control the flow of ideas.

Liberal pressure groups are using strong-arm tactics on textbook manufacturers to remove language, ideas, and traditions they find offensive. This has been going on for years, as you may know. Publishers and the testing agencies that design student exams have generated their own official lists of forbidden words and topics. One publisher has a list of verboten words spanning 161 pages.[22]

Here's a good one.

You can't mention "birthdays" because some kids don't have birthday parties—or might never be invited to one. We don't want them to be *offeeended* or feel left out. You can't say "snowman" (now changed to "snowperson"), "owl" (some cultures associate it with death), "brotherhood" (for obvious reasons of sexism), "busboy" (now "dining room attendant"), nor can you use "senile," "crazy," "heroin," or "swarthy" (as in swarthy Middle Easterner).

Words like "mountain," "ocean," and "forest" are pulled because they reflect a regional bias. The only exception is "rain forest" which replaces "jungle" to make the eco-nuts happy. This is stupidity of the worst kind. Or take "lumberjack." These manly men have gotten the ax and are now "woodcutters." I imagine "lumberjill" might be okay. And watch out: You dare not say "primitive" or "backward" when describing a backwards country.

Stop right there.

I find that particularly offensive. Why?

One of my master's degrees was in anthropology. I've spent *years* travelling and studying in the South Pacific Islands (Fiji, Samoa, Tonga, Tahiti, the Marquesas) going back to 1969. I have great respect for primitive cultures. But they certainly aren't equal to what we have achieved in our nation. There's no comparison. I don't care what argument the Left may make to justify extolling "primitive civilization." The fact is, when a country doesn't have running water, modern medicine, sewage treatment, and things of that nature, they *are* primitive.

To continue this nonsense and promote the idea that mat-weaving is somehow equivalent to building a rocket is intellectual dishonesty of the lowest order. Such semantics are designed to denigrate our achievements while masking the shortcomings of Krapistan.

Many of the barred words fall under the category of stereotypes. So that means you'd better not portray Asian Americans as being especially intelligent students. That's a stereotype. You're not allowed to portray African Americans as great athletes. That's a stereotype. You're not allowed to have women for secretaries, teachers, or housewives.

In fact, the word "housewife" is banned. A mother cooking dinner for her children can't be shown or described because it's sexist—and, for those with two daddies and no mommies, that image borders on a hate crime.

You must not show an old person who is sickly or feeble, using a cane, walker, or toting an oxygen tank. Older folks are supposed to be active and pictured running marathons, playing tennis, or jogging. Speaking of sports, girls must be shown *playing* sports, not *watching* sports. And men are no longer to be portrayed as plumbers, lawyers, doctors, or other professionals.

Yes, thanks to the word police, everybody pictured is the same as everybody else with a slightly different skin color and age. Here's the irony. The Left lectures us on diversity, but then we're not allowed to describe anything that makes us a diverse people!

Better read that again.

This hypocrisy is further proof extreme liberalism is a mental disease. Of course, California is a whole separate story. The self-appointed state censors have informed textbook publishers to drop references to "unhealthy" foods.[23] That means you can forget about pizza, soda, bacon, butter, hot dogs, ketchup, coffee, French fries, mayonnaise, cheese, cake— you get the picture.

So let me understand the logic here. A kid can't read about ketchup or fries in a textbook, but it's okay for them to read those same words on the lunch line menu board? What's next, banning McDonald's?

Diane Ravitch, a professor at New York University who served as assistant secretary in the federal Education Department under George W. Bush, studied this censorship trend for three years. The dumbing down of the education kids are getting disturbs her.

Ravitch says students are presented "stories that have no geographical location. Stories that have no regional distinctiveness. Stories in which all conflicts are insignificant. Stories in which men are fearful and women are brave. Stories in which older people are never ill."[24]

These same thought police are also working to have entire books banned from the classroom. You'll be astonished to see what's on the blacklist today. *The Little Engine that Could* was derailed because *the train was male*. Now, if he were a white male train, he'd be headed for the scrap yard.

What about *The Friendly Dolphin*?

No way. Kids who don't live by the sea could be offended.

Listen to this one. You can't mention Jews in an Isaac Bashevis Singer story about pre-war Poland. You can't mention blacks in Annie Dillard's memoir of growing up in a racially mixed town. Kind of cuts the heart out of the story. Even Mickey Mouse was sent packing with his tail between his legs. Is nothing sacred?

FACT-FREE ZONES

Textbooks today are rapidly becoming "fact-free" zones. Let's say a historical passage referred to the "Founding Fathers." Nope. Can't have that. The reference must be changed to the "Framers" because "Fathers" is exclusionary, sexist, and insensitive to Mary who has two mommies. Never mind the fact that historically speaking all of the Founding Fathers of the Constitution were male.

But let's not let facts get in the way of diversity and inclusion. Kids will just have to learn to call them by the gender-neutral term, the "Framers"—which sounds more like a group of carpenters to me.

Let me give you another heads-up. Your kids won't learn about Mount Rushmore. On the face of it, George Washington, Thomas Jefferson, Theodore Roosevelt, and Abraham Lincoln made the mistake of being men. That said, there is another reason this national monument was jackhammered. Evidently, the Black Hills of South Dakota are viewed by the

Lakota Indians as sacred prayer grounds. They think the sculpture is "an abomination." Off with the heads on the mountain!

Worse than these efforts to decapitate history and alter reality are the deliberate and willful *revisions* of history. More often than not, textbooks position the United States as the mean-faced bully of the world, while brutal dictators and those whack-jobs in headscarves are made into sympathetic characters.

Look at what's happening with the portrayal of Islam in our schoolbooks. Gilbert Sewall works for the American Textbook Council. He filed a detailed report called "Islam and the Textbooks." In it, he documents the outright manipulation of history, one that puts the best spin on those who perpetuate violence against America.

Sewall discovered, "On controversial subjects, world history textbooks make an effort to circumvent unsavory facts that might cast Islam past or present in anything but a positive light. Islamic achievements are reported with robust enthusiasm. When any dark side surfaces, textbooks run and hide."[25]

How are students supposed to address the very real threat of Islamic aggression when they have no factual basis for a discussion in the classroom? According to Sewall, textbooks today "omit, flatter, embellish, and resort to happy talk, suspending criticism or harsh judgments that would raise provocative or even alarming questions."[26] Even the most obvious word, "jihad" (which in the classic sense means armed warfare against non-Muslims), has been reduced to nothing more than engaging in minor altercations.

And here I thought we were the ones who lived in a free society. I thought we had the freedom of speech to have substantive conversations on even difficult issues. This censorship of current events is nothing short of an educational dictatorship. Our children have a right to know that radical Islam may attack our shores at any time.

Radical Islam has waged a guerilla war against America.

Radical Islam hates our way of life and us.

Radical Islam wants to convert the world to their religion!

Those are the facts.

Why are leftist America-haters in the publishing world doing this? Why have they joined the Enemy Within and compromised genuine, fact-based education? Sewall asserts, "[T]extbook editors routinely adjust perspective and outlook to advance the illusion of cultural equivalency and demonstrate cross-cultural and global sensitivity."[27]

That's part of it.

But greed is at the heart of it.

It all boils down to avoiding even the faintest whiff of controversy so that state education boards will continue to approve a textbook for student use. It is, after all, a $9 billion industry. The four major textbook producers want a piece of the pie, and they'll do anything to avoid offending a handful of well-placed liberal censors.

Bottom line? Thanks to the language police, you can say goodbye to Shakespeare, Hemingway, and Chaucer.

Even *Huckleberry Finn* is finished.

So is meaningful debate on important topics.

Instead, this censorship board has created a host of boring, lackluster, colorless textbooks that no kid in his right mind would ever want to read.

With or without the aid of Ritalin.

TONGUE-TIED

It's bad enough our schools have textbooks nobody wants to read. But it is alarming to me thousands of students can't even read them in the first place. I'm not talking about reading proficiency. I'm talking about the widespread refusal to learn to speak or read English by immigrants.

Let me give you the perfect example of how liberals are further abusing our tax dollars in defense of multi-culturalism. English is the language of the United States. When you go to school, shouldn't it be your goal to learn English if you want to get ahead in this country?

This you're not going to believe. Not long ago I read a story in California's *Orange County Register*. The reporter claimed no adult can speak fluent English in one-out-of-ten Orange County households. Isn't that nice?

They can speak Spanish.

They can speak Vietnamese.

They can speak Korean or another Asian language.

But they can't speak English. They are functionally illiterate in American society. Why bother to learn to speak and read English? They can spit on the flag and still get a welfare check.

And a driver's license.

And free health-care.

And free ACLU care.

Since parents are't making an effort to learn English, they fail to set the example for their children to learn it. That's why their kids come to school without the ability to understand a word of what the teacher is saying. Unless, of course, they're in sex-ed class where dildos and condoms are used to communicate.

This isn't isolated to one county in California.

In the Naples, Florida area, "there are more than 6,000 Collier County students whose home language is not English."[28] That is obscene. Ten years ago the number of students whose language of choice was something other than English was just 284.

So what does the brilliant school board do?

They hire an army of language translators. And taxpayers have to pick up the tab for this willful delinquency. The school is paying $20,000 annually for each of the 117 bilingual "tutors" to personally explain what the teacher is saying. Isn't this just wonderful? There are 93 Spanish translators, 22 Haitian Creole, 1 Portuguese, and 1 Canjoval.[29]

Even in non-border states like Georgia, we're seeing this trend towards linguistic anarchy. Gwinnett County School Board hired three translators to, as a spokesbabe whose name doesn't matter said, "meet the growing needs of a diverse community [and] to enhance communication with limited-English proficient parents."[30] So, if you speak Spanish, Korean, or Vietnamese, you need not assimilate and become an American.

Am I the only one who thinks this is insane?

Of course, this is now a booming cottage industry for the language translators' union. Walter Bacak, executive director of the American Translators Association, reports this has been wonderful for his business. Not in so many words, but that's the reality. His own membership has tripled in just ten years to more than nine thousand people. He said, "These are newly created jobs all over the country."[31]

Gee, isn't that great? We've found a new way to improve the economy while enabling those who expect us to wait on them hand and foot to retain their native tongue. It's no longer: "When in Rome, do as the Romans do." It's now: "When in America, make Americans do as you do."

THE KANSAS CITY EXPERIMENT

As long as I live, I'll never forget the day I first walked into a classroom to teach. You might not have known that about my background. In addition to my various academic credentials, I spent some time teaching. I'm talking about a long time ago. Maybe I'll write a book about it one day. You know, something for the students. I could call it *The Savage Guide to Surviving High School*.

Back then I didn't look much older than the students. I had graduated high school at sixteen, which means I, in turn, graduated college at a very young age. Frankly, I decided to grow a goatee to look older than the junior high school kids in my class. I remember my foot froze when I raised it to step over the curb that first day of teaching junior high school. I actually stopped mid-stride. The students were racing past me to get to class, and I was standing there as stiff as a statue.

I had no idea I had a fear of teaching. But I did. If you think teaching is an easy job, try it someday. It's probably one of the toughest jobs on earth if you do it right. So when I'm critical about the teaching profession and the teachers' union, don't get me wrong. I fully recognize it's a tough drill. At the same time, there are legitimate abuses in the schools these days on which I must comment.

Here's a big one. I must tell you about the Kansas City Experiment. Why? Because it's likely you have been seduced by the NEA into believing throwing more money at our failed school system is the best way to fix things. The alarmists on the Left tell us there's no money for school lunches and kids are starving from malnutrition. They say there's not enough money for politically correct textbooks and basic school supplies. They insist the teachers are hamstrung.

Teachers are underpaid.

Teachers are overworked.

Teachers don't even have chalk.

So the clipped-haired, educational czarinas wag their cucumbers at you, the greedy taxpayer, and lecture you for not coughing up enough dough. You are the problem. If only you weren't so selfish and paid more taxes to fund education, our kids would have a fighting chance to learn.

Really?

Nothing could be further from the truth.

According to Secretary of Education Rod Paige, we're spending more than $400 billion a year on education.[32] He's on record as saying, "No idea in politics has hurt children more than the false and misleading idea that the quality of education is determined by how much we spend."[33] Amen, brother! Paige had the guts to point out that a lack of accountability and the use of "unproven fads for instruction"[34] are at the heart of the problem.

The fanatical, power-grabbing NEA union doesn't want you to hear that. They insist *more money* is the answer—not the testing and retraining of teachers who can't teach. To them, the only way to raise sagging test scores, low achievement, and anemic proficiency skills is to further punish the taxpayer.

Let's set aside the fact we're spending $7.4 billion to educate *illegal* aliens,[35] with the hardest hit states being California, Texas, and New York. We're certainly not going to change that anytime soon, primarily because the Stench from the U.S. Supreme Bench ruled in the 1982 case of *Plyler v. Doe* that public schools must educate children. All children. Regardless if they were smuggled across the border in the middle of the night.

Here's my concern. I imagine after listening to the NEA for decades, some of the sheeple might be persuaded to believe maybe we *do* need to spend more on education. After all, that is what the Demoncats shout every time they're running for political office. We're told it takes a gold-plated village to educate kids.

Which is why I must tell you about the Kansas City Experiment. You're not going to believe what a federal district RDDB judge did in 1985. According to a jaw-dropping report by the highly respected Cato Institute, this tyrant "ordered the state and district to spend nearly $2 billion over the next twelve years to build new schools, integrate classrooms, and bring student test scores up to national norms."[36]

In other words, acting as a stooge of the NEA, this judge, who will remain nameless, reached into the pockets of hard-working Kansas City taxpayers for a pet educational experiment. The city's educational leadership was invited to dream big. Money was no object, naturally. They were encouraged to picture the perfect utopia of learning where they could teach inner-city kids.

And dream they did. What was the $2 billion spent on? According to the Cato report:

- Fifteen brand new schools.

- Olympic-sized swimming pools complete with an underwater viewing area.

- Full television and animation studios.

- A robotics lab.

- A twenty-five-acre wildlife sanctuary.

- A zoo.

- Higher teacher salaries.

- Reduced class sizes with a twelve– or thirteen-to-one student-teacher ratio.

- "Field trips" to such far away places as Mexico and Senegal.

And my personal favorite: They spent tax dollars to build a model United Nations—just what every American school needs. Tear down the flagpole and build a UN building with multi-language translation functionality. This is unbelievable to me. But what do you expect from the NEA's new socialist order?

"But Michael," you might be wondering, "Did it work? Did scholastic achievement improve after a decade of spending $2 billion on fifteen schools?" In a word, no. This fiasco was an abject failure—not to mention a major embarrassment. Even the judge had to admit the experiment was a disaster. The Cato Institute reported: "Test scores did not rise; the black-white gap did not diminish; and . . . there was little to show for all the money spent."[37]

What's the lesson? The next time your local school district and the NEA scream for a larger share of your taxes for education, remember what happened in Kansas City.

HOMO HIGH

Everyone is a victim these days.

Everyone wants special treatment. Special rights. Special privileges. If you cannot speak English at school, you demand a personal translator—and get it. It only follows if you're gay, bi, trans, or just confused by the endless programming by the psycho sex-czars, there's a special place for you.

Your very own alternative: homosexual high school.

Leading the way into this cesspool of uncharted waters is New York City. In the fall of 2003, Harvey Milk High School opened its newly renovated $3.2 million building to about one hundred gay, lesbian, transgender, and bisexual students. It is the first full-time, sexual orientation–based school in the country.

What's this? There's such a thing as gay algebra?

If so, let's do the math.

Let's divide $3.2 million by a hundred students. That works out to a mere $32,000 a student. A real bargain, no doubt. It is comforting to know the Big Apple has such a big heart. Especially when 497 schools (that's 41 percent of the 1,200 in the New York City system) were handed a failing grade by the Department of Education on September 10, 2003.

I'd better say that again.

Almost *half* of New York City schools are considered academically deficient.[38] That, my friend, is a staggering failure. And yet, rather than spend $3.2 million to improve this dismal situation, they launch a country club for a handful of allegedly oppressed kids. They want you to believe this extravagant misuse of public funds is justified because only the sexually deviant experience taunts and snubs at the hands of their peers.

Ninfa Segarra was president of the New York City Board of Education a number of years ago. Back then, she lobbied hard to make Harvey Milk a haven for the sexually defined crowd. She claims, "This is not an indoctrination center. This is a school. This is a place that helps youngsters deal with real-life situations."[39]

Real life?

Real life is working through your issues, *not running from them*. It means standing up in the face of opposition to defend your ground when you elect to hold an unpopular or minority opinion. This scam is nothing more than an awful throwback to the bad old days of segregation.

Still, Mayor Michael Bloomberg applauded the school. He said, "I think everybody feels that it's a good idea because some of the kids who are gays and lesbians have been constantly harassed and beaten in other schools. It lets them get an education without having to worry."[40]

Worry about what?

Worry about the teasing and verbal jabs that have been a part of school life for centuries? How about the fat kids? How about the kids with chronic zits? How about the pregnant students? Or the "four-eyes" with glasses? Or kids with foreign accents? I could think of a hundred different reasons kids get poked fun at in school. That's life. I'm not saying I'm in favor of such taunting. I'm not.

But what is the answer?

Are we now supposed to open a new school for every subset of the population that feels it needs a safe and *suppoooortive* environment? Is that it? Then let's round up the kids who are called "fatso" or "pudgy" or "Goodyear blimp" and put them in one place so they can eat Twinkies without the fear of mockery.

I'm not buying this reckless social experiment. It's nothing more than another attempt by the radical gay fringe to peddle their loathsome agenda.

TAKING THE HIGH GROUND

Why do I keep fighting? Aren't the schools a lost cause? Aren't we conservatives outnumbered by the Left? Isn't crushing the NEA an uphill battle? Let me answer those questions with one of the most important lessons I learned as a child on the streets of New York City.

I lived in a tenement in the Bronx. My street was Longfellow Avenue. Above me, just up the hill, was another group of tenements with blocks and blocks of buildings. There were more people on that block than in an average town. That was Bryant Avenue.

Next to us was an empty, steep lot that had been denuded of trees. All it had was dirt. Of course today, because of Al Gore and the language goons, you would have to say "soil" or "earth." We called it dirt.

Every once in a while, we would play "king of the hill." A "war" would break out between the guys on Bryant and the kids on Longfellow. I'm talking kids five, six, seven, maybe eight years old. It was like *Lord of the Flies* all over again. The gang on my block, the Longfellow gang, would take garbage can covers and storm the hill. I was by no means the leader.

The leader was an old guy, maybe nine.

He'd shout "Charge!" and we would run up the hill and try to make it to the top so we could throw the other gang down the hill. They had garbage can shields, too. So we're charging the hill, and they're throwing ash down on us. The ash was like lava rock.

In those days there were no pollution controls, so everyone would cook the garbage from each apartment in an incinerator in the basement. The dregs left behind looked like molten ash that turned into hard, lava-like rock.

It was basically melted-down garbage.

So, the other gang would hurl these ash rocks at us like in *Gladiator*. It looked like something from the Middle East ten thousand years ago. I'm holding a garbage can lid as a slew of stones rains down on us out of the air. I'm talking a regular meteor shower. Something like a hundred rocks were flying in our direction. If you didn't use your shield, you'd get hit in the head.

I was the guy who always seemed to get a rock in the head. I don't know how. It would always sneak in. To this day, I think someone in that gang hit me in the back of the head when I wasn't looking. My head would be split open two or three times, and the blood would trickle out. I knew my mother would get so upset, so I would go to my aunt's apartment and clean up first. Aunt Bea was the calm one who never freaked out.

I guess she knew boys would be boys.

I remember thinking as tough as the other guys were, we could beat them. I really believed it. We could knock them off the hill if we tried hard enough and didn't give up. Sure, we'd have to endure a few nicks, cuts, and scrapes. But when we did, I'm telling you, there was nothing like the feeling I got when we finally toppled the enemy.

The question is this.

What are you fighting for?

Why did your ancestors come here? What did they seek? What opportunities did they pursue so your children could go to a good school and then on to college, which were once institutions of higher learning and now are debased institutions of lower living? Where drug usage is rampant and polluted sexuality is not only accepted but encouraged. Where anti-Americanism is thought to be trendy.

I ask you, is this what your ancestors fled Europe or Asia or Africa for? Is this what America should be? Is this the America you want it to be?

I doubt it.

The America you and I cherish is one where our children receive the best education. One that will properly prepare them to pursue their dreams, their hopes, and their greatest potential. That, my friend, is worth fighting for.

As you have read what the Left has done to our schools, I don't blame you if you feel powerless and frustrated. That is their goal. They are the bullies with lava. They want us to feel like a bunch of wet-behind-the-ears neophytes. We're not. It's time to shake off those feelings of caving to their neo-Bolshevik agenda. It's time to stop tuning out and giving up. You must shake free of their brainwashing.

They don't hold all of the cards.

They just want you to think they do.

These hard-Left unions, the radical mad dog activists, and the special interest czarinas have an Achilles heel. I can give it to you in one word. To them, it is the most threatening word in the English dictionary.

Choice.

You can *choose* to put your children in a good private or charter school that's not run by the NEA. You can *choose* to homeschool your kids. You can *choose* to run for a spot on the local public school board and change how things are done in your community. You can *choose* to vote for candidates who favor school vouchers. You can *choose* to expose the wackos in the industry who are dumbing down our schools with bogus textbooks. And you can *choose* to fight the slutification of the sex-ed curriculum.

Or you can choose to sit by with a dunce hat on as the last nail is driven into the coffin of freedom.

It's your choice.

NINE

COLLEGES:
HOUSES OF PORN AND SCORN

Some of you won't like what I'm about to say. Others won't believe it. So before reading further, I must warn you to brace yourself, especially if you are in a public place. If you're reading this on an airplane, in a bookstore, library, or some other place where unsuspecting people are within earshot, consider moving to a less conspicuous location. What you're about to read will most certainly cause you to gasp, faint, or tremble uncontrollably with rage.

While that is not my intention, it's an almost certain by-product of the Savage truth. You see, you may not know it, but you are fighting for the survival of your country. You are in the midst of a cultural civil war against the Enemy Within—and you are losing. You and I did not ask for this war. But everything we hold dear is being stripped away from us.

As I have demonstrated thus far, degenerate bums on the Left are systematically poisoning our courts, military, health-care system, houses of worship, schools, and now they've made a mockery of higher education.

Radicals have turned our institutions of higher learning into cesspools of lower living!

Most sheeple don't understand how successful the Enemy Within has been in transforming our colleges and universities into houses of porn and scorn. Far too many of these formerly respected institutions have become intellectual wastelands dominated by dominatrices who invite prostitutes as guest speakers, think there's nothing odd about assigning pornography for homework, and encourage class trips to strip clubs.

It is bad enough these institutions have been turned into factories of reckless socialist programming. What's worse, most decent, God-fearing Americans don't even know how thoroughly these dregs of society, who fancy themselves to be on the "cutting edge" of education, have shredded all we treasure. As you will see, they attack morality and substitute Marxism.

They attack America and substitute anarchy.

They attack truth and substitute trendy lies.

They attack purity and substitute perversity.

Let's take that last one first. I warn you, if you prefer living like an ostrich with your head in the ground, skip the rest of this chapter. It'll be one of the most difficult things to read—at least if you care about the direction of our colleges and the future of our country.

Everything you're about to read is the pathetic and hideous condition of academia today. Having said that, you are in for a bumpy ride.

SEE NO EVIL

I grew up studying under liberal professors who tried to teach me that black-and-white issues don't exist in this world. Of course, I disagreed, and I said so. Today, they would just flunk you for disagreeing. Most students go to college with a pretty clear understanding of right and wrong. As our young people enter the campus, the deconstruction of truth begins.

From day one, professors tell students to open up their minds. To set aside outdated, quaint ideas of right and wrong. There is no good and evil, you see. No up and down. There's just a large gray zone, and they intend to fill it up for you with all of their lies. They'll make sure you're so confused by the time you graduate you'll be remolded into their image of the twenty-first century woman or man.

Such is the environment at the San Francisco Art Institute (SFAI), a school that prides itself on pushing the lunatic fringe. This institution of lower learning produced such infamous alumna as a "performance artist" whose idea of performance art was to strip naked on stage, smear her naked body with chocolate sauce, and invite the audience to lick it off for twenty dollars.[1]

Of course, this was too appetizing for the Ivy League to pass up. Big surprise that she was invited to bring her performance shtick to Yale[2] and has been a guest speaker at Harvard.[3] But let's set that aside, except to say the San Fransicko Art Institute (which benefits from your tax dollars) continues to produce students who are taught to lower and lick the bar.

You see, rather than creating a painting or sculpture that stands the test of time, today's crop of neophytes view their works in terms of how much they can shock the senses of a morally jaded audience. How? By pulling off outrageous stunts in public and then convincing the sheeple it's really *arrrrt*.

Frankly, I don't think there's a delicate way to tell you what happened on the campus of SFAI, so I'll just state the facts. On January 25, 2000, a 24-year-old student of darkness dreamed up and performed what must be the vilest display of performance art on a college campus in this century.

According to several published reports, he told his unsuspecting classmates he needed a volunteer for his class project, something he called *Art Piece No. 1*. He got one. This "artist" led the male subject to an empty room where he handed the volunteer a consent form to sign before they proceeded.

The volunteer was not provided any details of what he was about to do in the name of art. The consent form only indicated the performance art might contain acts "including and up to a sexual or violent nature."[4] If he still wanted to participate, he had to sign a release waiving all rights to sue afterwards.

This should have sparked at least a red flag, but the volunteer signed on the dotted line. After all, one of the fundamental pillars of his liberal indoctrination is that right and wrong don't exist. There is no good and bad, so what could possibly be the objection?

Signature in hand, the artist led his volunteer, his class of about twenty students, and his art professor to a public area on the SFAI campus. What happened next was performed on an open-air stage for the benefit of his peers and whoever strolled by. In what is nothing short of a dereliction of duty, the professor stood by as the following events unfolded.

The artist started his ten-minute performance bit with a little bondage, probably something he learned from late-night cable. He proceeded to engage in oral sex on his bound subject and then used enemas to exchange excrement.

This degenerate who, incidentally, had a scholarship to SFAI later described what happened this way: "He was tied up. He had a blindfold and a gag, but he could see and talk through it. He had freedom of movement of his pelvis. I engaged in oral sex with him and he engaged in oral sex with me. I had given him an enema, and I had taken a sh— and stuffed it in his a—. That goes on, he sh—s all over me, I sh— in him. There was a security guard present. There was an instructor from the school present. It was videoed, and the piece was over."[5]

Instead of applying his mind to the study of Picasso, Michelangelo, Ruben, or Rembrandt, this debauchee tossed aside his oils and paintbrush and used fecal matter and other bodily fluids in the creation of his "art." He defended this putrescence claiming he intended the piece as "an exploration of the notion of master-slave dialectic in Hegel."[6] This whack-job is exhibiting classic signs of mental illness, or at the very least derangement.

And the professor didn't raise a pinky to protest.

He should have been fired on the spot!

This obscene behavior didn't come as a complete surprise to one of the student's former instructors. Dodie Bellamy, his writing teacher, said, "Everything he wrote for me was about raping or mutilating babies."[7]

What was the college's response when the volunteer later had misgivings? They placed the "artist" on academic probation and told him no more public sex for a while. I'm not sure which is more obscene—the public insanity or the institute's flagrant mishandling of the incident.

In the old days, both artist and his nutty professor would have been tarred and feathered. Instead, the brilliant administrative narcissists running that vanguard of weirdness expressed *concerrrrn* about the dangerous risk of the art. They felt exchanging bodily fluids in the name of art was problematic.

Really? So everything would have been fine had he used a condom. Imagine that. We're supposed to forget about his public display of oral sex. He just didn't play safe. Now, don't try to figure out how a condom would work to protect the anal exchange of excreta. It can't. And never mind that this farce was videotaped and copies are probably for sale on-line. The show must go on . . . as long as proper care is given for high-risk activity.

Am I shocked? No.

Outraged? Yes. But I'm not shocked. This is what happens when you jackhammer the Ten Commandments, silence those who would pray in public school, and allow the ACLU to remove every semblance of faith from public view. Students no longer have a moral center from which to make decisions. In turn, a college cannot hold students to standards that don't exist.

Is this case the exception?

No. While this rectal gymnastics performance was the most egregious display of obscenity at a taxpayer subsidized college, the number of flagrant, public displays of sexual deviancy on campus—often for credit— has been creeping up over the last few years.

SEX-CRAZED "PERFORMANCE ART"
ON CAMPUS

The San Fran-Freako Art Institute fashions itself as being on the cutting edge of artistic expression, particularly in the area of performance art. But they are by no means alone in the pursuit of the obscene. Four recent examples demonstrate the cultural civil war in which we are living.

- New York University held a conference on May 1 and 2, 1998, entitled, "Queer Publics/Queer Privates." Author Roger Kimball reported "the conference culminated in a 'keynote performance' by a Los Angeles drag queen known as Vaginal Crème Davis." At one point in "her" performance, "The audience of students and faculty roared with laughter as 'she' pranced about, dispensing campy pornography, throwing fried chicken on the library floor and pretending to channel a character she called Saint Salicia Tate, an itinerant preacher of the gospel."[8]

- Candace deRussy, a trustee at the State University of New York (SUNY), attended a 1997 conference at the New Paltz campus of SUNY called, "Revolting Behavior: Challenges to Women's Sexual Freedom."[9] She describes "a performance by a stripper from a bisexual bathhouse, who simulated sexual acts including sadomasochistic anal sex with a character representing a Hasidic Jew, who was whipped on stage."[10] The conference was funded in part by your tax dollars supplied by the National Endowment for the Arts.

- A former porn star, enrolled at the University of Southern California, was working toward her major in fine art and gender studies. As part of her "performance art" she undressed and "had sex with two women and two dildos in class for credit."[11]

- Photos of sadomasochistic sex featuring an "artist" and his lover ejaculating were displayed in the gallery of the Robeson Student Center at

Rutgers University in 1998. Gallery director, Kathy Schnapper, defended the display. She said, "I wanted to evoke the back room of a leather bar . . . I wanted it to be frank and raw and about a certain kind of sexuality. I wanted to give the full range of the private life of the artist."[12]

Now, before I review a number of the outrageous classes professors are teaching today, I must share a personal story. This is especially important for the Ivy League frat boys who are being squeezed into conformity.

You see, there's a lot you can learn from a dog, especially compared to what they teach in college these days. So consider this a friendly tip from Dr. Savage that will take the pressure off. One day you'll thank me for what I'm about to tell you.

FAT PAT AND TIPPY THE DOG

When I was a boy, my parents moved us from our Bronx apartment to a small row house in Queens, New York. At the time we had a dog named Tippy. Tippy the dog was a ferocious chow who, when I was eleven, ripped my foot open. I'm not talking a scratch here. He treated my foot like a lamb shank. I actually had to be hospitalized and get stitched up. I still loved Tippy the dog, even though the doctor was trying to get us to take it to the pound to be gassed.

Tippy was a male, which might explain his crazy temperament. The truth is I happen to prefer owning a male dog. Why? I don't know how to say this in a delicate manner. You know, every once in a while a female dog has a thing happen to her, and it's a mess. And, no, I don't believe in having a dog "fixed." I didn't buy a pet to spend all my time and money at the vet.

Now, aside from taking a bite out of me, the worst thing Tippy ever did when he was little was doo-doo in the house. Dog owners know that's what happens until they're trained. You get used to that. However, when a dog grows up and knows how to do its business outside, another problem surfaces. Once or twice a year, Tippy would go into heat. He'd jump on my father's friends' legs. Whoever came into our house, Tippy would try to mate with them.

This was a real problem because people were always coming to our house. They all knew my mom loved to cook. Day and night they'd drop in on us. True, it was a different day and age. People could just stop by for conversation. It was not like today where you have an appointment a month in advance. For us, just about every night someone would knock on the door. My mother would make coffee; they would sit in the living room and talk for hours.

But when Tippy the dog was in heat, watch out.

One guy in particular drove Tippy insane. I don't know why Tippy focused on Fat Pat, but he did. Fat Pat must be dead twenty years now. This guy was like a character out of the *Sopranos*. You know, he had a size twenty-five neck. Rumor had it, he was a bookie. Fat Pat always seemed to have something shady going on the side, if you know what I mean.

Still, we kids loved him. He was just a lovable, giant sort of guy. Always laughing. Always good for a joke. Don't ask me why, but Tippy especially loved him. When Tippy went into heat, if Fat Pat was sitting in the living room, Tippy the dog would jump on Fat Pat's leg and grab it with his huge paws. The two of them would go crazy. Tippy would start rockin' and rollin' on Pat's leg. Pat would laugh his butt off.

Picture a fat guy rolling back, laughing as the dog's humping his foot. The women are screaming. I'm busting up. My mother gets a broom and starts hitting the dog. She chases Tippy with that broom like a Samurai warrior, yelling, "Get out of here, you animal. What are you, a dog?" We'd lock Tippy the dog up in the basement. He'd be barking and making noises like it was King Kong down there. Everyone would go back to coffee and cake.

There is a lesson here. Unlike humans, my dog went into heat once a year or whatever. But human males, especially those in college, think they're in heat every night. They've been brainwashed since kindergarten into thinking they're supposed to be in heat 24/7. And then they wonder why they're impotent half the time.

It's because they're not in heat.

They're not supposed to mate every night.

Animals are smarter than college students in this regard. They go in and out of heat, as you well know. And when they're in heat, they want a girl dog. When they're not, they don't.

But because of the brainwashing by the sex-ed, condom-on-cucumber crackpots, guys think they're supposed to be ready for action at a moment's notice. And man, if you're not, you must be gay. Or something's wrong with you. Or you're led to believe you're dysfunctional. You think you have to take a pill to spring into action.

Contrary to how you've been programmed, if you're not coming to life sexually it's because you don't want to. Period. And maybe, just maybe, you're smart enough to know there are more important things to do than chase skirts or create obscene art.

Like getting an education.

COLLEGE JUNK COURSES

Lest you think only the art community is overrun by depraved minds, read on. Spend a minute examining just a sample of the preposterous classes offered at some leading universities across America. Then, tell me liberalism isn't a mental disease that must be stopped before it hijacks what remains of our colleges.

For starters, undergraduates at the University of Nevada Las Vegas can take Sex, Dance, and Entertainment where "field trips to strip clubs, lectures by lap dancers and videos of breast-enlargement surgery"[13] are part of the "coarse" studies. If that class is full, students might consider either Porn in the USA or Sociology of the Sex Industry.[14]

Students at Carnegie Mellon University can take Sex and Death, which reflects upon "whether we need to liberate death now that (maybe) we have figured sex out."[15] Over at Cornell University, they offer Bodies Politic: Queer Theory and Literature of the Body, which examines important topics such as "How do concepts of perversion and degeneration haunt the idea of the social body?"[16]

Speaking of queer studies, in the fall of 2003, the University of Michigan in Ann Arbor offered How To Be Gay: Male Homosexuality and Initiation taught by Professor David M. Halperin. The course description posted on-line quotes professor Halperin as saying, "Just because you happen to be a gay man doesn't mean that you don't have to learn how to become one. Gay men do some of that learning on their own, but often we learn how to be gay from others."[17]

This class is advertised as dealing with the topics of "camp, diva-worship, drag, muscle culture, taste, style and political activism [as well as] the role that initiation plays in the formation of gay male identity."[18] Halperin has made statements in the past indicating his clear endorsement of pushing the radical homosexual agenda.

On the Left Coast, UCLA offers this gem: Death, Suicide, and Trauma, which *encourrages* students to explore the "definition and taxonomy of death; new permissiveness and taboos related to death; romanticization of death; role of individual in his own demise; modes of death"[19]—you get the picture.

Not to be upstaged, the University of California at Berkeley has introduced a full-fledged LGBT studies minor. That's "lesbian, gay, bi, and transgender" for readers who forgot their decoder ring. Again, this should not be a surprise. More than a hundred colleges and universities now have an on-campus LGBT center to further *sensitiiivity* and understanding and provide a safe place for the sexually confused to connect and network.

UC Berkeley also offers a "democratic education" or "De-Cal" lineup of 155 teacher-supervised courses led by student instructors, including The Religions of Star Trek, Journal Your Ass Off, Breasts: Their Natural History, and Chemistry of Beer. Each is worth two credits toward graduation requirements.

One De-Cal male sexuality class caused a near meltdown when a group of students decided to go to a gay strip club as part of their final project. *The Daily California*, UC Berkeley's student paper, broke the story of the goings-on at the event. The paper wrote, "Having their nipples sucked during a field trip to a strip club and watching instructors strip or have sex at clubs like Sex Exchange in San Francisco are among activities that may deter some students"[20] from future participation.

Although optional, those attending this class bonding experience went to an after-class party. There they were encouraged to take Polaroids of their privates, exchange them with the others in the group, and then guess which photo belonged to whom.

In my day, we played charades at a party.

Again, none of this behavior is inconsistent with the breakdown of morality these kids learned from the time they entered elementary school. Which is why the student instructor presiding over this zoo, said, "In the class we don't say anything is right or wrong."[21] In other words, let's not get hung up on finding answers or comparing choices to a moral standard.

What about the supervising professor? That would be Caren Kaplan. Her job included overseeing the class in question. Her reaction was without excuse. She evidently could not be bothered to interfere with the curriculum. She said, "I don't police the content."[22]

Great.

Hand the keys to the inmates and let them run the show.

PROSTITUTION 101

As if offering a wide range of promiscuous classes isn't enough, the whacked-out lefties who control these institutions seek to enhance the *learrrning* of students by hosting school-sponsored "sex festival" events. I won't bore you with more than two quick and recent examples.

In November of 2002, the University of Arizona co-sponsored the Sex Workers Arts Festival which included workshops like "The Sacred Prostitute" and "Fisting: Pleasuring Your Partner with Your Hands."[23]

Although that particular live demonstration was held off campus (*wink, wink*), the implied endorsement of such perversity was impossible to miss.

In the spring of 2003, Dartmouth's Center for Women and Gender held a sex festival which, according to one reporter, included "an extensive assortment of sex toys . . . a dazzling display of silicone—including . . . life-like latex penises, a variety of strap-on apparati . . . a vibrator with a 'Hello-Kitty' head on it . . . The station also exhibited 'adjustable' nipple clamps."[24]

Why aren't the states funding these institutions holding them to a higher standard? Why aren't the alumni of these institutions cutting off funding, too? Am I the only one who believes our colleges are becoming nothing more than socially degenerate hellholes? You know, there was a time I might have dismissed Fairmont State Community and Technical College of West Virginia's new two-year major in ballroom dancing as ridiculous. But, given the alternatives, I'm not so quick to laugh it off.

This might surprise you. When I was young, I really thought I wanted to attend an Ivy League school. But, originally, I couldn't afford to go to a private college. Growing up in New York, I decided to go to Queens College. It was an incredibly great school at the time. Very competitive. Extremely rigorous. There were no puff grades. People were intelligent and hard-working. I had to keep my nose to the grindstone.

Now, if I would've gone to some out-of-town school, I probably would've gone wrong. That's the honest truth. There's a side to my nature that probably would have gone off the rails when I was younger. What I'm saying is let's not forget how impressionable students are at that age. Let's not lose sight of the fact their minds, values, and sense of well-being are still being shaped. As the leftists once openly said, let's win their hearts and minds!

What alarms me is thinking about those who end up in a class where the professor is a miserable SOB who hates himself, hates his country, hates his history, and wants everybody else to become as miserable and lost as he is. The horror is you slave your whole life to send your child off to a good college hoping they'll come out the other end with more than a nipple ring and green hair, and instead they end up sitting in Dr. Death's class.

No wonder there are so many Red Diaper Doper Babies coming out of colleges these days.

THE GRIM REEFER GANG

Up to this point we have looked at the rampant sexual perversity invading our college campuses. But that is just for starters. The far-Left, Grim Reefer crowd with their neo-Marxist and socialist views completely dominates the prominent teaching positions. They enjoy unfettered freedom to preach their left-wing orthodoxy.

That's a fact. And that's ironic.

Think about it. The Left pushes diversity in all areas of life, with two exceptions: ideology and politics. On campus, where libs are king of the roost, look at what they've done to the admissions process. Over the last few years, liberal colleges are demonstratively less concerned with academic qualifications for incoming students and are more preoccupied with whether or not ethnic quotas have been met.[25]

And forget about faculty diversity. While professors and administrators strive to maintain a student body that is a perfect hodgepodge of multiculturalism, the formula for the teaching staff is completely altered. In the end, professorships represent a homogenized blend of leftist thinking.

Just look at the dearth of diversity at Ithaca College. An eye-popping survey conducted in the spring of 2003 found of the 125 professors, "93.6 percent are registered as Democrats or Greens. Only 6.4 percent are registered as Republicans or Conservatives."[26]

That's not an anomaly.

In the spring of 2002, the Luntz Research Companies conducted an extensive survey in which liberal arts and social science faculty of Ivy League universities and colleges were polled. A mere 3 percent said they were Republicans compared to 57 percent who were Democrats. Look how they voted. Of those who answered the question, a full 61 percent voted for Al Gore, while George W. Bush garnered just 6 percent, barely a full point ahead of Ralph Nader at 5 percent.[27]

Now, I have often said if you are unsure whether you are a conservative or a liberal, just look at how you reacted to the 9/11 attack on America. A lib wants to *understaaaand* why America *deserved* to be attacked. Liberals buy books on radical Islam and then join sensitivity groups to better grasp the plight of the terrorist mind.

A conservative, on the other hand, grabs his AR-15 and vows to defend his home and nation against the filthy terrorists in dirty nightshirts who murdered three thousand of our people in cold blood.

Another way to pinpoint your political leanings is to note how you reacted after George W. Bush sent troops to liberate the people of Iraq. If your heart swelled with pride as Iraqis danced in the streets at the fall of Saddam's brutal regime, you're a conservative.

But if you condemned the president for this military action or if you secretly wished Saddam were still in power, you're a liberal. That's all there is to it. Using this formula, consider the reaction by the academic senate at UCLA to the liberation of Iraq.

Keep in mind the streets of Baghdad were flooded by a people who were savoring their first taste of freedom in decades. They celebrated because the torture chambers were closed.

The floggings had stopped.

The mass graves would no longer be used.

The raping of women on their wedding day by Saddam's sons was now history.

What did this prestigious body of learned men and women at UCLA do? They voted to "condemn America's invasion of Iraq" by a 180-7 margin. That is 95 percent of the faculty senate at UCLA.[28] Tragically, their twisted anti-America viewpoint is echoed throughout the halls of academia.

Listen to this Stalinist-leftover.

Professor Nicholas De Genova of Columbia University spewed a borderline seditious statement on April 1, 2003. He said, "U.S. flags are the emblem of the invading war machine in Iraq today. They are the emblem of the occupying power. The only true heroes are those who find ways that help defeat the U.S. military."[29] What's this? He wants to see our boys dead?

Did Columbia University become Jihad University?

Why does the man still have a job?

Hear me. I am all for free speech. But to advocate the murder of our boys on the front lines is beyond the pale. That lefty should be censured. A day after De Genova made his hate-America comments before a crowd of three thousand, Pamela Morgan, an offended citizen, dashed off a letter to Dr. Rod Paige, secretary of the U.S. Department of Education. She reports De Genova also stated, "Peace is subversive, because peace anticipates a very different world than the one in which we live—a world where the U.S. would have no place."[30]

I'm not sure who's worse: this creep, or Richard Berthold, a professor of history at the University of New Mexico. He said, "Anyone who can blow up the Pentagon gets my vote."[31] Chalk up a vote for bin Laden.

Or maybe we can give the dunce hat to Jennie Traschen, a physics professor at the University of Massachusetts. At a town meeting on September 10, 2001, she called the American flag "a symbol of terrorism and death and fear and destruction and oppression."[32]

Maybe she could share a bunk in an al-Qaida training camp with professor Barbara Foley of Rutgers University. This mental case claimed "whatever its proximate cause, its ultimate cause is the fascism of U.S. foreign policy over the past many decades."[33]

That, my friend, is just a partial list of comments from the Enemy Within our colleges.

I ask you, what are the implications for a student trapped in a liberal-infested institution where conservative ideals are anathema, where professors struggle not to snicker at the mention of George Bush, or, worse, where subversive despots and armchair socialists reign supreme?

I'll tell you what happens.

Conservative students are buried under an avalanche of scorn, both from their professors and peers. They're treated as if they're Cro-Magnons with bones in their noses. It only takes one or two rounds in the barrel before conservative-thinking students learn the local custom. They learn to keep their mouths shut if their viewpoints run contrary to the prevailing winds of liberalism in the classroom—or risk a failing grade.

BARBEQUING SACRED COWS

When I first moved to Hawaii, I'm talking many, many years ago, there were little things running all over the place called geckos. If you don't know, a gecko is a little lizard-like creature with scales and boney claws. And, boy, can they run.

Now, coming from New York City, not to mention my being an inner-city kid, I had never seen one. To me, you killed any reptilian creature running around your house. You brought out a rock or a baseball bat and smashed its head in. That's all I knew. Anything that crawled like that, you killed it.

Granted, I was an environmentalist in the sense of saving forests and plants and nature. But anything that crawled in a house where a human being was living, you killed it immediately. You simply did not let it run around your house because it could spread disease and viruses.

It could get in your bags of wheat.

I'm talking ancestrally. It was a primal instinct thing.

Now, I grew up in a clean house. My mother always cleaned the linoleum. She prided herself in that if food fell on her floor, you could still eat it. That's how I ran my house, too. So there we were our first week living in Hawaii. Imagine my surprise and reaction the first time I saw a lizard-like creature scurrying across the ceiling. My instinct was to get a 2x4 and crush the little thing. You know, then get the Windex, wash it up, and be done with it.

But my new Hawaiian friends explained to me in their view, a gecko was a good luck sign because it ate insects. You never touched it. You certainly didn't kill it. No way. To do so would be to commit a major offense. I'd say the gecko was the equivalent of a sacred cow in India. Those cows have the run of the place. They could crap in the town square, but you didn't touch it. If you did, the Hindus would murder you.

That's why you've got sacred cows walking around Calcutta mooing to their hearts content, blocking traffic, maybe dumping on a Mercedes. If you're the guy with the car, all you can do is fume. You might be the head of a major export company with seventy-five thousand sewing machines going in Madras, but you don't dare touch that cow no matter who you are. The mobs would kill you with bamboo sticks.

It was almost the same thing in Hawaii.

I didn't touch the gecko. I had to learn the customs of the locals. And I learned fast.

That's the way it is when your kid goes off to college. The entire artificial universe within a university has certain rules that govern your kid's existence. If they intend to survive, if they hope to thrive, they must take a dive into the pre-defined cultural customs of that place.

Of course, while geckos *are* wonderful creatures and should be protected, the liberal vermin are not.

What are the customs and sacred cows of college today?

1. Engage in sex. Anywhere. Any time. With anyone.

2. Disengage your mind. Muzzle all conservative ideals.

3. Hate America. Turn your back on your country for extra credit.

On day one, students are handed a safe sex kit by the campus condom fairy. They don't even make it to their dorm before they are accosted by a mean-faced, clipped-haired girl giving out condoms to the boys and a wink-wink, nod-nod to the girls telling them where the dildo dispenser is so they can do it with their sorority sisters.

Days two and three, they are herded to the LGBT center for sensitivity training and an invitation to participate in the try-it-you'll-like-it sexual lifestyle of choice. By day four, students are given an opportunity to attend *The Vagina Monologues* touring show . . . sponsored by the dean's office.

On day five, students are introduced to their professor who leans back in his chair with his legs spread apart so you have to look over his crotch to make eye contact. Within minutes of the start of class, he announces he was raised on a commune and believes America is the great Satan. Then, to round out the weekend, a festival celebrating "Sex Worker Rights" is held in the quad. That's basically the first week at colleges today.

I only wish I were exaggerating.

How many poor immigrant families in this country are under the impression that if they just work hard enough, scrape enough money together, and send their little daughter into Harvard, she is going to become something? Give the Ivy League that beautiful ethnic girl, and they'll be sure to turn her into a slut, if not a total pervert. Instead of teaching her how to learn to earn enough to *buy* an SUV, they teach her how to *contract* an STD.

So the Sominex Generation leaves high school, heads off to college, and spends four years learning how to become a sex-mad Marxist youth of today. How did the Left convert a whole generation to the Marxist youth mentality?

As demonstrated in this chapter, by giving them unlimited sexuality; by deconstructing any value system they may have had and replacing it with a busted moral compass; and by indoctrinating them with socialist ideals while silencing contrary positions.

And for good measure, the most vile music fills dorm hallways, drowning out any conscience, any small voice that may be in your head. You know, that still, small voice of which the Bible speaks? The sex drowns out morality and the ever-present, unregulated drug and alcohol consumption drowns out all connection to family and nation.

After four years of that, you've got a card-carrying Red Diaper Doper Baby!

GIVE UP OR SPEAK UP

I went furniture shopping the other morning. I went to one of those furniture stores that sells rattan and straw furniture. They carried your mainstream kind of Third World furniture. In a word, junk. My guess is most of the stuff was woven by underpaid slaves and sold to the San Francisco art crowd for $699.

As I'm moving down the aisles, my ear catches the song playing on the radio. Something about "going to San Francisco with a flower in my hair." At first, I wasn't paying attention to the words. I sort of liked the tune. I thought it was kind of catchy. You know, it conjured up images of living around cable cars.

But then, I started to panic. I felt as if I was headed into a time warp. I started thinking, "Are the sixties coming back?" If so, I knew I had an obligation to warn the next generation. The Left wants you to believe the sixties were great. That the sixties opened the doorway to liberty, freedom, and the summer of endless love.

Wrong. That decade was horrendous.

Come to think of it, was there anything positive the sixties gave America? No. Absolutely nothing. Just look at the devastation it brought this country. We have had decades of broken homes, single mothers, abortion on demand, venereal disease, herpes, AIDS, drug usage, and teen pregnancy. There was nothing the sixties gave the country that was any good.

And there is one other thing that decade of decadence gave us: the current crop of ultra-intolerant professors who dominate our colleges and universities. By and large, many of them are sixties holdovers who have somehow become tenured professors. They prey on impressionable young minds and fill them full of leftist ideals under the pretext of teaching literature and history.

Now, standing in that store without flowers in my hair, I knew I had a choice. I could either hum along with that tune and go on my merry way, or I could speak out. I could warn those who still have a chance to avoid repeating the terrible mistakes of the past. I chose to speak out.

There is a ray of good news. When *New York Times* reporter Chris Hedges launched into a self-serving anti-war commencement speech at Rockford College, he was booed off the stage. We are seeing signs of this awakening across the country. Conservative activists are rising up.

You might recall the student activism of the late sixties, which amounted to nothing more than taking over the dean's office to smoke weed at his desk. Today, bright, forward-thinking conservative students are forming organizations on campus. They're publishing newspapers to mount assaults on the liberal establishment.

I'm not talking boring geeks with pocket protectors for their pens. Many of these students are at the top of their class. Granted, we have an America that has been taught not to fight. Ever since grade school too many of our children have been drugged and taught to become pacifists.

But somehow, a few brave souls are emerging on our campuses. They are tired of the anti-Americanism. Tired of the propaganda. Tired of their inner hurt. And they are especially tired of being drugged into submission.

If you are a student in college today—or wherever you are—I encourage you to speak out. I don't care if you're in a supermarket line or on the telephone. Speak out. Because if the millions of us being oppressed by these left-wing perverts and vermin spoke out as one, we could retake the country.

If I have to be the last angry man who speaks out, so be it. Then I shall go out with a roar.

TEN

MINDS:
THE SILENCED MAJORITY

The liberal media elite operate like modern-day gangsters. They're like Chicago's notorious mob boss Al Capone, only on a larger scale. As you well know, Capone maintained full control of the bookie joints, brothels, gambling houses, bootlegging, nightclubs—and had many, if not most, of Chicago's police and politicians under his thumb.

For years, nobody could lay a finger on him. Why?

Aside from his network of spies, spanning from paperboys to the police, Capone's cronies cooked the books. Actually, his accountants maintained a double set of books. One set was designed to mislead the IRS. The other set contained the truth of his financial holdings, pegged at upwards of $100 million a year.[1]

So it is with the liberals in the major media. They control the airwaves, the press, and the film, television, and music industries with two different sets of books. They, like Capone, maintain a double standard in order to protect their empire.

Words such as "hate speech," "homophobe," "racist," "intolerant," and "fearmonger" are leveled at anyone with whom they disagree.

The other set of books they maintain is used to defend "friends" of liberal causes—the activist actors, pandering politicians, perverted professors, extremist enviros, and PC pundits. You see, membership has it privileges.

In the major media, if you're a lib, you're protected.

If you're a conservative, you're crucified.

Case in point.

I host the fastest-growing radio talk show in the country. I live in and broadcast my show from San Francisco, the epicenter of modern liberalism. A town so morally bankrupt, we underwrite sex change operations with taxpayer dollars for city employees but defund the Boy Scouts. That's liberalism for you. Fund the pervs and sickos, while sticking it to the boys who believe in God, country, and morality.

In the spring of 2003, I decided to take my message of borders, language, and culture into the dog-eat-dog world of television by signing a deal with the MSNBC cable network. I knew that move would be warfare. All around me the yapping, rabid mad dogs on the Left were foaming at the mouth.

From the get-go they fought to make my TV show a no-go.

The moment MSNBC announced they had hired me, the anti-speech, militant homosexual pressure group, GLAAAAD (Gay and Lesbian Alliance Against Any and All Disagreement), launched an aggressive boycott of my advertisers.[2] I had not even aired one show, and these arrogant bigots were already marching in their brown shorts.

Cathy Renna, a spokesmouth for GLAAAAD, said they resented the way I would be wrapping myself in the legitimacy of NBC news. Hold on. Who made NBC legitimate? Since when did NBC become legitimate? If you mean legit in the sense they have sizable audiences, okay, fine. But size doesn't matter. Renna should know that.

It's what you do with your platform that counts. NBC is as unbalanced as the other alphabet channels. With shows like *Will and Grace* and other pro-homosexual propaganda in prime time, they are way out of touch with Middle America.

In true Chicago-land gangster fashion, GLAAAAD blasted me with every label in the book to shut me down after an unfortunate exchange with a crank caller.

While MSNBC and I have put our dispute behind us, here is what happened.

OFF MIKE

As you know, we all make statements in private, as do politicians, business leaders, and newscasters. We make comments we would never say in public. Why? Is it because we are afraid our words might be monitored by a dictator who delights in cutting out your lungs if you dare utter an honest word? No. We are careful because not all conversations are meant for public consumption.

That is why parents argue behind closed doors—so kids don't get an earful. That is why bosses discipline employees in the privacy of an office rather than posting his or her job performance on the web. That is why, in part, we have laws against wiretapping. Only a fool would argue there is never a time and a place for a private conversation.

I am no different than any reader of this book. I know the difference between a private and a public exchange. You might not know this, but built into the production of live television broadcasting there exists a seven-second delay system. This feature is designed to prevent such private comments from going out on the air.

It is also supposed to protect broadcasters from bottom-feeders who get their kicks ambushing live TV shows with crank calls. On July 5, 2003, what actually happened on the air is much different than what was widely reported.

People claimed I was fired from MSNBC for telling a *routine caller* to get AIDS and die. As if I lack that much commonsense. The truth is, I was reacting to a vicious personal attack made *by a crank caller*. I signaled and thought this crank was cut from the air. But his insults continued in my earpiece. Understandably, I reacted to him personally, defending myself against his diatribe. My comments were aimed only at the caller and, for the record, when I uttered the infamous words, I believed I was off air.

I wasn't.

Let me repeat, I thought this interchange was between the setup caller and me. My words were not meant to reflect my views on the terrible tragedy and suffering associated with AIDS. I immediately issued a full and complete public apology for the inadvertent and unfortunate exchange.

I've spent my entire life in the field of alternative medicine trying to heal the world and bring comfort to the sick. I certainly didn't intend for my comments to bring pain to anyone. I must say, however, there was something rather queer about the sequence of events.

I had just completed an improvisational piece with several props. I had airline seats and two crash dummies dressed up as large passengers brought into the studio. I sat squeezed in the middle of the crash dummies. The moment I completed my airline horror story in a humorous fashion, the producer, rather unexpectedly, told me in my earpiece to "go to a caller."

Frankly, in the midst of the fun, I let down my guard.

I was blindsided by the malicious caller.

Even so, the seven-second delay should have been used to dump the entire exchange. The call-screener admitted this mistake to me. In addition, my producer, sitting three thousand miles away in New Jersey at MSNBC headquarters, had a censor button at his fingertips. He had used the censor button to edit profane comments by the setup caller but did not use the button to edit my reply comments. He should have gone to a commercial break. He failed to do so.

The rest is history.

It goes without saying there were many who rejoiced over and applauded MSNBC's decision to pull the plug. Not just on the Left, but on the Right, too. The question is why did so-called conservatives on the FOX network celebrate my defeat? The answer is: they are competitors. The truth is, my show started cutting into FOX's lead (see chart), and they didn't like that. Not in the least.

What is especially painful is two weeks prior to this incident, Erik Sorenson the CEO of MSNBC and a decent man, came out to San Francisco to have dinner with me. He told me, "We don't care about ratings. We think you're extremely creative. I think this relationship could go on forever and even develop into something much bigger."

I was told the inherent liberal culture within NBC, their parent company, had always been against hiring me. I understood that from the beginning. No surprise there. I also knew they were trying to change to a more balanced perspective, and I rose to the challenge. My show delivered the goods, as the numbers demonstrated.

In just two months, *The Savage Nation* television show was growing so fast it occasionally beat CNN during the same time slot. I even gave FOX News a run for its money, beating the network on June 29 in the fourth quarter hour. Talk about gaining traction.

More important than the numbers, my show broke new ground. I was the first one in MSNBC history to dig up the video of the gassed Kurds, buried by the media for years. Thanks to that show, Americans were able to see what that mass-murderer Saddam Hussein had really done. I am very proud of what I accomplished.

Nobody can take that away from me.

INVADING THE RATINGS

I clearly clobbered CNN and severely cut FOX's previous ratings *in half.*

DATE: June 7, 2003

	MSNBC	CNN	FOXNC
	Persons 25-54	Persons 25-54	Persons 25-54
Saturday 5:00-5:15 P.M.	214,000	83,000	267,000
Saturday 5:15-5:30 P.M.	168,000	137,000	230,000
Saturday 5:30-5:45 P.M.	161,000	133,000	226,000
Saturday 5:45-6:00 P.M.	156,000	132,000	264,000

I beat FOX TV in the fourth quarter, a fact that a certain no-spin, backstabbing conservative from FOX does not want you to know.

DATE: June 29, 2003

	MSNBC	CNN	FOXNC
	Persons 25-54	Persons 25-54	Persons 25-54
Saturday 5:45-6:00 P.M.	138,000	127,000	121,000

I beat CNN to a pulp on my last show.

DATE: July 5, 2003

	MSNBC	CNN
	Persons 25-54	Persons 25-54
Saturday 5:00-5:15 P.M.	34,000	22,000
Saturday 5:15-5:30 P.M.	40,000	23,000
Saturday 5:30-5:45 P.M.	54,000	34,000
Saturday 5:45-6:00 P.M.	70,000	66,000

The early and swift success of my show enabled me to engage in talks about doing something much larger, perhaps on network television. I had sent the management team a proposal for a comedy sitcom about a radio talk show host that received a lot of interest at the highest level.

Of course, this has all gone up in smoke. Why? All because of a nasty interchange where a vicious crank setup caller insulted me and I responded with a reaction that should never had been broadcast. For my part, I have apologized. Unequivocally. Publicly. And without hesitation. When was the last time you heard a sincere apology from the Left?

WHEN THE SHOE IS ON THE LEFT FOOT

MSNBC was real quick on the trigger to dump me. If only they had been as quick to dump the prankster. In a way, I'm not surprised. The brown shorts have been relentless in their efforts to censor my free speech. It was a matter of time. So we move on. But in the interest of higher education, I want you to compare what happened to me to what *hasn't* happened to others who, by all appearances, need a refresher course in sensitivity training.

When "friendlies" fill the airwaves with liberal hate speech, media gangsters refuse to take them to task. A few examples of this double standard, this flagrant hypocrisy, will suffice.

National Public Radio's Nina Totenberg resented Senator Jesse Helm's assertion that the government spends far too much researching the problem of AIDS. She whined, "I think he ought to be worried about what's going on in the Good Lord's mind, because if there is retributive justice, he'll get AIDS from a transfusion, or one of his grandchildren will get it."[4]

Last time I checked, this death-wishing, mad vulture still files reports on NPR between classical music clips.

Julianne Malveaux, a hard-Left *USA Today* columnist publicly yearned for the *death* of Supreme Court Justice Clarence Thomas. This clipped-haired, mean-faced African-American lib spouted, "You know, I hope his wife feeds him lots of eggs and butter and he dies early like many black men do, of heart disease. Well, that's how I feel. He is an absolutely reprehensible person."[5]

The reaction from *USA Today?*

Not a peep of protest. The spineless editorial board should have trashed her column faster than a bag of stale pork rinds.

George Clooney took a drive-by potshot at Charlton Heston's battle with a terminal disease. He mocked the former head of the National Rifle Association, saying, "Charlton Heston announced again today that he is suffering from Alzheimer's."[6] What kind of lowlife would take aim at a guy in the midst of a personal health crisis? Nice touch, Looney. Where was the media outcry on that one?

Billionaire Ted Turner fashions himself a humanitarian and self-appointed advocate for religious tolerance—unless you are Catholic and it is Ash Wednesday. "What are you," he asked a group of CNN staffers, "a bunch of Jesus freaks? You ought to be working for Fox."[7]

Imagine the public lynching if Jerry Falwell labeled a group of Muslim's practicing their faith "a bunch of Allah freaks?"

Then again, why should we be surprised with Turner's bigotry? This intolerant lefty labeled pro-lifers "bozos and clowns" and a number of years ago pronounced Christianity a religion for "losers."[8] His pattern of hate speech transcends more than a decade.[9]

And there's plenty of religious bigotry from the Left to go around. Take CBS's former morning mouth and host of *The Early Show,* Bryant Gumbel. He had a few choice words for Family Research Council's Robert Knight. Knight, an advocate for traditional family values, defended the Supreme Court's decision to back the Boy Scouts' ban on homosexual troop leaders.

As he was leaving the set, Bumbel mumbled, "What a f—-ing idiot!"[10] There was no mistake about it. The TV camera caught Bumbel's unguarded moment. Still, CBS stood by its man. Outrageous!

Actor Alec Baldwin had his own personal meltdown on the *Conan O'Brien Show.* A red-faced, vein-popping Baldwin shouted, "If we were in other countries, we would all right now, all of us together—all of us together would go down to Washington and we would stone Henry Hyde to death! We would stone him to death! Wait! . . . I'm not finished. We would stone Henry Hyde to death and we would go to their homes and we'd kill their wives and their children! *We would kill their families!*"[11]

Where is the outcry from the Left?

And what about it, NBC? Why didn't you yank Conan—or slam him with a hefty fine—for allowing Alec to incite his audience to murder? Hear me: If an actor made those kind of comments on Pat Robertson's *700 Club*, a pack of RDDBs would have filed lawsuits the next morning charging Pat as an *accessory* to hate speech.

Tell me, where were the media bloodhounds when former Democratic Senator Carol Mosely-Braun, an African-American nut case from Illinois, slandered George Will as being a member of the Ku Klux Klan? She said, "George Will can just take his hood and go back to wherever he came from."[12]

Speaking of the Klan, Charles Rangel, the New York congressman representing Harlem, painted all Republicans as racists saying: "They are afraid to come out from under their hoods and attack us directly."[13]

And MSNBC's Keith Olbermann ripped North Carolina's conservative senator, Lauch Fairthcloth, with this gem: Lauch was "one of the junior Grand Wizards of the vast right-wing conspiracy."[14]

None of these socially reprehensible gaffes stooped as low as Geraldo Rivera's flagrant endangerment of our troops during the Iraq war. Remember this beauty? Geraldo, the Jerry Springer-of-journalism-turned-FOX-correspondent, divulged U.S. troop movements on international television.

Maybe Geraldo was bored. Maybe he did it in the interest of multicultism. Maybe he's really French. Whatever his reasons, he played a dangerous game.

For the benefit of non-English speaking Iraqi soldiers huddled around their TVs, the mustachioed buffoon actually drew a sketch in the sand of his position with the Army's 101st Airborne Division as well as where they were likely to strike next. Brilliant. Right on par with Homer Simpson. His irresponsible actions endangered the lives of our soldiers and could have compromised the mission.

Did FOX News fire Geraldo? No.

My comments on MSNBC pale by comparison to Geraldo's infraction. Why does he still have a job? Because he is a useful idiot in the grander scheme of the leftist agenda. Because the media gangsta thugs view Geraldo as the true yellow lib he is. He's one of them. I'm not.

ENEMIES WITHIN THE NEWSROOM

The question remains, was I set up?

Were there people working inside MSNBC who wanted to get me? I'll let you decide. We do know that activists in the radical student grassroots group MoveOn recently bragged at protest-organizing meetings in Washington DC that they have members working within the newsrooms at CNN, ABC News, and NBC (which supplies news feeds to their sister organizations including MSNBC).[15]

We're not talking about Boy Scouts wanting to serve the country here. We're talking about a far-Left group of radicals who organized in 1998 to defend Clinton against impeachment. Today, they claim they have more than 1.4 million members.[16] Forget Capone. These guys have mobilized an army.

MoveOn volunteers employed by the news industry work as content editors and produce TV network websites. They've also taken positions as low-level production assistants and have research jobs with the news divisions. One MoveOn anti-war activist said, "We're affecting news coverage of this war. We know it because our friends are telling us we're affecting it."[17]

Affecting news coverage? What business do they have to tinker with the nightly news? Whatever happened to journalistic integrity? Surely Peter Jennings is above this, right? Wrong. Another ultra-Left MoveOn organizer bragged, "At CNN and ABC we know that the producers and the anchors have been really receptive to our message. Peter Jennings even put our people on the air with no opposing view. He loves our message."[18]

These friendly insiders might explain the network bias and some other goings-on. Are you beginning to see the picture here? The Enemy Within is real. They cover each other's backs. They take no prisoners. They make no apologies about manipulating the news. Worse, they fashion news in their own image and to their own liking and then pass it off on the American sheeple as truth.

They have no shame.

THE SILENCED MAJORITY

I like to bicycle every day. Don't get me wrong. I am not one of those skinny-butts who wears a jester outfit to display my privates. I'm just a regular guy who likes the fresh air.

One afternoon I'm on my bicycle. I go down to the mall where I like to hang out for about an hour and just watch the people racing in and out. You got the moms juggling their babies and young kids. You got secretaries on lunch break grabbing a slice of pizza and a drink. And then there's a bunch of high school kids playing hooky in the middle of the day.

So there I was. I was standing near my bicycle minding my own business. Not talking to anybody. Just observing anonymously. Off to my side, I spotted a group of white kids. Some were standing; some were sitting on the curb. One of the punks had two earrings and a nose ring. His pants were hanging down below his underwear.

The truth is, if you get past the hoodlum image, he's actually a nice-looking boy, nothing wrong with him. I'm thinking in another generation he could have played Audie Murphy in *To Hell and Back*. But here he is, walking around in oversized pants. Every time he stands up his super-sized-pants fall down. The kid grabs his waistband and holds up his jeans to keep them from falling below his underwear.

I start to boil inside. You know, somebody should have smacked this kid at home and said, "I'm your father and you are not dressing like a crack addict; I'll burn your pants." Of course today the kid would sue his parents for emotional duress and win.

In a way, I don't blame the kid for dressing like a crack dealer. He's just the product of not having a father around. Now I'm fuming. I call Mrs. Savage on my cell and start fuming about what I'm seeing.

She said, "There's the next generation. That's what's gonna protect the country. That's what's supposed to pay Social Security when we retire. Those are the brains that are supposed to protect us from the illegal swarms amongst us." And we're on a roll. I feel the hair on the back of my neck start to bristle.

A minute later, the kid with the nose ring starts checking me out. He's over at the car with his friends, pointing at me, looking me over. Before I know it, he walks over. I'm thinking he either wants to bum a quarter to play a video game or he's looking to provoke a fight.

As he approached he said, "Are you Michael Savage?" I said, "Yes." He cracked a big smile and said, "I love you man. I have a Michael Savage fan club at my high school." I started to laugh. I said, "You're making this up, right?" He pulled his pants up again and said, "No, I'm not how I look." I said, "You're not how you look? Why are you dressing like that? Why don't you dress how you look?"

He said, "I'm actually very conservative." I said, "With two earrings, a nose ring, and with pants falling below your underwear? You're conservative?" He said, "Yes, yes, yes. I've read your book, too." I said, "Let me ask you something. Don't get me wrong, but tell me why are you dressing like a crack dealer? Aren't you embarrassed?"

He looked at me with disbelief.

I realized in that instant none of his politically correct teachers would ever say to him, "Why don't you dress like a normal human being, instead of dressing like a bum, an inner-city dope who sells crack on a corner?"

No teacher would dare say that to a kid today. Which is another reason why so many young people are so screwed up. None of the adults in their lives is willing to set any standards. So, by default, if baggy pants are good enough for gangster rappers, they're good enough for them.

A minute later, his friends decide to come over. These are all middle-class white kids. As they get up, their pants fall down on cue. All of them grab their belts and pull their pants up over their underwear. I said to myself, *I know where the style came from. This came from drug dealers who are boasting about their jail time.* In jail, they take away your shoelaces and your belt. These white suburban children are imitating not the best and the brightest but the worst and the dumbest.

Then it hit me.

There is tremendous pressure on these kids to look and act the part, to tow the liberal line—that is, if they want to fit into society. Here's a kid, a good kid, and a real thinker. He is attracted to my conservative message probably because it runs contrary to everything he's been taught by hate-the-family, hate-the-church teachers at school.

In his head, he doesn't go along with the pack of lies from the libs. But he knows he's outnumbered, so he conceals his true colors by looking like "one of them." If he dared to open his mouth, if he dared to speak his mind, if he dared to steer his convictions upstream and go against the flow of liberalism, watch out. He'd be dead in the water. The liberal gangsters would shoot down his ideology in a heartbeat.

And he probably understood that.

That's exactly the way it is in the public square of ideas. Today, the keepers of the media, the left-wing extremists who dominate the press, attack like a pack of hungry coyotes anytime a conservative speaks or a contrary viewpoint is expressed. I know. I deal with the pressure to conform to this narrow-minded leftist agenda everyday.

But it wasn't always this way.

America used to be a diverse country where the free exchange of viewpoints was encouraged. Our Founding Fathers understood the need for and worked to preserve the role of freedom of speech. Franklin D. Roosevelt trumpeted that precious treasure, saying, "We look forward to a world founded upon four essential human freedoms. The first is freedom of speech and expression—everywhere in the world."[19]

I'm telling you it is rare a lib calls my show and says, "Michael Savage, I respectfully disagree with you," and then offers a reasonable argument. I don't have a problem with arguing the issues.

I *do* have problems getting the shaft from, well, you know the type. From the crank callers. From the so-called caring, compassionate, understanding, unconditionally loving liberals who love to hate. Apparently there is only room for a certain kind of person on their planet.

When did vocalizing disagreement with a particular viewpoint become hate speech? Who managed to pull the wool over our eyes? The Enlightened Ones in the media, with the help of the Brown Shorts and the RDDBs in the ACLU, that's who. These thugs managed to manipulate the rules of the game while the rest of the sheeple were busy watching TV with their hats on backwards.

In the end, the only speech the media elite consider to be acceptable is speech that agrees with their viewpoint. And by throwing around buzz phrases like "hate speech," they have, in effect, created a chilling environment for dissent.

Wake up, America. To disagree is one of the cherished freedoms upon which this country was founded. Or did your history teacher conveniently skip that lesson? Our forefathers disagreed with the notion of paying taxes to England. They disagreed with the concept of a state religion. They disagreed with the demand to bow to the English throne.

Yes, they disagreed. And, so we do not forget, they fought for the right to not be silenced. What about you? Do you understand your right to freely and publicly engage in a vigorous exchange of ideas is at risk? Do you understand there are forces working to silence the voices of freedom? Do you think I am overstating the threat?

Why do you think we hear all of this talk about starting a liberal radio network and a liberal TV network? What is that all about? Why do they even need it? The majority of teleprompted talking heads wearing pancake makeup are already controlled by the libs. Their goal is obvious. They have mounted a full frontal counterattack to stop conservative talkers.

That's me. That's Rush. The next stop on the bus is to stop the conservative thinkers. That's you. If the Enemy Within has their way, you will soon be the Silenced Majority.

I was undermined from within. I made one regrettable error, and I got thrown off the air. I made the mistake. I gave them the power to destroy me—so they think. But at the end of the day, they have emboldened me because they made me more widely known than ever before. And, unlike those high school kids with nose rings at the mall, I refuse to hide my true colors in order to fit in.

Because I represent the voice of the majority of the people, I will not be silenced by the Enemy Within.

AFTERWORD

A CONSERVATIVE REVOLUTION IS CALLED FOR

I t should be clear to you by now the RDDB lawyers of the ACLU, the yap-ping dogs of hate, the militant Brown Shorts, the unfettered judicial oli-garchy, the clueless Hollywood Idiots, the activist journalists, the pony-tailed Marxist professors, and the neo-socialist education czarinas have seized power in this country. These subversive forces are nothing more than a collective criminal enterprise.

They're the head of the snake.

For forty years, they have slithered into every state of the union, every community, every classroom, every living room, every closet, spreading their filth, chaos, and anti-American venom. Look at the legacy of the Left. Their America is one where criminals have been given more freedom than cops.

Where junk lawsuits proliferate in the courts.

Where the United States Constitution is becoming subservient to international law.

Where too many school children, even though they have been taught

231

how to put a condom on a cucumber, can barely add, spell, read, or write.

Where pornography has penetrated every home with a television or computer.

Where violence has become the national sport.

Where athletes, who were once role models, have become models of ghetto trash.

Where unborn babies are slaughtered and their body parts sold for profit by the factories of death.

Where diseased and criminal illegal immigrants are flooding America with minimal effort to stop them.

Where illegals are given medication and education.

Where white males are considered the incarnation of evil.

Where voting is rigged and turnout is falling to new lows.

Where free speech is disappearing on our campuses.

Where thought crimes are now being created.

Where the military is undermined.

Such is the pathetic legacy of the Left.

How did America's brilliance become so tarnished?

As you know, the Statue of Liberty is the symbol of America's independence. Today, after decades of holding up her lantern of freedom, she is covered by a very deep patina. Some would argue the patina and detritus are beautiful. I don't agree. The patina makes her look decadent.

To me, the patina of age on Lady Liberty represents the natural progression of an unguarded nation towards neglect, corruption, and the loss of idealism. It is symbolic of what happens when a nation looks the other way while the Enemy Within compromises her borders, language, and culture. That, my friend, is how America the Beautiful has lost her brilliance.

Albert Einstein once said, "The world is a dangerous place to live; not because of the people who are evil, but because of the people who don't do anything about it." For far too long, that has been the story of America.

We're apathetic when we should be alarmed.

We're indifferent when we should be outraged.

We're sluggish when we should be vigilant.

We're defensive when we should be on the offensive.

I say it's time we fight back. We must strip off everything that hides our greatness, beauty, and unique national identity. We must rebuff the dullness of apathy. We must scrub away the filthy lies of the Left and get back to those freedoms *with their inherit limitations* which distinguish us from the rest of the world. And we must act while there is still time to reclaim our former glory.

The mouthpieces of the Left would have you believe they, along with their programs and agenda, are the answer to what ails America. They're wrong. Extreme liberalism, as I have demonstrated, is either treason or insanity. Take your pick. Either way, left unchecked, we are finished.

From my perspective, America is beginning to understand her life and soul hangs in the balance. She's under attack from without and—more insidiously—from within. These pages have documented a simple truth: There is no way to compromise with the Enemy Within.

It's defeat them, or be defeated by them.

Beat, or be beaten.

Strike, or be stricken.

To the Left, I say you are wrecking this country and there will be a day of reckoning. America is waking up to your tricks, your lies, and your hatred. You've crossed a line. You've stretched the goodwill and patience of the people too far; they are about to snap.

I'm ever optimistic this book (as well as *The Savage Nation*) will encourage citizenry of all ages to work diligently to remove the patina, to begin the laborious process of stripping away the detritus hiding the sheen of liberty. Such unified determination to confront the Enemy Within is our only hope the shining symbol of our freedom will glisten once again.

PREFACE

1. Eric Lichtblau, "U.S. Uses Terror Law to Pursue Crimes from Drugs to Swindling," *The New York Times*, 28 September 2003.
2. "Celebrities urge Bush to avoid Iraq war," United Press International, 10 December 2002.
3. Lichtblau, "U.S. Uses Terror Law to Pursue Crimes from Drugs to Swindling."
4. Lichtblau, "U.S. Uses Terror Law to Pursue Crimes from Drugs to Swindling."
5. Lichtblau, "U.S. Uses Terror Law to Pursue Crimes from Drugs to Swindling."
6. Harvey Klehr, "A Family Affair," *The Weekly Standard*, 27 September 2003.

CHAPTER ONE

1. "Feminists Celebrate as Patricia Ireland Takes the Helm at Y.W.C.A.," National Organization For Women, press release, 2 May 2003. "YWCA should reject Patricia Ireland as new leader," Traditional Values Coalition, press release, 6 May 2003.
2. "United Way in Dade ends Boy Scout funding," *The Miami Herald*, 14 May 2003.
3. "Pro-infanticide prof awarded ethics prize," WorldNetDaily.com, 12 July 2003.
4. Anita Vogel, "Calif. Offers Textbook Case of Political Correctness," Fox News, 30 April 2003.
5. Lawrence Morahan, "Psychiatric Association Debates Lifting Pedophilia Taboo," CNSNews.com, 11 June 2003.
6. "Attorneys General Want High Court To OK Pledge," Associated Press, 11 June 2003.

7. "Get a MoveOn," *American Spectator* Online, 24 March 2003.
8. "Split Ruling on Affirmative Action," NPR, 23 June 2003.
9. "Supreme Court strikes down Texas sodomy law," CNN.com, 27 June 2003.
10. Robert Bartley, "Open Nafta Borders? Why not?" OpinionJournal.com 2 July 2001.
11. "Supreme Court Strikes Down Gay Sex Law," Click2Houston.com, 26 June 2003.
12. "Candidate Clinton wants to expand health-care eligibility for children," CNN.com, 19 July 2000.
13. "Daschle criticizes Bush tax cut, offers economic boost plan," CNN.com, 4 January 2002.
14. "Rev. Jackson Proposes African Growth Policy for Bush's Upcoming Trip," Rainbow/PUSH, 3 July 2003.
15. "Focus on Gays, Lesbians & Bisexuals," 2000-2001 New Member CD, NEA.org
16. "Pelosi Remarks to NAACP," DemocraticLeader.house.gov, press release, 13 July 2003.
17. Mary Jo Anderson, "Sex-ed programs designed by prostitution advocates," WorldNetDaily.com, 6 October 2003.

CHAPTER TWO

1. Linda Bowles, "Democrats Expose Themselves," NewsMax.com, 6 February 2001.
2. George Gilder, "Slouching, Still," *American Spectator*, July/August 2002.
3. "Legal Scholars, Religious Leaders Decry 'Litmus Test' for Judges," CNSNews.com, 3 September 2003.
4. Report for the U.S. Commission on Civil Rights, April 1977, p. 102, quoted in "Ruth Bader Ginsburg's Feminist World View," *The Phyllis Schlafly Report*, Vol. 26, No. 12, Section 1, p. 3.
5. Report for the U.S. Commission on Civil Rights, quoted in *The Phyllis Schlafly Report*.
6. Bowers v. Hardwick, 478 U.S. 186 (1986) (USSC+).
7. Bradley R. Gitz, "The Ginsburg doctrine," *Arkansas Democrat-Gazette*, 10 August 2003.
8. "Justice: Can Constitution make it in global age?" WorldNetDaily.com, 7 July 2003.
9. Robert H. Bork, press release announcing release of *Coercing Virtue*.

10. Bork, press release.
11. Hans Bader, "The California Civil Rights Initiative Goes to Court," The Federalist Society, 2001.
12. Greg Hoadley, "'Pledge' Judge No Stranger to Controversy," Center for Reclaiming America, 3 July 2002.
13. Martin Kasindorf, "Appeals court ponders whether to reexamine halt of recall vote," *USA Today*, 16 September 2003.
14. Mike Branom, "Fla. Judge Rules Woman Must Shed Veil In Photo ID," *The Boston Globe*, 7 July 2003.
15. http://www.princeton.edu/~lawjourn/Spring98/ferraro.html.
16. Dana Parsons, "This Just In, Judge: There's No Cultural Defense for Child Abuse," *Los Angeles Times*, 28 April, 2002.
17. Macella Monk Flake, "The Impact of Culture on U.S. Law," Yale-New Haven Teachers Institute, Curriculum Unit 96.01.08.
18. Doriane Lambelet Coleman, "Individualizing Justice Through Multiculturalism: The Liberals' Dilemma," *Columbia Law Review*, June 1996.
19. Lana Whited, "Cross burning, flag burning: First Amendment burning?" Roanoke.com, 27 January 2001.
20. William Booth, "Court Delays California Recall Vote," *Washington Post*, 15 September 2003.
21. Art Moore, "Amazon sells 'deadly' pedophile magazine," WorldNetDaily.com, 20 September 2003.
22. Moore, "Amazon sells 'deadly' pedophile magazine."
23. "ACLUM Agrees to Represent Nambla in Freedom of Speech Case," http://www.aclu-mass.org/legal/namblareinstein.html.
24. Moore, "Amazon sells 'deadly' pedophile magazine."
25. "ACLUM Agrees to Represent Nambla in Freedom of Speech Case."

CHAPTER THREE

1. Dick Gephardt, Democratic Debate in Columbia, South Carolina, 3 May 2003.
2. Al Gore, Speech to the Democratic National Convention, 18 August 2000.
3. Hillary Clinton, Senate debate in Manhattan, 8 October 2000.
4. Kerri Houston, "Canada's health care is ailing," *Dallas Morning News*, 1 May 2000.
5. Sarah Lyall, "In Britain's Health Service, Sick Itself, Cancer Care is Dismal," *New York Times*, 10 February 2000.

6. Stephanie Strom, "Gates charity reshapes world health," *International Herald Tribune*, 15 July 2003.

7. "San Francisco will foot bill for city employee sex change operations," Reuters, 2 May 2001.

8. Rachel Gordon, "S.F. Set to Add Sex Change Benefits," *San Francisco Chronicle*, 16 February 2001.

9. "Adult Mortality, Profile of the Nation's Health," CDC Fact Book 2000/2001, p. 73.

10. "Adult Mortality, Profile of the Nation's Health," p. 37.

11. Phil Valentine, *Right from the Heart* (Nashville: Cumberland House, 2003).

12. Valentine, p. 45.

13. http://www.stopaids.org/program/events/index.html.

14. "CDC: Take Sex Out of AIDS Workshops," *OutIn San Francisco*, 25 June 2003.

15. "AIDS groups warn Bush against CDC 'censorship,'" *AIDS Policy and Law*, 22 July 2003.

16. Fred Bridgland, "Fighting stigma with a Muppet," *Sunday Tribune* (Ireland), 29 September 2002.

17. Bridgland, "Fighting stigma with a Muppet."

18. Alan Gustafson, "Inmate gets benefits citizens are losing," *Statesman Journal* (Salem), 5 May 2003.

19. Bryan Robinson, "Condemned Prisoner May Get Kidney Transplant While Law-Abiding Citizens Wait," ABCNews.com, 28 May 2003.

20. Jon Dougherty, "Court: State must cover care for illegals," WorldNetDaily.com, 26 August 2003.

21. Dougherty, "Court: State must cover care for illegals."

22. "California 'Drag Queen Law' and Attack on Normalcy Legislator Says," NewsMax.com, 12 July 2001.

CHAPTER FOUR

1. Bret Stephens, "Our Media Jihadis," *The Jerusalem Post*, 4 October 2003.

2. Carl Limbacher, "CBS TV Star Compares America to Nazi Germany," NewsMax.com, 2/3 2003.

3. David Konig, "Oh, that Robin!" NationalReview.com, 2 April 2003.

4. Stephen Dalton, "It's no walk in the park," *The Times* (London), 21 January 2002.

5. Trish Deitch Rohrer, "Don't Tread On Janeane," *Buzz*, 1993.

6. "No Cheers for Woody," FoxNews.com, 12 August 2002.

7. Carl Limbacher, "'Idiocy Watch' Lets Norman Mailer Hang Himself," NewsMax.com, 21 November 2001. Emphasis added.

8. James Hirsen, "Attack on Mel Gibson Continues," NewsMax.com, 11 March 2003.

9. John Berlau, "Anti-war singers out of tune with public," WorldNetDaily, 7 May 2003.

10. "Second U.S. aircraft carrier leaves Gulf," Associated Press, 17 April 2003. This figure represents casualties during the war, and does not include post-war operations.

11. "Postwar Iraq likely to cost more than war," *USA Today*, 11 August 2003. This figure is reported by Dov Zakheim, the Pentagon's top budget official and accounts for the costs associated for the war in Iraq over a nine-month period (Jan. 2003 – September 2003). It does not include funds for rebuilding Iraq.

12. "Congress Heats Up Over Kennedy Remarks," FoxNews.com, 24 September 2003.

13. "Splitsville: Pat K breaks with dad over Iraq," *The Boston Herald*, 29 September 2003.

14. "Splitsville: Pat K breaks with dad over Iraq."

15. Carl Limbacher, "Hillary Hits TV with Wall-to-Wall 9/11 Bush Bash," NewsMax.com, 12 September 2003.

16. "Harrison Ford Slams Bush policy, guns," WorldNetDaily.com, 28 August 2003.

17. USDOT, Press release, 17 July 2003.

18. "Democrat Congressman: Media's Bias 'Is Killing Our Troops,'" NewsMax.com, 22 September 2003.

19. Audrey Hudson, "Sharpton calls Bush L.A. gang leader," *Washington Times*, 7 July 2003.

20. Ron Fournier, "Democrats take turns bashing Bush," Associated Press, 5 September 2003.

21. Sarah Schaerr, "Professor Forces Students to Send Bush Anti-War Letters for Credit," *Accuracy in Academia*, April/May 2003.

22. Schaerr, "Professor Forces Students to Send Bush Anti-War Letters for Credit."

23. Schaerr, "Professor Forces Students to Send Bush Anti-War Letters for Credit."

24. Ellen Sorokin, "Anti-Americanism blamed on college teachers," *Washington Times*, 10 March 2002.

25. Sorokin, "Anti-Americanism blamed on college teachers."
26. Steve Sexton, "Anti-American 9/11 Day at UC Berkeley," *The California Patriot*, 6 September 2002.
27. Miral Fahmy, "Iraqis Cheer Fall of Baath on Anniversary of Coup," Reuters, 17 July 2003.
28. Fahmy, "Iraqis Cheer Fall of Baath on Anniversary of Coup."
29. Stephens, "Our Media Jihadis."
30. David Asman, "The Way to Win Is . . . to Lose?" FoxNews.com 16 September 2003.
31. Maureen Dowd, "Drunk On Rummy," *New York Times*, 28 September 2003.
32. Fahmy, "Iraqis Cheer Fall of Baath on Anniversary of Coup."
33. James Tarranto, "Veteran Intelligence Professionals for Sanity," OpinionJournal.com, 16 July 2003.
34. Josh Grossberg, "Celebs Open Up Online About Attacks," Eonline.com, 26 September 2001.
35. L. Brent Bozell III, "Gere, Stone Behind the Curve," Creators Syndicate, 30 October 2001.
36. Dan DeLuca, "Vivid lesson on curbs placed on free speech during crisis," *Philadelphia Inquirer*, 30 September 2001.
37. Limbacher, "'Idiocy Watch' Lets Norman Mailer Hang Himself."
38. Bozell, "Gere, Stone Behind the Curve."
39. "Barbie A Threat To Morality?" Associated Press, 10 September 2003.
40. "Muslim slays daughter in 'honor killing,'" WorldNetDaily.com, 29 September 2003.
41. "Sisters axed in Muslim 'honor killing,'" WorldNetDaily.com, 11 September 2003.
42. Terri Judd, "Execute me, pleads Muslim who killed his daughter over her Western lifestyle," Independent.co.uk, 30 September 2003.
43. "Soros calls for 'regime change' in US," *BBC News*, 30 September 2003.
44. Glen Elsasser, "Religious Pluralism is Newest Theater for Military Action," *Chicago Tribune*, 6 July 1999.
45. Jerry Seper, "Arrested Muslim activist helped pick chaplains for U.S. military," *Washington Times*, 1 October 2003.
46. Solomon Moore, "Religion; Fiery Words, Disputed Meaning," *Los Angeles Times*, 3 November 2001.
47. Seper, "Arrested Muslim activist helped pick chaplains for U.S. military."
48. Niles Lathem and Brian Blomquist, "Khadafy Cash Shock," *New York Post*, 30 September 2003.

49. Rowan Scarborough and Steve Miller, "Airman accused of terror spying," *Washington Times*, 24 September 2003.

50. Barbara Starr and Chris Plante, "Muslim chaplain's arrest prompts U.S. probe," CNN, 22 September 2003.

51. Susan Schmidt, "Armed Forces Directed to Radical Muslim Web Site," *Washington Post*, 29 June 2003.

52. Schmidt, "Armed Forces Directed to Radical Muslim Web Site."

53. Edward E. Plowman, "Rubber-stamping Islamic chaplains?" *World*, 11 October 2003.

54. "Pentagon Fears Terrorist Spies Have Infiltrated U.S. Military," NewsMax.com, 4 October 2003.

55. MTVNews.com, 5 February 2003.

56. Aparisim Ghosh, "Iron Maiden Found in Uday Hussein's Playground," *TIME* magazine, 19 April 2003.

57. Stephens, "Our Media Jihadis."

58. Stephens, "Our Media Jihadis."

59. "Department of Peace," *Summit Daily News*, 8 April 2003.

60. Ian Hoffman, "Congress sharpens spending debate; Feinstein takes moral stand; Republicans cite strategic needs," *Daily Review*, 16 September 2003.

61. Ken Guggenheim, "Senate votes to end ban on developing low-yield nuclear weapons," *The* Associated Press, 20 May 2003.

CHAPTER FIVE

1. Dan Rather, "Saddam Interview Airs In Iraq," CBSNEWS.com, 20 March 2003.

2. George Rush and Joanna Molloy, "Moore Bush-Bashing From Film Flake," *Daily News*, 13 May 2003.

3. Steve Dunleavy, "And the Oscar for Idiocy Goes to . . ." *New York Post*, 4 February 2003.

4. Dunleavy, "And the Oscar for Idiocy Goes to . . ."

5. Richard Roeper, "Iraq flak: Some actors don't know their roles," *Chicago Sun-Times*, 30 January 2003.

6. Andrew Coffin, "Attention deficit," *World*, 5 April 2003.

7. Greg Pierce, Nation; Inside Politics, *Washington Times*, 14 April 2003.

8. Glenn Garvin, "When Hollywood entertains a political opinion—run," *Miami Herald*, 3 April 2003.

9. Garvin, "When Hollywood entertains a political opinion—run."

10. Alan Caruba, "Who Should Run America? Hollywood or the White House?" CapitalismMagazine.com, 20 March 2003.

11. Caruba, "Who Should Run America? Hollywood or the White House?"

12. "Actor George Clooney frustrated by U.S. war drive," Reuters, 23 February 2003.

13. "Actors Grammer, Priestley and Duvall Denounce Anti-War Celebs," Media Research Institute, 29 April 2003.

14. "Names in the news," *Philadelphia Inquirer*, 3 July 2002.

15. Patrick Goldstein, "Leaning to the left, buy why?" *Los Angeles Times*, 25 March 2003.

16. Gethin Chamberlain, "Madonna Joins the Anti-War Bandwagon with Video Protest," *The Scotsman*, 11 February 2003.

17. "Richard Gere criticizes Bush in anti-war attack," Ananova.com, 10 February 2003.

18. Abdul Latheef, "From Elizabeth Taylor to Madonna, from Gore Vidal to John le Carre, many celebrities are voicing their frustration over Washington's apparent rush toward a war against Iraq," *Canadian Press Newswire*, 15 February 2003.

19. Sean Penn, iFilm.com.

CHAPTER SIX

1. Gene Robinson, press conference covered by CNN, 6 August 2003.

2. "Fears of split follow gay bishop vote," CNN.com, 6 August 2003.

3. "First Gay Episcopal Bishop Interview with Reverend Gene Robinson," *Good Morning America*, 6 August 2003.

4. "S.Africa's Tutu Dismisses Gay Bishop 'Fuss,'" *New York Times*/Reuters, 10 August 2003.

5. Ken Connor, *Washington Update*, Family Research Council, 24 April 2003.

6. Paul Simao, "HIV Cases Climb Among Gay, Bisexual Men in U.S.," Reuters, 28 July 2003.

7. Daniel Webster, from a discourse delivered at Plymouth, December 22, 1820.

8. David R. Guarino, "Kerry raps Pope: Senator fuming over gay marriage order," *Boston Herald*, 2 August 2003.

9. Guarino, "Kerry raps Pope: Senator fuming over gay marriage order."

10. "ACLJ: Federal Judge Upholds Constitutional Right of Suspended PA Teacher's Aide to Wear Cross Pendant," *Business Wire*, 25 June 2003.

11. Benjamin Franklin, *The Works of Benjamin Franklin*, Jared Sparks, Ed., (Boston: Tappan, Whittemore and Mason, 1840) X: pp. 281-282.

12. "YWCA Should Reject Patricia Ireland as New Leader," Traditional Values Coalition, 6 May 2003.

13. Adam Liptak, "Courts Weighing Rights of States to Curb Aid for Religion Majors," *New York Times*, 10 August 2003.

14. John Cheves, "Demoncrat Enlisted Help from Conservative group; Ten Commandments," *Lexington Herald Leader*, 7 May 2003.

15. William J. Federer, *America's God and Country Encyclopedia of Quotations* (Coppell, Tex.: Fame Publishing, 1994), p. 411.

16. "Cardinal's speech upsets university," *Sydney Morning Herald*, 23 May 2003.

17. Paul Brent, "Great SUV divide: Anti-sports utility vehicle movement worries automakers," *National Post*, 10 March 2003.

CHAPTER SEVEN

1. "Court says monument violates Constitution," Southern Poverty Law Center Report, December 2002, Volume 32, Number 4.

2. "Alabama chief justice defies court order to remove religious monument," *Agence France Presse*, 22 August 2003.

3. Alan Keyes on *Hannity & Colmes*, FOX News, "Keyes lambastes clique of 'lawless' judges," reported by RenewAmerica.us, 22 August 2003.

4. Alan Keyes, text from a speech delivered at a Ten Commandments Rally in Alabama, 16 August 2003.

5. Manuel Roig-Franzia, "Ala. Justices Symbolically Conceal Commandments; Partitions Put Up Briefly to Comply With Order," *Washington Post*, 22 August 2003.

6. "After 300 Crosses Taken Down in Churches across America, Muslim, Jewish & Christian Scholars and Leaders Confront Barriers to Peace," *U.S. Newswire*, 20 August 2003.

7. Vince Morris, "High Court Ruling Hits 'Dirty' Art," *New York Post*, 26 June 1998.

8. "Brooklyn museum photograph depicting Jesus as naked woman angers mayor," Associated Press, 16 February 2001.

9. Witherspoon, *Works*, III:42, from "The Dominion of Providence over the Passions of Men," delivered at Princeton on May 17, 1776.

10. Adam Miller, "Art Wouldn't Irk Jesus, Rev. Al Says," *New York Post*, 18 February 2001.

11. "PETA'S 'Animal Holocaust' Billboard Banned in Mobile," PETA, press release, 9 September 2003.
12. Diana Lynne, "PETA Likens Chickens to Holocaust victims," WorldNetDaily.com, 25 February 2003.
13. PETA's Masskilling.com, 1 August 2002.
14. Matt Prescott, "Letter to the Jewish Community" at http://www.masskilling.com/lettocomm.html.
15. Prescott, "Letter to the Jewish Community."
16. Duncan Osborne, "Sustaining the Marriage Drive Attorney Evan Wolfson focuses on political, educational efforts outside the courtroom," *Gay City News*, 10 March 2003.
17. Elisabeth Bumiller, "Why America Has Gay Marriage Jitters," *New York Times*, 10 August 2003.
18. "Bridal magazine promotes homosexual weddings," WorldNetDaily.com, 28 July 2003.
19. Uwe Siemon-Netto, "Solo Marriage is a Sign of the Times," *United Press International*, 28 May 2003.
20. Stanley Kurtz, "Beyond Gay Marriage," *Weekly Standard*, 4 August 2003.
21. "Bush wants marriage reserved for heterosexuals," CNN.com, 31 July 2003.
22. Philip Pullella, "Pope Tells Catholics to Defend Traditional Family," Reuters, 8 June 2003.
23. "Vatican Warns Against Gay Marriages," Associated Press, 28 July 2003.
24. "Mother of Muslim GI held in base attacks says he is being accused because of his faith," WorldNetDaily.com, 25 March 2003.
25. Joseph Farah, "Radical Islam's 'plan' to take over America," WorldNetDaily.com, 4 August 2003.
26. Paul Sperry, "FBI invites Muslim scholars to preach," WorldNetDaily.com, 30 July 2003.
27. Sperry, "FBI invites Muslim scholars to preach."
28. ACLU Letter to Reps. Smith and Scott on H.R. 4623, the "Child Obscenity and Pornography Prevention Act of 2002," 8 May 2002.

CHAPTER EIGHT

1. NEA Resolution I-13 on Family Planning; adopted in 1985; amended in 1986; ratified every year since.

2. Debra W. Haffner and William L. Yarber, editors, "Guidelines for Comprehensive Sexuality Education; Kindergarten – 12th Grade," National Guidelines Task Force, 2nd Ed., Sexuality Information and Education Council of the United States (SIECUS), 1996.

3. Haffner and Yarber, p. 3.

4. Haffner and Yarber, p. 14.

5. Haffner and Yarber, p. 16.

6. Haffner and Yarber, p. 30.

7. Haffner and Yarber, p. 30.

8. Haffner and Yarber, p. 32.

9. Haffner and Yarber, p. 14.

10. Haffner and Yarber, p. 16.

11. Haffner and Yarber, p. 35.

12. Haffner and Yarber, p. 16.

13. Haffner and Yarber, p. 34.

14. "Students get sex-ed without parents OK," WorldNetDaily.com, 10 September 2003.

15. Cathi Herrod, "Sex Education Bill in the Arizona Senate," Center for Arizona Policy (AzPolicy.org), 22 April 2002.

16. Herrod, "Sex Education Bill in the Arizona Senate."

17. Herrod, "Sex Education Bill in the Arizona Senate."

18. Robert Rector, "Sex Ed or Porn 101?" *National Review Online*, 2 September 2003.

19. National Center for Health Statistics, "Births: Final Data for 2000," *National Vital Statistics Report*, Vol. 50, No. 5, 12 February 2002, p. 46.

20. Robert E. Rector, Kirk A. Johnson, Ph.D., and Lauren R. Noyes, "Sexually Active Teenagers Are More Likely to Be Depressed and to Attempt Suicide," Center for Data Analysis Report, Heritage Foundation, 3 June 2003.

21. Candi Cushman, "Unsafe at Any Grade," *Citizen*, December 2002.

22. "Dick and Jane don't teach bias; STRAIGHT A'S," *Contra Costa Times* 2 June 2003.

23. Arnaud de Borchgrave, "Big Brother's new classroom; Political correctness takes over education," *Washington Times*, 29 April 2003.

24. "Companies Shirk Responsibility for P.C. Textbooks," NewsMax.com, 19 August 2003.

25. John LeBoutillier, "Poison Textbooks," NewsMax.com, 8 May 2003.

26. LeBoutillier, "Poison Textbooks."

27. LeBoutillier, "Poison Textbooks."

28. Ray Parker, "Translators help schools communicate with growing immigrant population," *Naples Daily News*, 5 September 2003.
29. Parker, "Translators help schools communicate with growing immigrant population."
30. David Fein, "Georgia School District's Hiring of Translators 'Misguided' Says Group," CNSNews.com, 5 June 2003.
31. Parker, "Translators help schools communicate with growing immigrant population."
32. Rod Paige, "More spending is not answer," *USA Today*, 10 January 2003.
33. Paige, "More spending is not answer."
34. Paige, "More spending is not answer."
35. Jon Dougherty, "Illegals busting education budget," WorldNetDaily.com, 24 August 2003.
36. Paul Ciotti, "Money and School Performance: Lessons from the Kansas City Desegregation Experiment," Cato Policy Analysis No. 298, 16 March 1998.
37. Ciotti, "Money and School Performance."
38. Carl Campanile, "41% of Apple Schools Get 'F,'" *New York Post*, 11 September 2003.
39. Tracy Dell'Angela, "Gay high school charts new territory," *Chicago Tribune*, 8 September 2003.
40. "NYC To Open First LGBT High School," Associated Press, 28 July 2003.

CHAPTER NINE

1. Joel Stein, "Q+A: Karen Finley," *Time*, 20 July 1998.
2. Brian Mullin, "Karen Finley forces a new definition of art," *Yale Daily News*, 21 January 2000.
3. Beth Potier, "Karen Finley provokes, reveals in lecture," *Harvard University Gazette*, 14 February 2002.
4. Matt Smith, "Public Enema No. 2," *SF Weekly*, 23 February 2000.
5. Smith, "Public Enema No. 2."
6. Nina Willdorf, "Performance Involving Defecation and Oral Sex Sparks Controversy at San Francisco Art Institute," *The Chronicle of Higher Education*, 1 March 2000.
7. "Bondage Act Steps Over Cutting Edge," *San Francisco Examiner*, 7 March 2000.
8. Roger Kimball, "What Next, a Doctorate of Depravity?" *The Wall Street Journal*, 5 May 1998.

9. "Embattled Head of SUNY College Quits," *The* Associated Press, 29 August 2001.

10. Candace deRussy, "Sex and Bondage 101," *The Women's Quarterly,* http://www.iwf.org/pubs/twq/su98b.shtml.

11. Carina Chocano, "Scholars of smut," Salon.com, 5 October 1998.

12. David M. Herszenhorn, "Explicit Photos Touch Off a Debate at Rutgers," *New York Times,* 23 March 1998.

13. Susan Carpenter, "Exploring sexuality on the strip," *Los Angeles Times,* 5 June 2003.

14. Carpenter, "Exploring sexuality on the strip."

15. Andrea Billups, "Dirty Dozen exposes absurd college courses," *Washington Times,* 7 September 2000.

16. Billups, "Dirty Dozen exposes absurd college courses."

17. George Archibald, "'How to be Gay' course draws fire at Michigan," *Washington Times,* 18 August 2003.

18. Archibald, "'How to be Gay' course draws fire at Michigan."

19. Billups, "Dirty Dozen exposes absurd college courses."

20. Brittany Adams, "Continuation of Sexuality De-Cal Classes Uncertain," *Daily Californian,* 15 February 2002.

21. Adams, "Continuation of Sexuality De-Cal Classes Uncertain."

22. Adams, "Continuation of Sexuality De-Cal Classes Uncertain."

23. Daniel Cucher, "Sex festival showcases skewed ethics," *Arizona Daily Wildcat,* 19 November 2002.

24. Joseph Rago, "Collis Sex Festival: Deviance on Tap," *Dartmouth Review,* 23 March 2003.

25. "Illiberal Education," http://www.dineshdsouza.com/illiberal.html.

26. Jim Sparkman, "Ithaca College Faculty 94% Liberal, and Think It's OK," *ChronWatch,* 18 April 2003.

27. "Diversity Dishonesty on College Campuses," *Eagle Forum,* Vol. 35, No. 9, April 2002.

28. David Horowitz, "The Campus Blacklist," FrontPageMagazine.com, 8 April 2003.

29. Daniel Pipes and Jonathan Calt Harris, "Columbia VS. America," *New York Post,* 1 April 2003.

30. Pam Morgan, letter to Dr. Rod Paige, 2 April 2003.

31. David Abel, "America Prepares Domestic Impact; Campuses See a Downside to Unity Civil Rights Stifled, Some Professors Say," *Boston Globe,* 6 October 2001.

32. "Towers of Intellect," *Wall Street Journal*, 5 October 2001.
33. "Towers of Intellect."

CHAPTER TEN

1. "Al Capone," Chicago Historical Society, http://www.chicagohs.org/history/capone/cpn1a.html.
2. "Al Capone," Chicago Historical Society.
3. Data compiled from Cable Network Daily Comparagraph, Nielson National People Reader, Nielson media research, June/July, 2003.
4. Comment made to Tina Gulland on *Inside Washington*, 8 July 1995.
5. *To the Contrary*, PBS, 4 November 1994.
6. Bill O'Reilly, "Mean Talk Could Derail Clooney's Ride," *Sun-Sentinel*, 25 January 2003.
7. Brit Hume, The Political Grapevine column, FoxNews.com, 7 March 2001.
8. Marie McCullough, "Marking the 4th With A Rite of Free Speech," *Philadelphia Inquirer*, 5 July 1997.
9. Don Kowet, "Hi! It's Ted and Fidel having fun in Havana," *Washington Times*, 25 June 1990.
10. *The Early Show*, 29 June 2000.
11. Jeff Jacoby, "1998: Another Year of Liberal Slanders," *Boston Globe*, 31 December 1998.
12. Jacoby, "1998: Another Year of Liberal Slanders."
13. Jacoby, "1998: Another Year of Liberal Slanders."
14. Jacoby, "1998: Another Year of Liberal Slanders."
15. "Get a MoveOn," *American Spectator* Online, 24 March 2003.
16. Michelle Goldberg, "Progressive popularity contest," Salon.com, 24 June 2003.
17. "Get a MoveOn."
18. "Get a MoveOn."
19. Franklin D. Roosevelt, annual message to Congress, Washington, D.C., 6 January 1941.

SPONSOR
THE
PAUL REVERE SOCIETY!

A Non-Profit 501(c)(3) Organization

Federal Tax Exempt # 91-1786633

Your sponsorship will help make your voice heard,
By helping our educational organization make our voice heard
To the people who need to hear our message concerning this
Great Nation's Borders, Language, and Culture.

Your Sponsorship includes our Generous Package of
Free Merchandise, Not Available in Stores, which has a Value that
Exceeds the Sponsorship Fee, along with Your Numbered
Unique Sponsorship Card.

COMPLETE THE FOLLOWING FORM.

SUBMISSION INSTRUCTIONS FOLLOW.

THE PAUL REVERE SOCIETY, INC. SPONSORSHIP FORM

Name _____

Address: _____

City: _____ State: _____ Zip: _____

Optional: Telephone (Home) _____ (Work) _____ (Mobile) _____

Payment Method (Circle one):

Money Order   Check   Credit Card

I authorize The Paul Revere Society to charge the following amount to my credit card:

_____

(Circle your choice, please)

One-Year Sponsorship: $40; Two-Year Sponsorship: $70; Contribution: $_____

TWO-YEAR SPONSORSHIP ($70) INCLUDES:
- Official Paul Revere Society Sponsorship Card
- Discounts and Advance Notice for Future Events
- Free SAVAGE NATION Baseball Cap, Navy Blue with Embroidered Lettering ($24.95 Value, Made in USA)
- ADDED BONUS: Double CD Set, THE BEST OF THE SAVAGE NATION ($24.95 Value, Made in USA)
- The Honor of Helping to Build America's Premier Educational Organization

ONE-YEAR SPONSORSHIP ($40) INCLUDES:
- Official Paul Revere Society Sponsorship Card
- Discounts and Advance Notice for Future Events
- Free SAVAGE NATION Baseball Cap, Navy Blue with Embroidered Lettering ($24.95 Value, Made in USA)
- The Honor of Helping to Build America's Premier Educational Organization

HELP US GROW! I WANT TO CONTRIBUTE AN ADDITIONAL:
(Circle your choice) $100 $250 $500 $1,000   OTHER: _____

CREDIT CARD INFORMATION:
(Note: We utilize the secured Bank of America e-commerce online division for your protection. We will never share your personal information with anyone.)
NAME ON CARD _____
ADDRESS ON CARD _____
TYPE OF CARD: (Circle one)   VISA   MASTERCARD
CARD NUMBER _____
EXPIRATION DATE ON CARD _____

I authorize the Paul Revere Society to charge my credit card as follows (Circle one):
One Year Sponsorship $40; Two Year Sponsorship $70; Contribution $_____

Complete this form and send it with your payment (check, cash, money order, or credit card) to:
THE PAUL REVERE SOCIETY, INC
150 SHORELINE HIGHWAY, BLDG "E"
MILL VALLEY, CA 94941

TELEPHONE: 415-388-5921
THIS FORM MAY BE FAXED TO: 415-388-2257
(All information submitted will never be sold or shared with any other entity.)

PAUL REVERE SOCIETY MISSION STATEMENT

~

MICHAEL SAVAGE founded the Paul Revere Society (PRS). With a crisis of leadership threatening the United States, PRS stands for the reassertion of our borders, our language, and our culture.

Some say that the borders are arbitrary, English is only one of many languages in our new "Multicultural America," and that we share no common history or values. We believe in the Sovereignty of our Nation. That English is our national "glue." And that we all do share in the pillars of the *Bible,* the *U.S. Constitution,* and the *Bill of Rights.* These documents and what they stand for are our common cultural heritage.

The Paul Revere Society will assert the values inherent in these pillars of freedom. We will seek to educate the citizenry about our nation's freedoms.